The Echo of Things

The Echo of Things

THE LIVES OF PHOTOGRAPHS IN THE SOLOMON ISLANDS

Christopher Wright

Duke University Press ▪ *Durham & London* ▪ 2013

Library of Congress Cataloging-in-Publication Data
Wright, Christopher (Christopher J.)
The echo of things : the lives of photographs in the
Solomon Islands /
Christopher Wright.
p. cm. — (Objects/histories)
Includes bibliographical references and index.
ISBN 978-0-8223-5496-3 (cloth : alk. paper)
ISBN 978-0-8223-5510-6 (pbk. : alk. paper)
1. Photography in ethnology — Solomon Islands.
2. Solomon Islands — Pictorial works. 3. Solomon
Islanders — Pictorial works. I. Title. II. Series:
Objects/histories.
GN347.W73 2013
305.80099593–dc23
2013020979

CONTENTS

ACKNOWLEDGMENTS

I owe a great deal to many people in Roviana, Honiara, and elsewhere in the Solomon Islands, in particular Faletau Leve. I hope this book will serve as a monument to his memory. Other Roviana people include Ronald Talsassa and family, Chris Mamupio, Donald Maepio and family, Sae Oka, Josephine Wheatley and family, Reverend Robertson Bato, Annie Homelo, David Kera and family, Simon Sasae, Olive Talasassa, Lawrence Foana'ota, the Saunders and Poras families, Tepa, and Stanley (and everyone I played football with). Thanks to all those I worked with constructing the new school building in Dunde, the staff and students at the Sokogaso Learning Centre, and all those Roviana people who shared their knowledge and photographs with me in such a generous way. I am very grateful to the elders of the Dunde Council for their permission to work there. Thank you and *leana hola*.

In Australia and New Zealand I am very grateful to Peter Sheppard and his family, Christine Dureau, Takuya Nagaoka, Frida Wheatley and family, and Dom and Michelle.

In the United Kingdom, I owe a great deal to Chris Pinney, who has been helpful in more ways than I can count and has been a constant friend. Roslyn Poignant also provided a huge amount of support and productive critical input, as well as serving as the best possible source of inspiration. I have also benefited greatly from discussions with the following people: Elizabeth Edwards, Susanne Kuechler, Deborah Waite, Phil Burnham, Nicholas Saunders, Christopher Tilley, Daniel Miller, Lucy Norris, "Buck" Scheifellin, Haidy Geismar, Graeme Wear, Nicholas Thomas, Edvard Hviding, and Jari Kupiainen. The work of Edvard Hviding was a particular source of inspiration for my research, especially for the way in which he always privileges the voices of Solomon Islanders. His fieldwork always served as an excellent model. I have been lucky enough to have been involved in the intellectual project on anthropology and photography initiated by Roslyn Poignant, Christopher Pinney and Elizabeth Edwards in the 1980s, and my own work owes an inestimable debt to their examples. I have also learned a lot through presenting some of the ideas in this book in the form of papers at Goldsmiths, University College London, University of Manchester, and the AAA annual conference.

The members of the New Georgia Archaeological Survey, particularly Peter Sheppard, Shankar Aswani, Takuya Nagaoka, and Tim Thomas warmly welcomed me in Roviana in 1998 and have continued to provide strong collegiate support for which I am extremely grateful.

Staff at the following institutions provided a great deal of support: Royal Anthropological Institute, London (especially Sarah Walpole); Royal Geographical Society, London; Ethnography Department and Library at the British Museum; Cambridge Museum of Archaeology and Anthropology; Pitt Rivers Museum, Oxford; Mitchell Library, Sydney; Australian Museum, Sydney; Melbourne Museum, Melbourne; Powerhouse Museum, Sydney; Methodist Archives, Auckland (particularly Jill Weeks); National Museum, Honiara; Auckland Museum; Rautenstrauch Joest Museum, Cologne; National Library, Canberra.

I owe a huge debt to Nicholas Thomas for all his insightful and helpful comments — this book owes much to his intellectual inspiration and support. The staff at Duke University Press have provided a huge amount of support in seeing this book into production. In particular Ken Wissocker has been extremely patient and has always been there with excellent advice. Thanks are also due to Elizabeth Ault and Jessica Ryan for their consistent help, to Rebecca Fowler for some exceptionally good copy-editing, and to my anonymous reviewers of the original manuscript.

I owe most of all to my wife, Joanna, and to my sons, Beinn and Evan. This book would not have been possible without their enduring support and love.

. . .

Some of the material presented here has appeared in an altered form in the following articles and chapters:

"Material and Memory: Photography in the Western Solomon Islands," *Journal of Material Culture* 9, no. 1 (2004): 73–85 (SAGE Publications).

"'A Devil's Engine': Photography and Spirits in the Western Solomon Islands," in "Haunting Images: The Affective Power of Photography," edited by B. Smith and R. Vokes, a special edition of *Visual Anthropology* 21, no. 4 (2008): 364–80 (Routledge).

"Faletau's Photocopy, or the Mutability of Visual History in Roviana," in *Photography, Anthropology and History: Expanding the Frame*, edited by Christopher Morton and Elizabeth Edwards. © Ashgate, 2009.

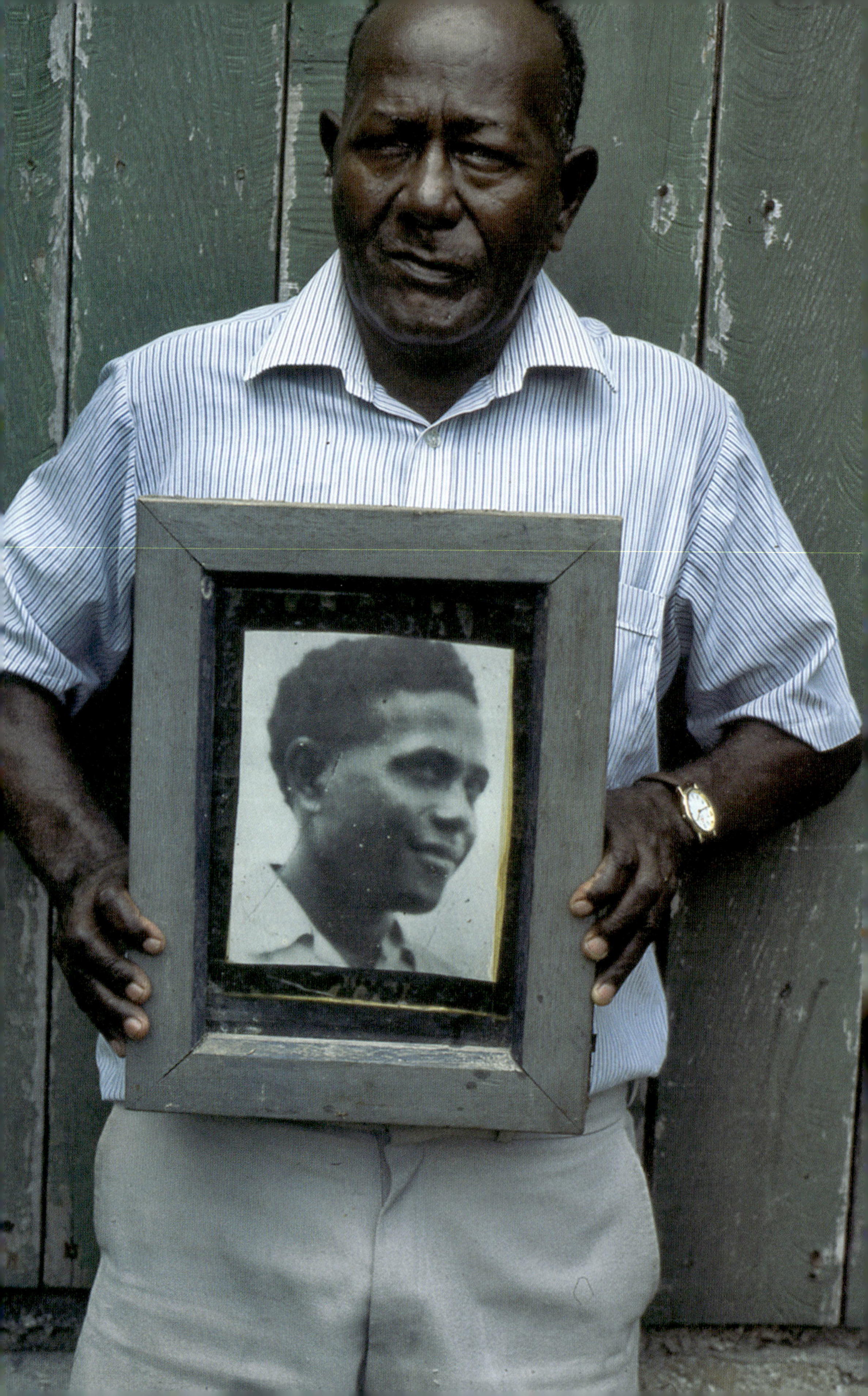

Prologue

FALETAU LEVE, FROM ROVIANA LAGOON IN THE SOLO-
mon Islands in the South Pacific, described to me the photograph
of himself that he was holding (figure P.1): "You can see the shadows of people in photographs. Something remains—it is the echo
of things. Your shadow is the photograph. The soul is like a mag-
netic thing—the photograph is the soul of a person. This photograph is my shadow."[1] The photograph, held in a wooden frame he
made, is the only image that he has of himself as a young man. He
went on to tell me stories that are connected to the photograph,
stories that bind him and this material object together, as well as
tracing lines of connection to other histories and places. The photograph was taken in 1957, when he first began working for the British
government—which controlled the Solomon Islands as a colonial
protectorate from 1893 to 1978. Faletau worked for many years as
a carpenter and boat builder in Gizo, a center of British administration on an island of the same name that lies to the west of Roviana. A friend of his from Fiji, Maepaza Gina—a fellow carpenter—took the photograph on Faletau's own camera, which he had
just bought with his first wages. Faletau wanted the photograph

FIGURE P.1 (*opposite*)
Faletau Leve holding a
photograph of himself
as a young man.

to send to his girlfriend at the time, Daisy. The idea of exchanging these kinds of "love photos," as they are known locally, came from American soldiers stationed in Munda whom Faletau had befriended during World War II in the mid-1940s. His powerful sense of physical attachment to this photograph—this object—seemed familiar; I have photographs of my own family and of me that exert a similar hold. The terminology that he used to describe the photograph—shadow, echo, soul—suggests his understandings of photography as a medium. This book is concerned with how Roviana people have been, and are, entangled with photography in various ways: through being the subjects of colonial photography, through their own uses and expectations of the medium, and through the role it can play in their ideas of history. It is an argument for an ethnographic approach to our understanding of photography, and for a focus on the particular kinds of magic that it works on us.

The conflation of two senses—vision and sound—that occurred when Faletau talked of the "echo of things" in relation to his photograph is entirely appropriate to this project. The idea of a direct physical connection between the photograph and the object—Faletau's notion of the image as an echo, a reverberation—is a key component of photographic magic, and of the way in which photography is thought to work in Roviana. It is these kinds of ideas about how a photograph is related to its subject that I am concerned with tracing in a context where photography is a technology introduced from elsewhere. Photography is not simply a technical process; photographs are social objects as much as they are visual images. Photography produces interconnected networks of objects, meanings, and social relationships, and in their social lives, photographs have as much to do with oral history, with the stories that circulate around them, as they have with any technological understanding or strictly visual meaning (Edwards 2005). These kinds of stories—themselves the echoes of photographic objects—are what I am also concerned with here: the way that such stories can reveal not just personal biographies and memories but also wider issues about what photography is and what it does for Roviana people. The notion of an echo contains the idea of a call and response, an aural reflection, similar to the visual one associated with photography, but similar too to the process of entwining stories and photographs.

Faletau brought his first camera—a Kodak Box Brownie—in 1957 from a Chinese store in Gizo. The camera cost him $1.70 in

Australian dollars and a roll of twelve shots of film cost $3.00, both of which represented considerable sums of money at that time. The price of the film included the cost of the store owner sending it to be developed and printed in Australia, and the process took at least two months, and sometimes longer, before a series of contact prints were sent back. Faletau never received negatives. The photograph of Faletau is an enlargement made from one of these contact prints by a friend who worked in the photographic darkroom run by the British administration in Gizo. This was a small rudimentary darkroom set up in Gizo in the 1960s as part of a research project on coconuts, and several Roviana people still possess photographs made in this darkroom. Faletau told me that the original print did not make him "come out good," so he persuaded a British friend to make an enlargement for him. He went on to explain that at that point Roviana people did not know how to "frame" or "pose" photographs, "so people's faces appeared strange; they did not come out good."[2] Roviana people had to learn what, and when, to photograph, as much as they had to learn how to use the camera in any technical sense. Similarly, new skills of framing subjects had to be learned when large numbers of people in Europe and North America, who had previously relied on photographic studios, began to take their own photographs at the end of the nineteenth century (Holland 1997, 128).

Older people whom I spoke to about photographs in Roviana often had difficulties recognizing anything in photographs other than whole bodies facing forward against a plain or relatively neutral background. Photographs that showed close-ups of faces, or bodies in action, were hard for these people to make out, and they complained that in these images people did not "come out good." Although they could recognize faces of individuals they knew if I drew attention to them—in several cases having to cover up other parts of the image—the older people clearly had their own set of expectations of photographs. As Anthony Forge notes regarding the Abelam of Papua New Guinea in the late 1960s: "When shown photographs of themselves in action, or of any pose other than face or full figure looking directly at the camera, they ceased to be able to 'see' the photograph at all. . . . Even when the figure dominates (to my eyes) the photograph I sometimes had to draw a thick line around it before it could be identified, and in some cases I had the impression that they willed themselves to see it rather than actually saw it in the way we do" (Forge 1970, 287).

In terms of his own motivation to take photographs, Faletau declared that he wanted to "keep every something," to maintain a physical closeness to people and events through getting hold of their images. But he pointed out that he ended up giving lots of photographs away to other people, like his brother, other family members, or to anyone in his large extended family group (*butubutu*). Faletau wanted to make an "album," but he ended up "sharing every something." He would also take photographs for other people too — at weddings and feasts, and he was known as a *matazona*, a Roviana term that refers to someone endowed with certain powers, including "good sight" and memory, but also implying a general sense of efficacy, of being able to make things "come out good." Historically, matazona were carvers and boat builders — key figures in constructing the large and elaborate trading and headhunting canoes called *tomoko*. They were also consummate oral historians. The role is hereditary, and contemporary matazona can trace the genealogical line through which they acquired their power through four or five generations. For Faletau his ability as a matazona is what enabled him to make photographs "come out good." Faletau originally learned how to use a camera from another Roviana man called Solomon Dakei, who had been educated in Fiji, but Faletau asserts that his ability to make people "come out good" and to frame a photograph is a direct result of his matazona power. He describes the photograph of himself as a young man as enabling "the memory of time," and although it is the only photograph he has of himself prior to the early 1970s, he laments the fact that the photograph does not show his whole body: "This is a special photo. [But] I cannot come out good. But I will be remembered. You can see that I remain [stap]."[3]

Faletau uses the Pijin word *stap* in the sense of "endure," but also in reference to being in the photograph. Although it is usually used in the more mundane sense of someone staying indoors — hemi stap lo haos — Faletau uses it here to indicate something physical that remains. Spirits are said to stap in certain places and features of the Roviana landscape, and this photograph contains something of Faletau. It seems amazing that for someone who owned a camera and was a keen and active photographer, Faletau should have so little in the way of surviving photographic images. This is partly the result of sharing photographs with others, but also reveals the way that photographs often do not survive long in the intense heat and humidity of Roviana. Photographs *spoilem* (are spoiled) very quickly —

fading to an abstract pattern of colors, or succumbing to mildew — a process that means that those that do survive acquire an extra aura. Faletau's attachment to this particular photograph, which sits on a shelf in his bedroom and is one of nine photographs in his possession, reveals the hold that photography has over Roviana people — it is important to stap.

I was in Roviana Lagoon on New Georgia, an island in the Solomon Islands group, in the late 1990s to carry out some research for an exhibition project I was involved in curating at the National Museum in Honiara, the capital of the Solomon Islands. The exhibition was a celebration of the twentieth anniversary of independence from British rule. I spent most of my time in Roviana talking to people and showing them a small collection of copy prints of nineteenth- and early twentieth-century photographs of New Georgia that I had taken with me. My intentions were to use the photographs as a collaborative means of gathering oral histories and biographies, and some of these accounts would then be used to "caption" the photographs for the exhibition in Honiara. I was also interested in what people's expectations of the photographs were in historical terms; what did they want from the photographs? I "exhibited" the photographs in many ways. This ranged from hanging a series of photographs by pegs from strings stretched between thatched huts in a village, or across a room, to pinning photographs and accompanying texts to walls. Exhibitions often took place in people's homes rather than in any public space. The practical processes involved with organizing these performances were often revealing as people discussed what photographs should be shown, and how they should be arranged.[4] As well as giving prints to specific individuals and families, and leaving copies of all of them with a local *kastom* (custom) school — I produced several small booklets for local distribution with photocopies of photographs and texts in Roviana. These kind of simple objects often have a considerable impact — they can be given out free, whereas books have to be purchased.

In one village along the shore of the lagoon, Bulelavata, a large crowd gathered in the welcome shade of a large communal cooking hut to look at the prints that I handed around. Old men talked about the kastom revealed in a photograph taken by a British naval lieutenant, Henry Somerville, during a hydrographic survey of Roviana and nearby Marovo Lagoon that was carried out in 1893–94 by the Royal Navy (figure P.2). The large earrings, shell valuables,

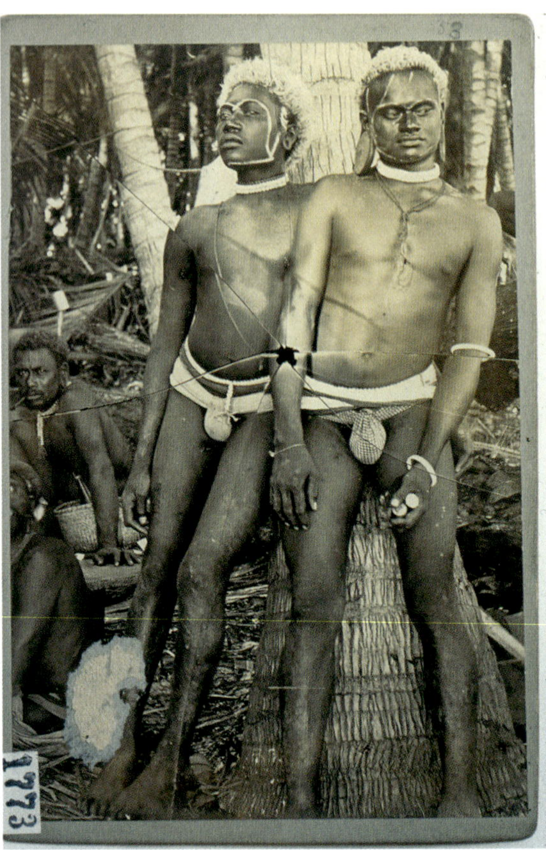

FIGURE P.2 Two young New Georgian men. Photograph by Henry B. Somerville, 1893. Courtesy of Royal Anthropological Institute, London. No. 1773

limed hair, clothing, and body decorations depicted in the image all identified it as a photograph from "before." Although the apparent newness of the copy I had, in comparison to the very worn condition of the few photographs that Bulelavata people possessed, was commented on, people considered it an object connected with the past. Some people suggested that the photograph might have been taken "at the time *Royalist*," a reference to a historically significant attack made by the Royal Navy ship HMS *Royalist* on Roviana villages in 1891, a few years before Somerville's visit. This was put forward as a probable reason for the visible crack in the photograph, which was thought to be the result of the photograph itself having been shot during the attack by the *Royalist*. People constantly turned the copy over to see if the hole went right through the print, and my discussion of a broken glass negative—from my own understanding of the process of making a print from a negative on a fragile sheet of glass—was met with indifference.

Several older men speculated about how it might be possible to trace the living ancestors of the youths in the photograph by comparing their faces to contemporary people. Middle-aged men were more concerned with the photograph's ability to comment on the present and animatedly talked about their teenage sons, who had finished school and now hung listlessly around the village avoiding the subsistence work of gardening and fishing. These teenage boys, whose sunglasses, knotted red bandanas around their heads, and oversized baggy trousers showed the influence of reggae and ragga musical subcultures, laughed dismissively at the photograph. Yet, in later conversations — out of parental sight — that included discussion of photographs of themselves and images cut out from Australian music magazines, they expressed more curiosity. Middle-aged women, who looked at the photograph together in a large raucous group, pointed out that, like Somerville's subjects, teenagers today had an obsession with their physical appearances. Laughing loudly, they talked about the ruf boys of the village and made a series of thinly disguised innuendos and jokes about teenagers' interest in sex. As the photographs were passed from hand to hand, they became the subject of many different kinds of conversations, revealing the multiple frames and histories that revolve around each photograph — their echoes. What I am concerned with in this book is not just what is depicted in the photograph, what it might be thought to contain in any fixed historical sense, but also what goes on around it, its life. The photograph is transformed through processes of recontextualization, changing despite its apparent material fixity (Thomas 1991). In moving beyond its forensic capacity, these performances of the photograph reveal its ability to be absorbed into other histories and trace a wide range of connections between past and present (Edwards 2005).

Geographically, Roviana consists of a large lagoon and string of barrier islands that runs for some twenty miles along the southern coast of the main island of New Georgia in the western Solomon Islands (map P.1). One of the best descriptions of the environment of the lagoon remains that provided by Somerville himself in 1893–94:

> We now come to [the New Georgia group's] most striking, and probably unique feature — its barrier island and lagoons. . . . Following the southern shore of Main Island [New Georgia] to the eastward . . . there is a long chain of barrier reef and islands which

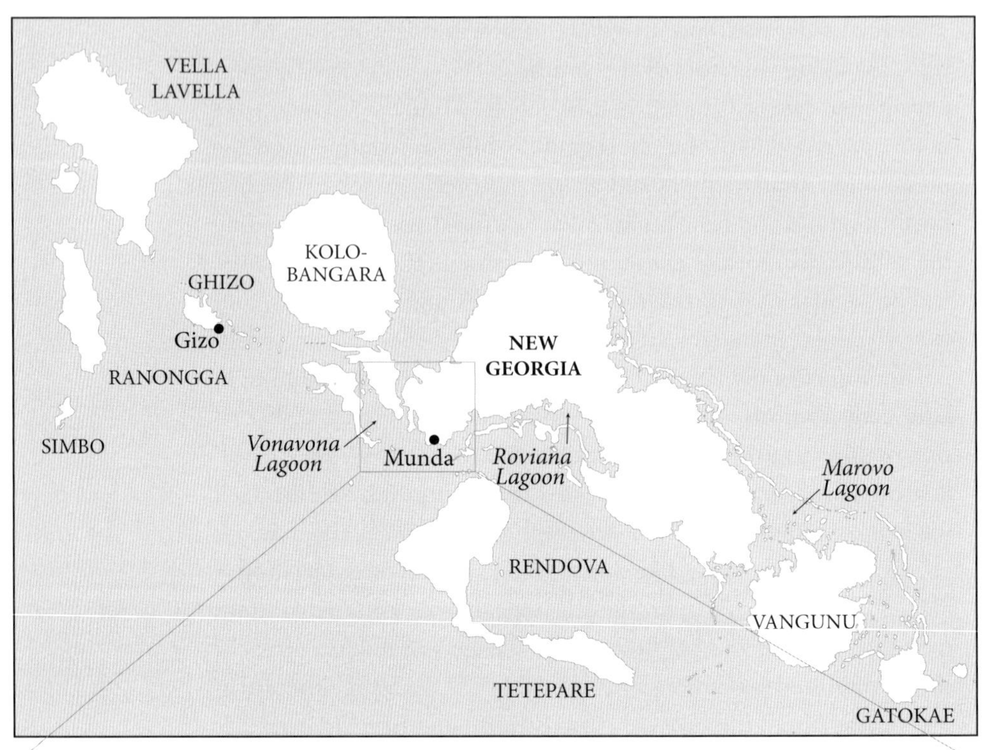

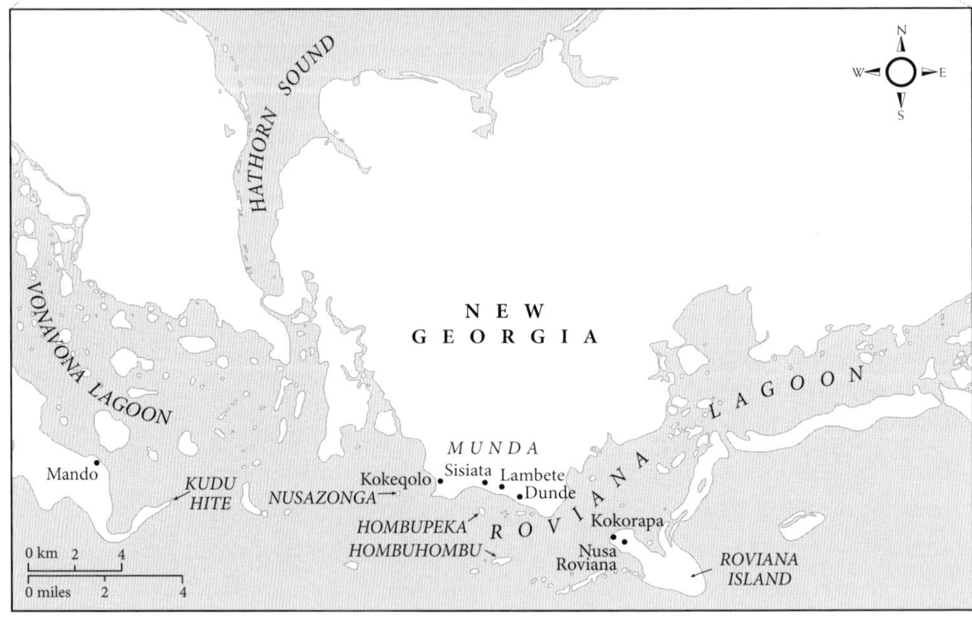

MAP P.1 Map of the New Georgia group and Roviana.

enclose the Rubiana [Roviana] lagoon. On its inner beach is built the largest settlement in the group, a series of villages holding probably between 3000 and 4000 inhabitants, the chief of which gives its name to the lagoon. . . . To look down upon the lagoon from the summit of any of the hills of the large islands is to have spread before one the strangest and most picturesque scenes imaginable. The splendid luxuriant bush close round forms a foreground of the highest interest, edged at the waterline by the white sand, or dark green mangroves of the coast, with perhaps a brown thatched native village standing among its coconut palms, and canoes plying about beyond on the calm water. The middle distance is filled with the lagoon itself, dark blue in the deeps, pale blue in the shallows, light brown over the labyrinthine reefs — a feast of colour. (Somerville 1897, 359–60)

Although this excerpt suggests a certain colonial desire for a commanding view, it does describe some of the enduring physical beauty of the lagoon environment (figure P.3). Despite the "discovery" of the islands in 1568 by the Spaniard Alvaro de Mendaña, who sighted two islands of the New Georgia group, it was not until 1787 that a European vessel came within close proximity to the islands (Jackson 1978, 43). For Roviana people there followed a history of increasing contact with Europeans, which led finally to the declaration of the Solomon Islands as a British protectorate in 1893, followed by the arrival of traders, and then, in 1902, the Methodist mission. Historically, the villages that Somerville encountered in 1893–94 had been established in the late sixteenth or early seventeenth century when previously inland populations moved to the coast (Aswani 2000). Life in Roviana as Somerville found it was, and to a large extent still is, based around the subsistence activities of fishing and gardening. But, despite the endurance of the physical landscape and certain features of daily life, Roviana has undergone huge changes both before and after colonialism. As Edvard Hviding argues, the cultures in Roviana "did not consist of a static society existing more or less in a 'timeless present' before the arrival of Europeans. Shifting alliances, migrations and territorial displacement were common features . . . prior to European contact" (Hviding 1996, 101–2).

The early decades of the twentieth century saw large-scale change in Roviana as a result of missionary work and economic development, but in the late 1950s a local breakaway movement from the

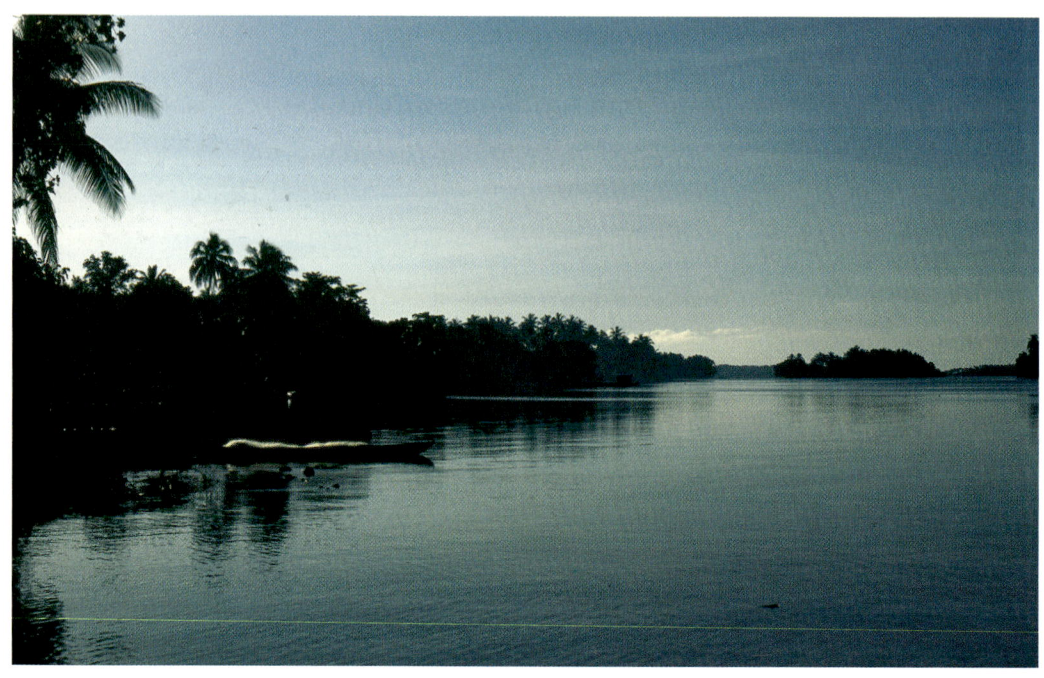

Methodist Church was formed, called the Christian Fellowship Church. This was a highly syncretic movement founded by a local "prophet"—Silas Eto—and the majority of Roviana people today belong either to the Methodist Church or the Christian Fellowship Church (Harwood 1971). Independence from British control was granted to the Solomon Islands in 1978, and although there were subsequent moves to establish an independent western Solomons state (political ideas that were once again the topic of much conversation during my research), Roviana currently remains politically part of Western Province and the Solomon Islands (Premdas, Steeves, and Laramour 1983). During the time of my research, from 1998 to 2001, the ongoing "ethnic tensions" and what was effectively a military coup in Honiara in June 2000 were having a considerable impact on the people of Roviana. The violence and upheaval, which revolved mostly around long-standing rivalries between people from the island of Malaita and those from Guadalcanal, eventually resulted in the Australian government being instrumental in sending in a pan-Pacific peace-keeping force in the form of the Regional Assistance Mission to the Solomon Islands (RAMSI) in July 2003. The last Papua New Guinean armed contingent of this force only left the Solomons in April 2013. In early 2000 many refugees from the violence in the capital had moved back, semipermanently, to Roviana and this had caused a resurfacing of many persistent local problems over land and access to resources. These problems and others related to authority and law and order were often referred to by Roviana people in direct relation to the upheavals that resulted from the actions of the officers and crew of the HMS *Royalist* in 1891. The way in which this particular historical event reemerged and was linked to current events was facilitated or provoked by discussions of photographs like Somerville's.

Photographs are revealing of wider cultural concerns, and Pierre Bourdieu has argued that "the most trivial photograph expresses, apart from the explicit intentions of the photographer, the system of schemes of perception, thought and appreciation common to a whole group" (Bourdieu 1990, 6). But photographs also reveal fractures and cannot be taken as straightforward reflections of culture. What is required is an intimate understanding of how they function as a medium in practice — a practice that is both historically and culturally situated. What is needed is an ethnography of the uses of photographs. This book is a study of the uses of photographs in Roviana Lagoon that will look at both contemporary photographic practices and consider people's reactions to historical photographs of Roviana made in the late nineteenth and early twentieth centuries. It is an ethnography of photography that argues for a new and fuller anthropological engagement with photographies.

Transforming photography into the plural — photographies — highlights the need for this ethnographic approach to understanding the medium. The great bulk of the previous research on the intersection of anthropology and photography has looked at the photographic representation of other cultures produced by colonial regimes (see Alloula 1987; Edwards 1992; Green 1984). Christopher Pinney has argued that photography and anthropology share a "parallel history," and, while productively problematizing the relationship, he has shown how the positivism ascribed to photography in the name of scientific endeavor found fertile ground in the early positivism of the anthropological project (Pinney 1992). The writing on colonial photography has often treated it as an unoccluded mirror of colonial attitude and, in focusing solely on a formal critique of the images, it has largely failed to investigate the political complexities and historically situated practices of production and consumption that are involved in photography's entanglement with other cultures. But in addition to understanding the historical context of anthropology's involvement with photography, questions about contemporary anthropological approaches to the medium also need to be reconsidered.

Anthropology cannot treat photography as some kind of neutral technology or tool, and the discipline needs to come to terms with questions about photography's identity as a medium if it is to engage with it as an object of study and as a force that produces certain kinds of selves and social formations, as well as whole constellations of imaginaries and networks of many kinds. Photography is productive of these formations, not simply a reflection of previously existing attitudes. There needs to be a focus on other photographic traditions in addition to considering photography as a tool for representing anthropological knowledge. Marcus Banks and Howard Morphy have argued that contemporary visual anthropology can be divided into two strands. The first involves the use of visual media in the gathering and presentation of research, and the other the study of visual media themselves as part of "visual systems" (Banks and Morphy 1997, 21). The latter potentially makes photography an object of anthropological study in itself. Banks and Morphy go on to propose that "the focus of visual anthropology includes both the properties of the anthropologist's own representational systems . . . and the properties of those visual systems studied by anthropologists in the field" (21). Anthropologists can potentially contribute much to the debates about media such as photography, the identity of which, despite its 150 years of history and its global reach and ubiquitous presence in our lives, is still very much a source of contention (Batchen 1997).

The photography critics John Tagg (1988) and Victor Burgin (1982) argue that there is no such thing as photography in the sense of a singular medium with a unified or universal identity, only a myriad of discontinuous photographies. Tagg's famous statement that "photography as such has no identity" is founded on the notion that photography's status as a technology is dependent on the power relations that invest it. Photography has no meaning in itself, no nature, but is a "flickering across a field of institutional spaces" in which the meanings of any individual photograph are dependent on the context of its use by state institutions, such as the police, and the medical profession (Tagg 1988, 63). Tagg sees photography as a technology of surveillance. A similar carceral approach has been adopted by recent commentators on anthropological uses of photography, and this view has become the main theme in many critical studies of colonial photography (Alloula 1987; Green 1984; Faris 1992, 1997). The problem with this kind of formal approach is that photographic images are solely seen to reflect, in an uncomplicated way, the concerns and political dispositions of those who made the images, and the complexities of the actual historical circulation and consumption of the images are sometimes ignored.[5] In summarizing current debates about the identity of photography, Geoffrey Batchen (1997) contrasts Tagg with formalist proponents of the medium such as Peter Galassi (1981), for whom photography is the outcome of a long tradition in Western art and has a specific nature of its own. However, both Tagg and Galassi understand photography in relation to wider cultural spheres and practices, only differing as to whether they are of social history or art history.

In taking photography as its object, this book considers the interrelationship between indigenous and Euro-American practices without collapsing one into the other. The book does so to directly question the normative value of Euro-American models of photography and to "provincialize" these through an ethnography of Roviana photographic practices (Chakrabarty 1992). Consequently, the book will reveal certain similarities and differences in photographies in both geographical locations and will tackle questions about photography's identity that are important and productive for how anthropology approaches and uses the medium.

Early ethnographic accounts from the western Solomons, such as Arthur Hocart's fieldwork in Simbo and Roviana in 1908, make intriguing passing references to other visual worlds, suggesting in one instance that Simbo people thought that the soul could be "caught in a camera" (Hocart 1922, part 1). In addition to resonating with popular Victorian ideas about spirit photography—the fixing of phantasms on photographic plates—Hocart's example raises questions about local ideas of photography's mimesis and its ability to capture and reveal a self, and this study will ask what photography makes visible, and what it obscures, for Roviana people.

Siegfried Kracauer has argued that "modern photography has not only considerably enlarged our vision but, in doing so, adjusted it to man's situation in a technological age" (Kracauer 1980, 251). It seems generally accepted that photography has profoundly altered our perception of, and relation to, the world. Kracauer goes on to suggest that photography has been responsible for "the dissolution of traditional perspectives" and a revolution in perception that brings "our vision, so to speak, up to date" (252). Michel Serres has talked of how the camera has influenced modes of perception, forms of cognition, and systems of knowledge, in effect transforming the basic means through which we encounter the world. Photography is frequently seen as a key element of modernity, and this has influenced arguments around the effects of introducing camera technologies into other cultures (Serres 1982; see also Faris 1992, 1993; Ginsburg 1994; Michaels 1991, 1994).

In terms of the impact of new visual media on Solomon Islanders, Geoffrey White has studied the role of VHS tapes, noting that intermittent screenings of Hollywood and Hong Kong action films are a feature of life on Santa Isabel Island, particularly for teenagers (White 1991b). Although he is discussing the situation in 1988, White suggests that an interest in "Western images" had already led to the development of new forms of Solomon Islands dance and music using "Western forms." James Weiner's polemic on "televisualist anthropology" raises important issues for the situation discussed by White, and for any consideration of vernacular photographic practices in Roviana (Weiner 1997). Aside from the new imagery involved, do Western forms such as video and photography bring with them their own metaphysic? Talking in particular about indigenous media, Weiner proposes that visual representation has to be considered in relation to "the particular metaphysic that is reposited in our image-producing technologies, a metaphysic that is just as much a part of our culture and the social relations through which we live it and just as accurately descriptive of it as the djukurba, or 'Law' or 'Dreaming[,]' is a theory of Walbiri culture" (Weiner 1997, 198). Since it entails the adoption of a foreign metaphysic, Weiner sees the introduction of visual media such as video into other cultural contexts as effecting "the replacement of genuine historical, linguistic, social, and cultural difference with an ersatz difference among electronic images" (Weiner 1997, 208). For Weiner one negative effect of the introduction and adoption of new media is a transformation of the self. Within the visual economy of Roviana, photography potentially represents new opportunities and experiences of self-imaging, as well as a new way of seeing the world. But, although photography is an externally introduced technology, the extent to which it is new or represents a revolution in vision needs to be demonstrated rather than assumed. As Pinney has shown, photography is not new in India: "Partly because of [a] semiotic and lexical slippage, the 'photo' is not clearly marked as 'modern' because its functions are duplicated by so many other forms of palpably ancient representation" (Pinney 1997, 112).

In addition to potentially modernizing our vision, photography has altered our sense of the past, and in looking at photography in Roviana, I will consider its entanglement with perceptions of past and present. For Alan Trachtenberg the utility of photographs to history lies not just in what they show but in how they construct their meanings: "The historical value of photographs includes depiction but goes beyond it" (Trachtenberg 1989a, xiv). It is the way that photographs allow different kinds of histories to surface and articulate the relationship between past and present, memory and history that makes them so useful, as the photograph that Somerville took demonstrates. As Edwards suggests, the realism in which our historical hopes for photography are invested is surpassed when they are absorbed into alternative histories (Edwards 2001). Andrew Lattas has discussed the way in which memory becomes problematized within the context and aftermath of the colonial encounter; memory becomes subject to various rewritings and becomes an object of contention (Lattas 1996a, 262). He stresses the importance of "mnemonic regimes" — the ways in which memory is organized — in the Pacific, and he is concerned with "the techniques, practices and contexts within which memory and forgetting emerge as forces for mediating and constituting present existence" (257). This anthropological approach argues that in order for a people to control how they define themselves in the present, it is necessary for them to control how they define their past. Memory is mediated by the structures through which communities apprehend and render time and history significant, and in the Euro-American experience, photography is a central mediating structure. This book will ask how the relation between photography and memory is figured in Roviana and will suggest ways that it is connected to preexisting Roviana processes of memorialization.

During the time I spent in Roviana between 1998 and 2001, there was increasing emphasis on the use of computers; there were several people, mostly expatriates, with Internet access, and the kastom school with which I worked had one computer, although it only functioned intermittently and had no Internet access. There were some strange anomalies that accompanied this process of mediatization — stories of schools provided with a single computer through foreign aid, but with no Internet access and no books. But the proliferation of digital media that is such a powerful and all-consuming feature of contemporary Euro-American experience was, at that point, having relatively little impact on Roviana people, and certainly very little impact outside the capital, Honiara. No Roviana person had a digital still camera and no one had a mobile phone; one local guesthouse catering mainly to expatriates had a computer with Internet access. On the occasions when films were played, they were still in the form of VHS tapes and shown on television sets powered by diesel generators. The relatively small-scale impact of digital media was partly due to the political and public-order problems that were a feature of the Solomon Islands at that point — problems that led to a sharp decline in interest from external media providers such as Australian and Southeast Asian telecom conglomerates. But the limited impact was also due to a lack of infrastructure. Digital images were largely inaccessible to local people because of an absence of a physical support or substrate for the images — no phones or computers to view them on, and no printers to produce hard copies of photographs. In contrast, the copies of archival photographs that I took to Roviana with me, along with the few photographs in people's possession, had a reassuring sense of physicality; they could be passed from hand-to-hand and held lovingly. This will no doubt change and digital media will perhaps become more widespread, a process that highlights the need for ethnographic studies of mediatization in cross-cultural contexts.

During my time in Roviana, I used the archival copy prints of photographs that I took with me to talk to people in a wide variety of contexts, as individuals and as groups of women, men, and teenagers in both formal and informal contexts. Often groups would form that replicated wider social structures; teenage boys would look at the photographs among themselves (figure P.4), or elderly women would sit on mats in the shade (figure P.5). The photographs circulated through a wide range of different encounters, from excited and confusing groups to individual moments of quiet reflection. My aim in taking these photographs to Roviana was not to fill in the historical blanks or uncover the history behind the photographs to give them a more complete caption. I wanted to explore their opening up into a whole range of

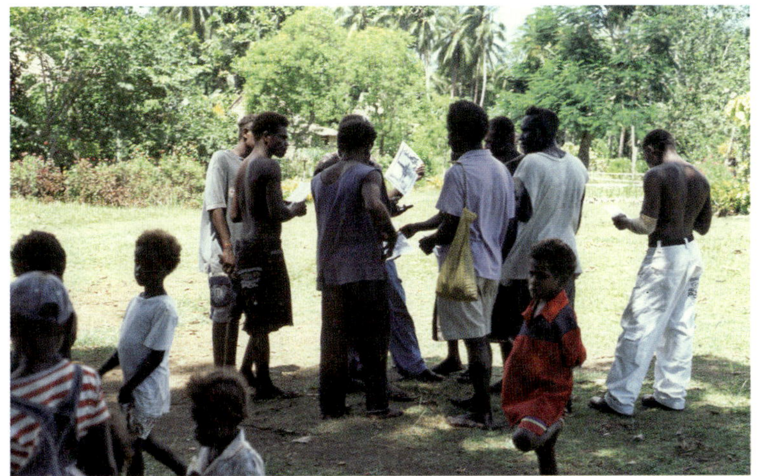

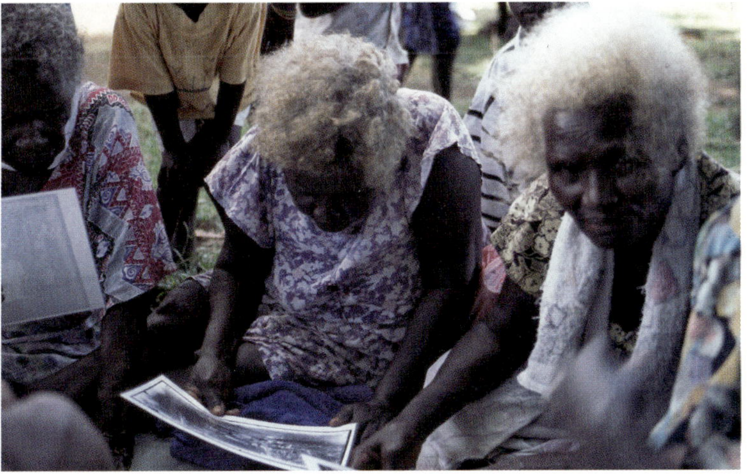

FIGURE P.4 Teenagers looking at photographs, Vona Vona Lagoon.

FIGURE P.5 Older women looking at photographs, Vona Vona Lagoon.

uses. Many of these photographs were on the edge of "living memory" and, although the photographs are undoubtedly refigured and reanimated — they acquired a life — through the process of being "returned," they sometimes also revealed what was lost. This book explores this process of reanimation alongside contemporary photographic practices in Roviana and broader ideas of what photography is for Roviana people. The book does so through an ethnography of photography in Roviana that pays close attention to the words of local people, and this book is really a series of extended conversations about photography, and about particular photographs, between myself and Roviana people, alongside and entangled with conversations they had among themselves.

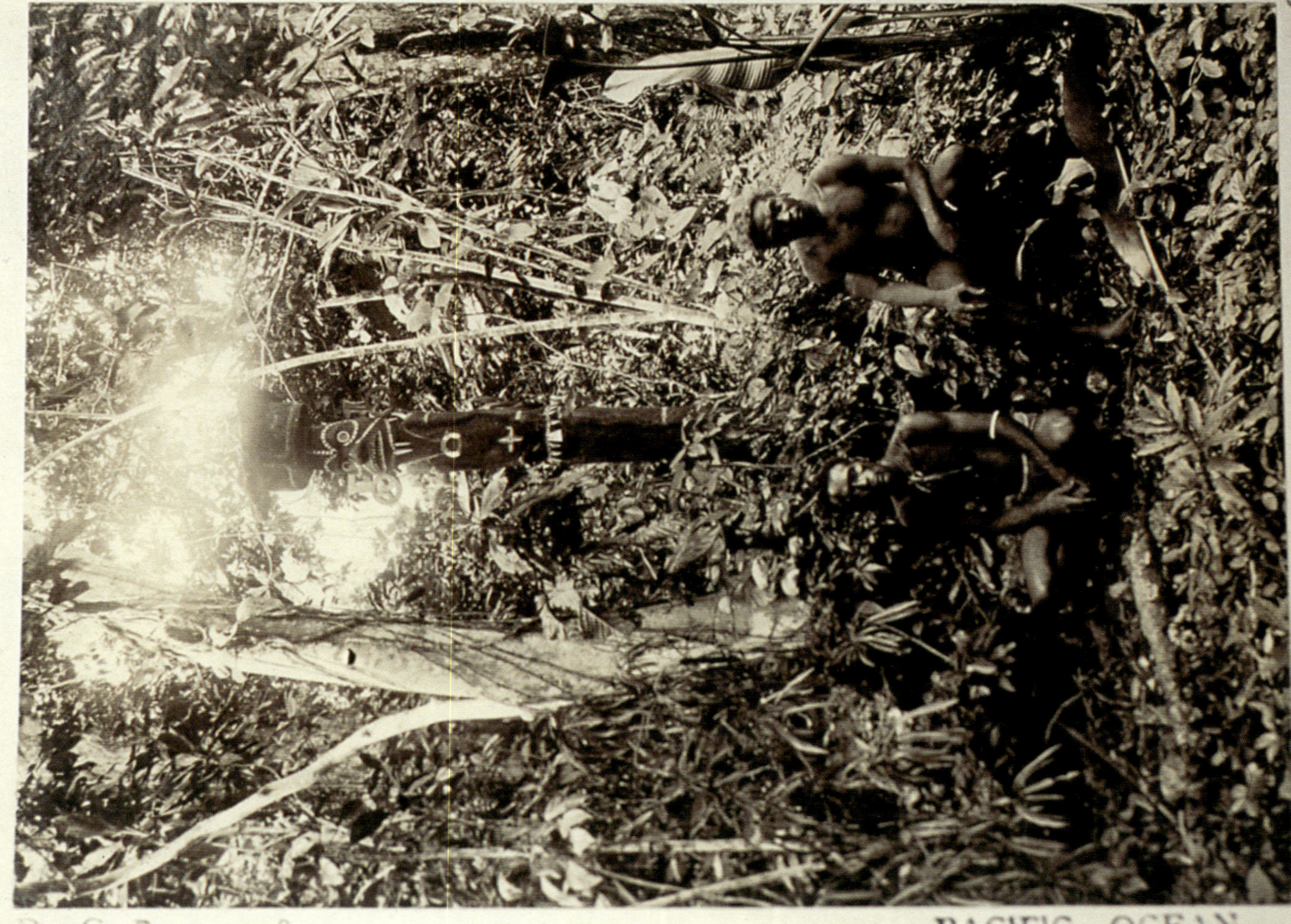

Sacred image in bush, Rubiana, New Georgia Solomon Is.

Phot. Rev. Dr. G. Brown 1899.

PACIFIC OCEAN—

Sacred image in bush, Rubiana, Solomon Islands

6 MAR 1900 LONDON

Tie Vaka— The Men of the Boat

FROM THE BEGINNING OF ANY REGULAR EUROPEAN contact with the people of the western Solomons in the early and mid-1800s, headhunting—an important ritual, social, and economic feature of local cultures—was key to the kinds of imaginings that informed textual and visual representations of Roviana and its people. From the other side, referring to them as *tie vaka*—the men of the boat—Roviana people treated these visitors as potential trading partners, and they were not subject to any particularly strong prohibitions or forms of religious incorporation. Instead they were dealt with in a largely pragmatic way. Perceptions among members of both groups were heavily influenced by specific instances of contact, which were relatively sporadic, and for Europeans the encounter with headhunting was a powerful and enduring factor in how Roviana people were seen. Following a visit to Simbo Island in the western Solomons in 1844, the European trader Andrew Cheyne wrote this account: "[I] visited the Head-chief's village this afternoon on the low island, and on landing the first thing that met my view, was the wall plates of a large canoe house strung with human heads, of both sexes, and apparently of all ages. Many of them appeared to have been recently killed, and the marks of the toma-hawk were seen in all" (quoted in Shineberg 1971, 303–4).

Cheyne was undoubtedly playing to the European abhorrence of headhunting, and it is unlikely that he could have discerned the gender of victim's skulls or that any skull displayed was "recent"—all skulls were ritually prepared prior to display. But his account does demonstrate the emotive language used to describe headhunting—language that defined colonial visions of a perceived Roviana savagery. However, despite featuring so largely in written accounts of all kinds, from logbook entries to published volumes, headhunting features in few actual photographs. There were of course many problems associated with obtaining any such images, especially the available technology and the impossibility of taking photographs in the dark interiors of canoe houses (*paele*) where skulls were ritually displayed.[1] But, importantly, it was also necessary for the Europeans to negotiate any access to evidence of headhunting with Roviana people themselves. In the absence of direct evidence, photographs of Roviana warriors holding spears or axes and wicker shields, or of the large canoes (*tomoko*) used in headhunting raids (but also for trading expeditions), often operated as visual stand-ins for headhunting.

The only photograph of skulls taken during a headhunting raid that I have come across in my research is by Charles Woodford (figure 1.1). Woodford became the first Resident Commissioner of the British Solomon Islands protectorate in 1896, but in early October of 1886, he was visiting Roviana Lagoon as a naturalist and geographer and stayed for two weeks to collect specimens of fauna for the Natural History Museum in London. As well as taking his own photographs, Woodford collected those of others, and his collection "was certainly the best ever obtained in the islands," according to Henry Brougham Guppy, who was commenting on Woodford's lecture to the Royal Geographical Society on March 26, 1888 (quoted in Woodford 1888, 376). However, to date I have been unable to locate any trace of the collection. In the accounts he published two years after his visit to Roviana in the *Proceedings of the Royal Geographical Society*, Woodford notes that Roviana people "are the most notorious head-hunters and cannibals," and that during his stay he visited a small island in the lagoon, Hombuhombu, that, although occupied by a European trader, "belongs to the natives of Sisieta; they will not sell it, as they use it for their cannibal feasts. I was told that six bodies were eaten here a fortnight before my visit" (1888,

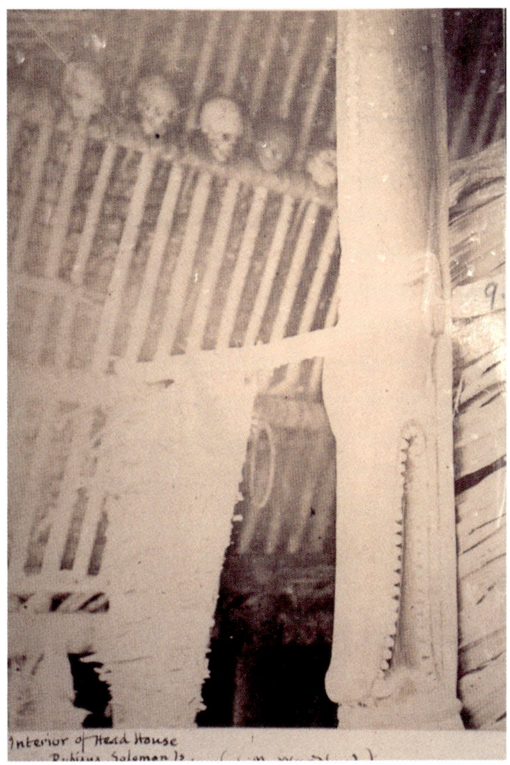

FIGURE 1.1 Skulls inside a canoe house (*paele*), Nusa Roviana. Photograph by C. Woodford, 1886. Courtesy of Solomon Islands National Museum, Honiara. Another print of this image exists in the photographic collections of the British Museum. Cabinet Card OC/B34/23

360). Woodford proceeded to the island of Nusa Roviana, where he found that most of the men were away on a headhunting raid to Santa Isabel. He then "photographed the interior of a tambu house, the post of which was carved to represent a crocodile. Along the rafters was a row of heads. [He] also took a photograph of a collection of sacred images, near to which was a heap of skulls, upon every one of which [he] noticed the mark of the tomahawk" (360). Woodford also wrote of visiting Inqava's paele in Sisiata: "The house contains two large canoes and several smaller canoes. In racks above my head are stowed away all sorts of gear; fishing nets . . . are suspended by wooden hooks from the roof. Bones of fish, pigs' jawbones, and turtles' heads are hung along the rafter of one side, and from the other a row of eight human heads look down upon me" (Woodford 1890b, 152).

During the remainder of his two weeks in the lagoon, Woodford reports that he saw an additional eight heads in another canoe house, and thirteen in yet another. And, when the Nusa Roviana men returned from Santa Isabel, they brought with them the heads of three men and two women. Woodford recounts, "during the fortnight that I spent in the lagoon I heard of no less than thirty-one heads being brought home" (152). Woodford also comments on the cannibalism associated with headhunting: "Not only will the New Georgian natives eat the bodies of those killed in battle, or prisoners, they will exhume the bodies of those recently buried for their disgusting purpose." He goes on to say that cannibalism was "a matter of constant occurrence" and headhunting was "a perfect passion" (1888, 374). Although, as Woodford points out, various punitive raids had been carried out against Roviana villages by British gunships in an attempt to suppress the headhunting, and several white men had recently been murdered on the island of Rendova; heads were required by a local prominent *banara* (chief) for the launching of a new canoe. Woodford was so concerned about the level of headhunting that he wrote to Sir John Bates Thurston, the British High Commissioner for the Western Pacific, on the matter. Returning to Roviana in March 1887, Woodford stayed with two local banara, Inqava and Wonge, and he reported that six heads had recently been brought back from Bogotu on Santa Isabel Island, one of which was the head of a native teacher from the Melanesian Mission located there (Woodford 1888, 361).

William Arens has famously argued that the "myth" of cannibalism was a device that justified racism and imperialism and was a means of establishing difference, and Peter Hulme has suggested that the figure of the cannibal served as an Other for the modern subject as well as a legitimating trope for cultural appropriation (Arens 1979; Hulme 1986). The cannibal is the inverse of the European subject, but the cannibal also represents the dangers of reverting to a state of barbarism. Bronwen Douglas discusses French reactions to an eighteenth-century Kanak reenactment of cannibalism: "We cannot know whether the French reactions were those intended by the Kanak protagonists—textual inscription was certainly not one of them—but I am convinced the performance was consciously intimidatory and contestatory, a deliberate and successful psychological assault to exploit the evident horror of cannibalism previously expressed by these strangers" (1999, 81). The Kanak tease the French colonialists, feeling their arms and legs as a way of threatening a more powerful enemy and asserting their own agency and sense of humor. Douglas suggests that "merely to condemn colonial texts and deplore their tropes as repulsive is to re-empower them and endorse the continued, if now largely negative, discursive hegemony of colonialism" (92). In considering colonial visions of Roviana headhunting, we must remain aware of the possibilities of local concerns and local performances — notoriety might have been something that local Roviana polities actively aspired to.

So although, from one perspective, Woodford's photograph of skulls displayed in the interior of a canoe house on Nusa Roviana provides an illuminating illustration of so-called Roviana savagery, the canoe house is also a Roviana space of display. The skulls are lined up in the rafters for visitors to view, and they demonstrate the efficacy of the local banara. Woodford complains that although the banara allowed him to photograph this display of skulls, they did not allow him to photograph any of the "sacred images" on or near shrines (1888, 360).

Showing Woodford's photograph to Roviana people in 2000 and 2001 provoked a range of ambivalent reactions. Although the feats of headhunting ancestors belong to the *taem bifo* (time before) — they are a feature of the "darkness" of Roviana life before the arrival of Methodist missionaries in 1902 — there was also a sense of pride in the fact that their ancestors and banara were "strong" and had *mana* (efficacy). Woodford's photograph was intended to reveal the savagery of headhunting, but for Roviana people, the display of enemy skulls demonstrated the power and efficacy of their banara. At the time the photograph was taken, Woodford's horror may have been seen as a positive outcome of the encounter, and in 2000 it evoked a range of emotional responses, from pride to apprehension to amusement.

Woodford's photograph was evidence of headhunting, and although he did not include the image in his book *A Naturalist among the Headhunters*, published in 1890, it was an object destined for the collection or the archive. Given that the publication and circulation of accounts and representations of Roviana headhunting were also intended to legitimate increasing British juridical and administrative interest in the area, it seems strange that Woodford's photograph was not published widely. Engravings based on some of his photographs, including one of the exterior of a Roviana paele, appeared in the *Illustrated London News* on February 23, 1889, where they were printed to look like actual photographic prints that you could hold in your hands. Woodford was a naturalist and geographer who amassed large collections of Solomon Islands flora and fauna—more than seventeen thousand specimens—which are now housed in the Natural History Museum in London. He preserved the specimens collected in Roviana by placing the dead bodies of mammals and reptiles in glass jars of formaldehyde and pinning the bodies of butterflies, moths, and insects to boards—a different, yet strangely related, display of efficacy to that involved in headhunting.

In 1907, the nineteenth-century explorer and travel writer Ernest Way Elkington accounted for the savage practices of headhunting and cannibalism as a kind of "religious mania," and he compared Roviana people to the "prophets and priests of old" who believed in sacrifice (Elkington 1907, 97, 95). He argued that "they do not kill and eat human beings for the sake of their taste, or because they are hungry, as some writers will insist on having us believe. The cause is farther back than this; in nearly every case when human beings are killed and eaten, it is on occasions when such a sacrifice is necessary, according to the natives' religious beliefs" (95). Although Elkington comments that headhunting is "losing favour, particularly with the younger generation," he makes numerous references to the "duplicitous nature" of Roviana people in relation to this savagery: "When standing before a chief, who is smiling at you and treating you to all the courtesies his nature can conjure up[,] . . . it is difficult to realise that the same chief a week before was on the warpath, concocting the most devilish schemes, and carrying out the most fiendish atrocities on men, women, and children in his pursuit of heads" (97).

Another recurrent theme in late nineteenth- and early twentieth-century accounts of Roviana, both visual and textual, is an attempt to establish a firm connection between people's appearances and their intentions. Roviana people look savage and behave accordingly. But there is also an acknowledgment that appearances can be deceptive. Henry Guppy, who visited the Solomons as a surgeon aboard HMS *Lark* in 1881, writes of a headhunter called Mai from Santa Anna island: "The cunning and ferocity which marked his dealings were sufficiently indicated in his countenance" (1887, 19). The revelation of interiority through external appearances and characteristics was a common concern shared by a nascent anthropological science and also by popular nineteenth-century movements such as phrenology. The revelation was also one of the central concerns of photography of that period, both in terms of its popular use in portraits and in the service of anthropology. Johann Casper Lavater's science of physiognomy had an enormous impact on nineteenth-century anthropological and photographic desires for legible bodies and faces: "Lavater suggested that individuals' moral beauty could be judged on the basis of external characteristics. . . . Certain structural features of the face were codified in a system which permitted the literal and precise 'reading' of character and disposition from external features. 'The countenance is the theatre on which the soul exhibits itself,' he proclaimed" (Pinney 1997, 51).

Lavater was interested in discerning "national physiognomies," and this was certainly one of the concerns of early photographers in Roviana, but the reading of character from external appearances also informed more popular accounts. Elkington met the banara Inqava during his time in Roviana:

> The most notorious head-hunter in later years was Ingova of Rubiana lagoon. . . . He is old and wizened now, and his hand trembles as he lifts the glass of grog he begs from you, after telling a yarn of the good old days. . . .
>
> . . . His feeble limbs, his shaking hand, his bloodshot eyes. . . .
>
> Years ago Ingova's Euro [possibly a canoe house] was hung with skulls, hundreds of them strung in the cross-beams with staring, vacant eyeholes, which looked out of nothing and yet seemed to see everything. Their drooping lower jaws, showing sets of white teeth which glistened in the rays of the moon. (Elkington 1907, 98)

This visually descriptive passage contains many elements of European fantasies of headhunting, and here external appearances also form a narrative of historical change. The "dark" past is required to remain visible, a necessary counterpoint to the present. Elkington also points out the disastrous effects of alcohol on native populations, and his description of Inqava as old and malaria-ridden is intended to contrast with his, by then firmly established, reputation as the king of Roviana.

The photograph of Inqava (figure 1.2) standing next to his wife is one of several of Inqava taken by the Methodist missionary Reverend George Brown on a visit to Roviana in 1899, which he took with an intent to establish a mission there. Brown met the European trader Frank Wickham as well as Inqava, and Brown reported a visit to Rendova where he was told stories of cannibalism and headhunting. The photograph of Inqava does show an old man by Roviana standards, but according to Brown, the violence of the recent past is lurking just below the surface: "Mr. H. Cayley-Webster, writing of his visit to the Rubiana Lagoon as late as 1898, says; 'These natives are not only head-hunters and cannibals, but they make no secret of it. They are the most treacherous of all the people in the Southern Seas, and when apparently on the most friendly terms, are only awaiting a favourable opportunity to catch the stranger unawares, and to add one more head to their already huge collection.' These wild people are absolutely untouched by any Christian agency" (*Australian Methodist Missionary Review*, December 4, 1901, 4).

Both the missionaries and the colonial government in waiting had a stake in establishing a belief in Roviana savagery. When Sir John Bates Thurston visited Roviana as part of a tour of the Solomon Islands in 1894, just after the declaration of the islands as a British Protectorate, it was in his role as Commissioner of the Western Pacific, and he was there to preside over a court case brought by Inqava against a European trader named Edmund Peter Pratt over a land claim (Scarr 1967). This was a test case for the newly established jurisdiction of the Protectorate. Thurston was a keen amateur photographer who took many photographs of Fiji, and he also brought his camera to Roviana. One of the photographs he took during his stay (figure 1.3) depicts two lines of Roviana people arranged for the camera in a style that is typical of nineteenth-century colonial encounters with native populations. The taking of the photograph is itself an enactment of colonial power, and the imposition of order seems to suggest an imperial gaze. It is an official document and, like the written proceedings of the court, it is a record destined for the archive. But other photographs taken by Thurston at the same time complicate this gaze.

The Roviana tomoko was a type of prestigious large canoe that was used for long-distance trading as well as headhunting, and it was a symbol of chiefly power and mana. Tomoko are ubiquitous in photographic images of Roviana in the late nineteenth and early twentieth centuries; they were visually emblematic of headhunting and were a visual synonym for the "despicable practice" in the same way that carved wooden "cannibal forks" were for cannibalism in Fiji (Thomas 1991, 165–67). However, the photograph of Inqava sitting at the stern of a large tomoko (figure 1.4) is, at the moment of its inscription at least, concerned with a display of Roviana power

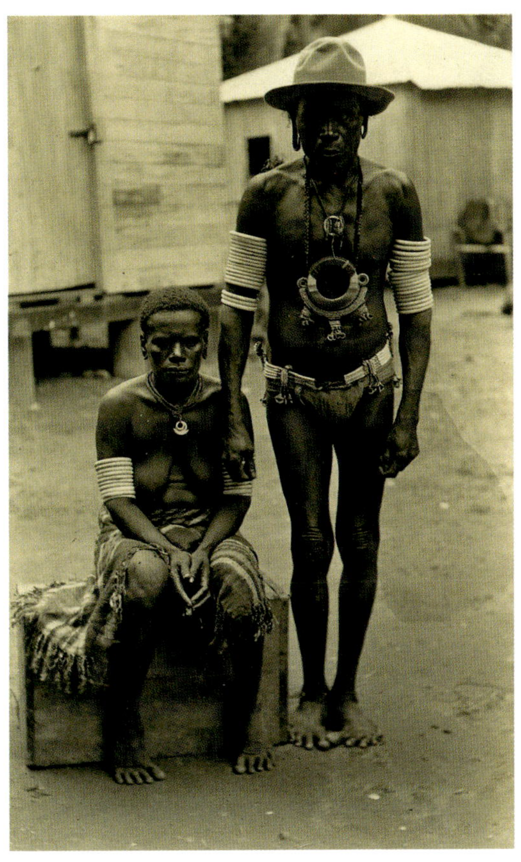

FIGURE 1.2 Inqava and his wife. Photograph by Reverend George Brown,
1899. Courtesy of Rautenstrauch Joest
Museum, Cologne. 9713_600

FIGURE 1.3 Roviana men and boys.
Photograph by Sir John Bates
Thurston, 1894. Courtesy of Royal
Geographical Society, London. B7952

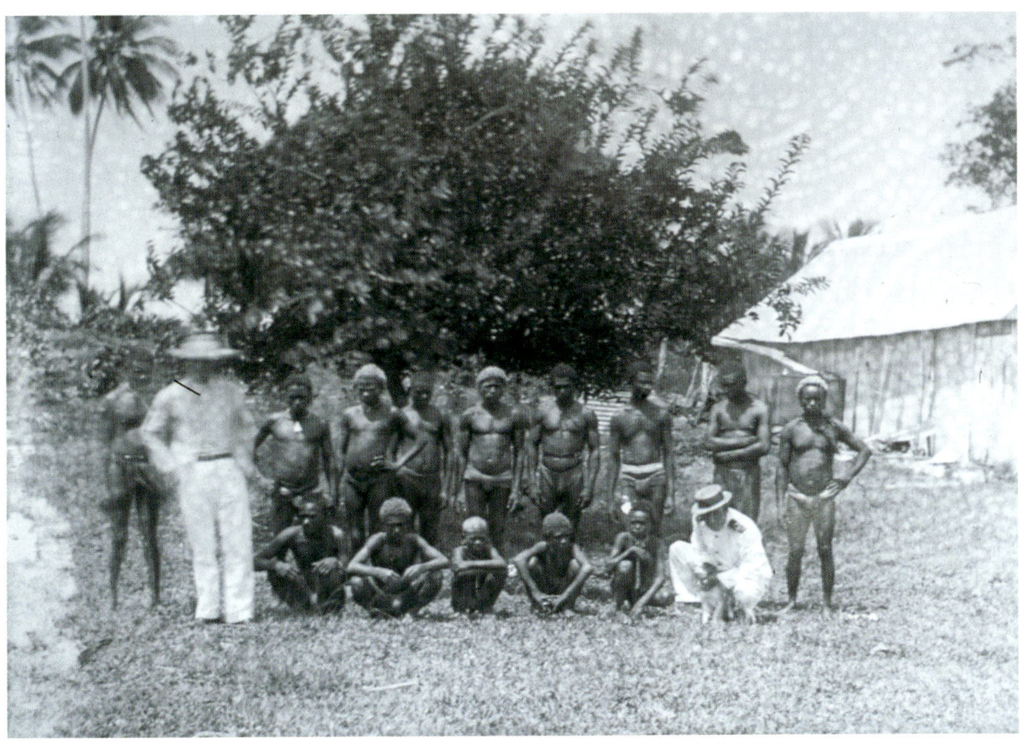

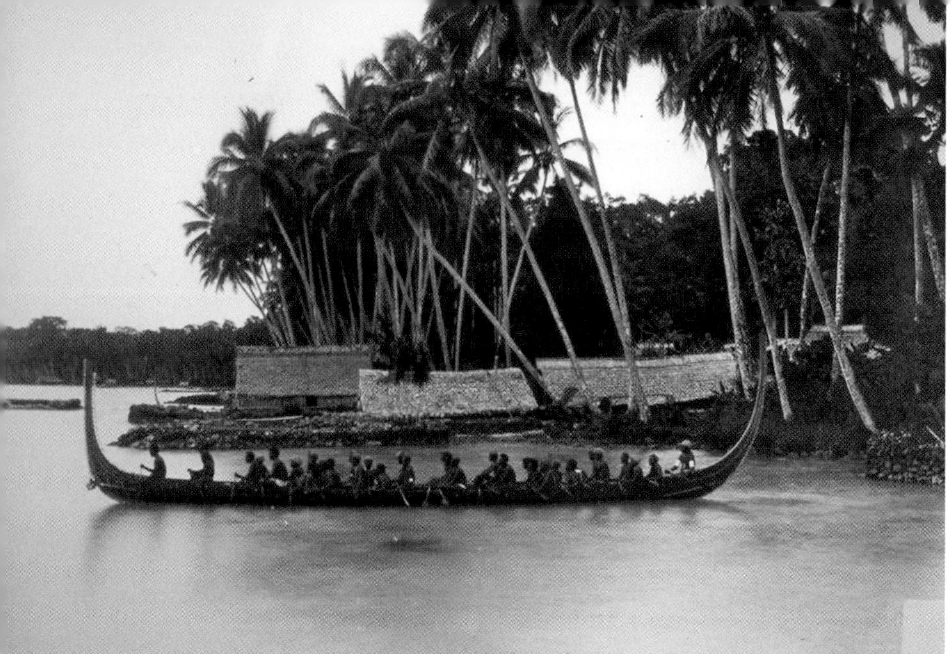

and efficacy. While this photograph may in one context represent the savagery of Roviana headhunters, in another it is concerned with Inqava's power; the size and decoration of the canoe function as visual representations of his authority and his mana. Photographs like this one, alongside Inqava's skills at dealing with the British, may well have contributed to the view of him as the king of Roviana.

Inqava demonstrated his ability to use the British administration to his own advantage when he initiated and won the court case against Pratt a mere two months after HMS *Curacao* visited Roviana in 1893 to declare the protectorate and hoist the British flag on Nusa Zonga Island, just off Munda.[2] Despite the fact that Pratt had tricked local banara into signing a deed of purchase for some land to the west of Munda, the British authorities chose to rely on Inqava's oral testimony and reputation as a "friend" and as the "king of Rubiana." Inqava's victory over a white trader certainly added significantly to his local status as a strong banara.[3]

Although the Roviana people that visiting Europeans encountered in the late 1890s were nominally "pacified" in the period following the declaration of the Solomon Islands as a British protectorate in 1893, local networks of trade and raiding continued, although in a much reduced form, well into the first decades of the twentieth century. Roviana people had been, and remained, very much concerned with maintaining a reputation for being strong (*ninira*). The possibilities for any localized acts of negotiation and resistance over representations need to be considered in this light. From popular travel accounts and newspaper articles about "heathen practices" to official reports and scientific investigations, images of Roviana both contributed to and were formed by contemporary ideas of South Seas savagery. But, as Nicholas Thomas argues, "what is true of the representation that reached a public in New Zealand, Australia and Europe is not true of the colonial encounter from which it derived" (Thomas 1994, 37).

The anthropologist Robert Ward Williamson visited Roviana, and also Kolombangara Island, in May 1910 and published an account of his visit in a book, *The Ways of the South Sea Savage*, in 1914 (Williamson 1914). Lacking the concentrated focus of his later work on the Mafulu of British New Guinea (Williamson 1912), Williamson's book resembles popular travel accounts in its mixture of amusing anecdotes and detailed ethnographic information about customs such as taboo markers. Williamson was a member of the council of the Anthropological Institute in London. He writes, "These Rubiana people are still extremely primitive, but little changed from what they were, undoubted cannibals, and most interesting to the traveller" (1914, 18). Williamson viewed the "Rubiana" natives as sly: "In countenance they are generally sinister, and they often have an underhand, treacherous expression, which does not tend to increase one's faith in them; this indeed is well in accord with their character, for a Solomon Islander will rarely meet an antagonist face to face in open hostility, if he can get a chance of secretly stealing up to him and striking him down from behind" (22).

While he was visiting the British administrative station at Gizo, Williamson met and befriended Norman Wheatley, a British-born trader who had been established in Roviana since 1892. Williamson notes that Wheatley was "a person of great power and influence in his district" (1914, 19). He continues: "Acting on the advice of Mr. Wheatley, I was always . . . careful not to walk or stand with a native immediately behind me" (70). Popular accounts of attacks on Europeans regularly featured stories of the axes that had just been exchanged in trade being used to cut down unsuspecting ship crews. Williamson could only communicate with people by signs and gestures, and was helped by Pana, a Roviana man employed by Wheatley, who spoke good Pijin English. Williamson's photographs, such as the one reproduced as figure 1.5, are informed by

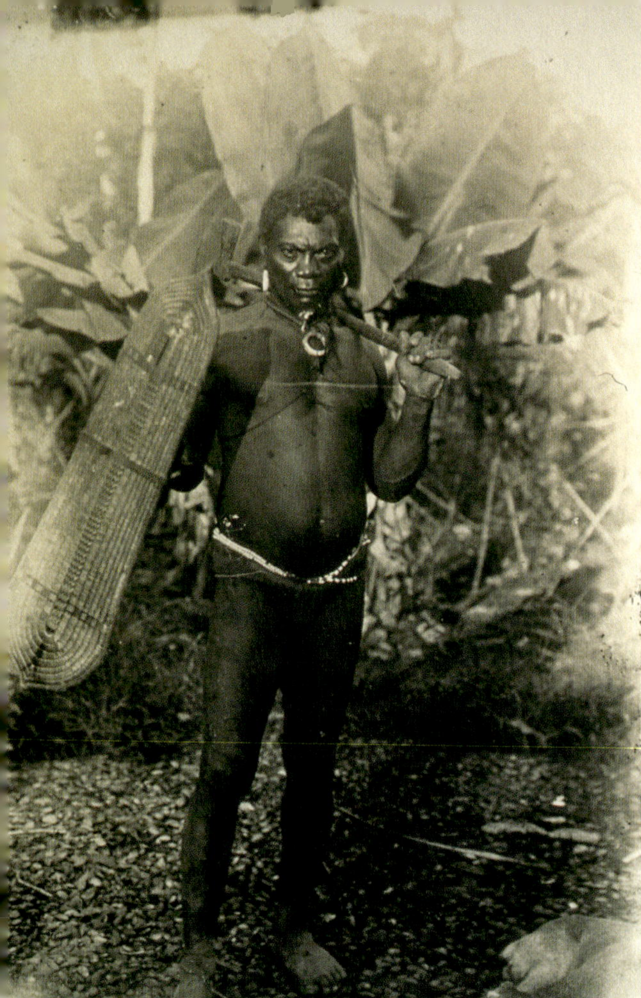

FIGURE 1.5 Roviana man. Photograph by Robert Ward Williamson, 1910. Courtesy of Royal Anthropological Institute, London. 11434

assumptions about the moral character of Roviana people and that character's relation to their external appearance, and for Williamson the encounters that took place on beaches along Roviana Lagoon were with an "authentic savagery" (19).

Williamson's and Elkington's focuses on savagery is symptomatic of many European imaginings of Roviana in the late nineteenth century. Roviana was considered so violent that Elkington identifies only two possible reasons for European interest in the area: "No doubt the extreme danger which has always attached to a visit to these islands has made the white man give them as wide a berth as possible, only going there when compelled to either for trading or scientific purposes. It is here that cannibalism flourishes, and the headhunters go forth on expeditions in all their savage grandeur to strike down the unsuspecting neighbour" (Elkington 1907, 94). The islands of the New Georgia group were seen by European traders, explorers, and colonial officials as rife with headhunting and cannibalism and were, like Fiji, referred to as the "cannibal isles." As Elkington suggests, Roviana Lagoon was viewed as the center of these "unspeakable practices": "The Rubiana natives are perhaps the most bloodthirsty of all the Solomon group, and, being both rich and powerful, they can descend on a village and overpower it by sheer force of numbers, even without the use of modern weapons, which are now owned by nearly all the important tribes" (1907, 97–98).

Although we are dealing with a series of European perceptions and imaginings, the ferocity of Roviana headhunters may well have been an image that to some extent they themselves promoted. Roviana people had a vested interest in appearing rich and powerful to other local polities and to Europeans. Gannenath Obeyesekere argues that cannibalism was "not only a discourse on the Other, but also constituted a complicated series of discourses between native populations and European interlocutors" (1998, 63). Cannibalism was frequently a "weapon of the weak" to dissuade European intrusion or to secure trading advantage over other "more savage" neighbors. Victims' skulls were displayed in canoe houses (paele), and also in men's ritual houses (*zelepade*) (Aswani 1998, 31), where they were intended as visual evidence of mana. Shankar Aswani has argued that "success in war made chiefs and warriors very powerful because the capture of more victims manifested the ancestral power of their fighting spirits and magic" (1998, 31). There was a desire to make ancestral power visible, and skulls, along with a range of shell valuables (*bakiha*) worn on the body, would have been proudly displayed (figure 1.6).

Consequently, a reputation as bloodthirsty or savage may in some instances have been actively pursued by Roviana people in their relations with Europeans. There is no evidence to suggest that Europeans were treated by Roviana people as anything other than an alternative "side"—another economically and politically motivated kinship-based group. Europeans were perceived as belonging to one side—hence the practice of exacting revenge on any available white man—and they were not perceived as a separate class of being (see Dureau 2001). Because they saw Europeans as potential trading or raiding partners, Roviana people might have sought to entangle Europeans in local economies of political prestige through visual displays of power and efficacy, and this might have included

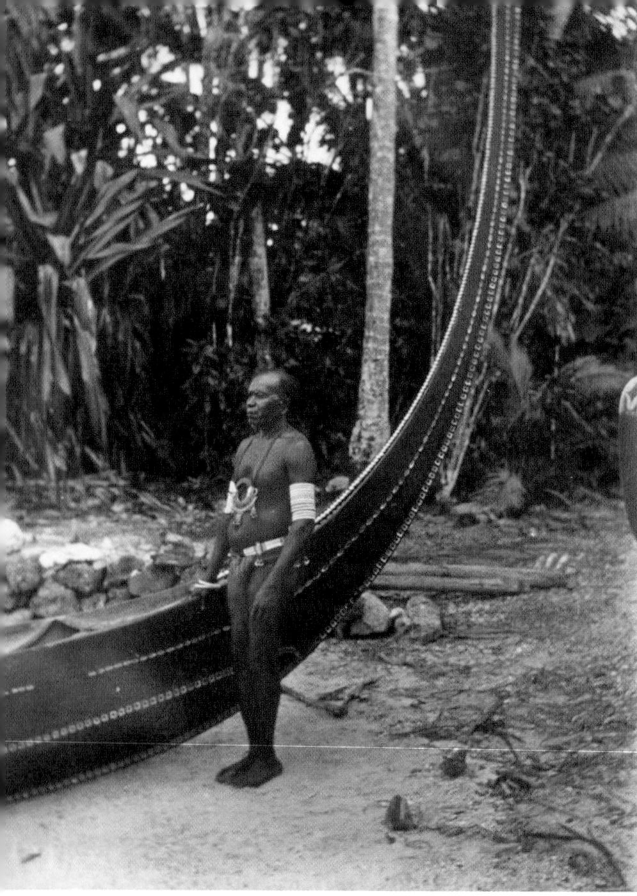

FIGURE 1.6 Inqava standing near the stern of the large canoe (*tomoko*) (shown in figure 1.4). Photograph by Sir John Bates Thurston, 1894. Courtesy of Royal Geographical Society, London. B7971

accounts of headhunting. Although this is a matter of conjecture, and the opposite was also the case—the alleged bloodthirstiness of others could be alluded to in order to warn Europeans away from them—what must be kept in mind is that it is not simply a matter of Europeans imposing their own fantasies, their colonial vision, on docile populations. In the early nineteenth century, a Simbo banara, Lobi, convinced the bêche-de-mer trader Cheyne that, although Simbo people were also headhunters and that evidence of this was seen by Cheyne, it was the people of Roviana who were truly treacherous (Bennett 1986, 27). Stories of the massacre of ship crews by Roviana people persuaded whalers to avoid the area for some years and allowed Simbo people to retain control of lucrative trade and effectively act as intermediaries for the rest of New Georgia. In a culture of prestige where appearing strong was important, Roviana people might have seen that their reputation was providing them with an advantage in trading with Europeans and not perceived it in negative terms at all. Roviana people managed to dictate many of the terms of trade and retain some of their long-established trading networks until the early part of the twentieth century (Dureau 1998). Such was their lack of influence over trade that Europeans were reduced to trying to imitate local forms of exchange—shell rings called *poata*—by having them mass-produced in porcelain in Germany (see Guppy 1887, 132).

Both headhunting and cannibalism were central to the European colonial vision of Roviana. The region was seen as dangerous and was never part of the "ethnographic pastoral," and was therefore not subjected to the kind of classical or arcadian constructions that other Pacific islands were. It was not considered an idyllic place. Bernard Smith argues that there were two basic tropes developed in representations of the Pacific in the period 1773–84: arcadia and savagery (Smith 1992, 188). The history of European contact with the western Solomon Islands means that there are no representations from the period that Smith is talking about outside the occasional mention in a whaling logbook. However, by the late nineteenth century, representations of Roviana were constructed almost entirely in terms of savagery.

The colonial project in Roviana, as elsewhere in the Solomons, involved the symbolic construction of this savagery: an essentialized native who was bloodthirsty and cunning. But, as Thomas argues, an Orientalist tendency in postcolonial studies has focused on "the will to dominate in imperial culture, science and vision, without investigating the ways in which the apparatuses of colonialism and modernity have been compromised locally" (Thomas 1999, 2–3). It is necessary to take account of the other side of the colonial encounter. European vision and indigenous vision are entangled with each other at certain conjunctures, and at other points they are autonomous. As Thomas suggests, we must remain aware of this "double vision," the possibility of "non-encounters" and moments when European and indigenous imaginings were autonomous and did not engage in dialogue: when others were imagined in a way that remained internal to existing imaginative purposes (Thomas 1999, 5).

Accounts from the logbooks of whalers from the early 1800s reveal that certain known sites in the western Solomons were considered safe places to trade and resupply, and the whalers initiated the trade in tortoiseshell. As the Atlantic whaling grounds gradually became less profitable, activity increased in the Pacific, and the Solomon Islands were on the migratory paths of sperm whales. The whalers also wanted access to local women, sometimes professional prostitutes, and Makira Harbor was known as a place where this could be arranged with the payment of a small gift (Bennett 1986, 29).[4] Although these encounters were infrequent—Judith Bennett notes an average of three visits from whaling ships a year at Makira Harbor for the period 1850–70 (29)—the image of the western Solomons that is constructed in whalers' accounts does have some of the attributes of arcadian fantasy. There were some occasional violent encounters, but for the most part the focus is on the benefits of trade and the abundance and availability of local produce and women. There is an erotic element to these accounts that contrasts with the way in which Melanesia was often "understood as a masculine domain rather than a feminine one[,] . . . characterized by the aggression of warriors, cannibals and headhunters rather than the seductiveness of 'woodland nymphs'" (Thomas 1993, 49). Roviana was never subjected to the kinds of photographic representation that was a feature of the sexualized portrayal of Polynesian women or women from Papua New Guinea (Wright 2003). The relatively late stage at which any visual representations of the people and culture were made or circulated meant that photographers visiting Roviana in the late nineteenth century, although they responded to earlier written accounts, were not producing images in relation to any well-established body of visual representations of the area.[5]

Prior to the mid-nineteenth century, Simbo was the major regional center for the western Solomon Islands (see Jackson 1978). It was here that whalers and ships on their way to Port Jackson in Australia stopped to resupply. The first European trader to visit the western Solomon Islands on a regular basis was Lewis Truscott, having discovered the possibilities of trade when captaining whaling ships in the 1840s. In 1851 he brought back a thousand pounds of tortoiseshell and some sperm oil to Sydney from New Georgia (Bennett 1986, 46). In the latter half of the nineteenth century, coconut oil (required for the manufacture of soap and explosives), and by 1876, copra, began to supplant the earlier trade in tortoiseshell, pearlshell, gold-lip shell, ivory nuts, and bêche-de-mer (used as a commodity in trading for tea in China) (Bennett 1986, 47). This was accompanied by a gradual shift in emphasis from Simbo to Roviana as the central focus of Euro-American commercial interests. But, although Roviana was on vectors of trade, it did not attract anything like the significant colonial presence that Fiji did. The numbers of Europeans permanently living in Roviana, and the western Solomon Islands as a whole, remained small, limited to a few traders. After 1893 there were occasional visits by British officials, and only after 1902 were there a handful of Methodist missionaries and South Seas pastors (mostly from Fiji) associated with the mission. The first reports of an expatriate trader permanently settled in Roviana refer to a Jack Brookfield in 1870, and it was 1880 before a second trader, Frank Wickham, also settled there (Bennett 1986, appendix 5). Despite belated attempts to encourage settlers from Australia, and further economic development in the 1920s (Quanchi 1997), the western Solomon Islands and Roviana never had a large expatriate population. The Solomon Islands were not declared a British protectorate until 1893, and up until that point British colonial interest in the western Solomons was largely limited to responding to the alleged outrages committed against expatriate traders, along with the occasional visit by an explorer or scientist.

By 1903 the Australian company Burns Philp was producing leaflets advertising tours of the islands aboard commercial vessels that stopped briefly at "Rubiana Lagoon" (Burns Philp 1903), but the number of visiting tourists was equally small. With no significant expatriate community to cater to, either resident or visiting, there was no call for commercial photographic studios of European origin to be set up in the Solomon Islands. This sharply contrasts with the situation in Fiji and other Pacific islands with a longer history of contact with Europeans and where there was a large expatriate community and a thriving tourist business. Brigitte d'Ozouville reports that the English photographer Francis Herbert Dufty maintained a studio in Fiji from 1871 to 1892 (d'Ozouville 1997, 34; see also Quanchi 1997). Alison Nordström notes that there were three resident photographers at work in Samoa's largest town, Apia, by 1890 (Nordström 1991, 272). Even though at least one member of the late nineteenth-century expatriate community in the western Solomon Islands was an amateur photographer, there were no commercially run photographic studios, and it was the mid-1950s before Chinese traders in the islands began to offer a postal service so that undeveloped film could be sent to Australia and prints sent back. Sometime shortly after 1902 the Methodist mission in Roviana set up a rudimentary darkroom at its headquarters in Kokeqolo, to the west of Munda, and produced prints for fundraising purposes back in New Zealand and Australia. They also gave prints to select local people, mainly those they wanted to impress, such as local banara or those directly involved in the mission's work. But the lack of any commercial studios in the late nineteenth century means that one of the main genres for photographs of people of the Pacific during this period—studio photographs—simply does not exist in terms of images of Roviana people. There are commercial studio photographs of Solomon Islanders taken by Fiji-based operators, but these are mostly of men from Guadalcanal and Malaita temporarily working in Fiji as indentured laborers on the plantations. They are predominantly rather formal posed images of men holding wooden clubs—sometimes from elsewhere in the Pacific and probably studio props—against a painted backdrop of "exotic" plants and often wearing Union Jack beadwork belts.[6] There are, however, photographs of Roviana people made in other European spaces, such as the decks of European vessels or the verandas of traders' or missionaries' houses, which function as containing spaces in the same way that studio backdrops did.

There are also relatively few commercial postcards or stereographs of Roviana, the main exceptions being some photographs taken by the Methodist mission that were printed as postcards in New Zealand in the early 1920s and some postcards of western Solomon Islands people acquired from unnamed photographers and printed by Kerry & Co. in Sydney.[7] Images of Roviana were not a significant part of the huge commercial circulation of postcards of the Pacific—by 1903 Kerry was producing more than fifty thousand postcards annually (Nordström 1995, 24)—but those images that did circulate in other formats certainly had a powerful impact on Euro-American perceptions of the people and their culture.

The earliest photographs of the Solomon Islands may have been taken by the Irish artist James Glen Wilson, who signed on as a clerk aboard HMS *Herald* at Chatham, London, on March 5, 1852. The *Herald* was to explore and survey uncharted areas of the Pacific, and its departure attracted much public attention after an article appeared in the *Illustrated London News* on May 15, 1852. This article reports: "[Wilson,] a young artist, has also been appointed to make drawings of objects likely to prove interesting in illustration of these islands, and the manners and customs of the people. . . . By order of the Board of the Admiralty he has been supplied with a photographic apparatus. Up to the present time we have had very few good drawings from this part of the globe that could be depended upon; but now that photography is to be employed, we may expect to have representations of a very superior description."

The *Herald* visited Makira Harbor on the island of Makira in 1854, and then toured the eastern Solomon Islands and other areas of the Pacific, not returning to the United Kingdom until 1861. Although there are two surviving photographs, one of Wilson and one of the captain and officers, no others from the voyage have so far come to light (see Black 1979, 270; the photographs are listed as "Private Collection"). The report from the *Illustrated London News* on Wilson's endeavor reveals that photography held out the promise of a "superior description," and this faith in its indexical qualities was the reason behind it being rapidly adopted as a surveying instrument. However, the numbers of visitors to the western Solomon Islands, with or without cameras, remained small until the last decades of the nineteenth century. The photographic record reflects this. As relatively late as 1881, Fred Fairfax, a special reporter for the Sydney *Daily Telegraph*, was still making watercolor illustrations of Roviana people rather than taking photographs.[8]

The intended destination for many of the photographs taken of Roviana in the late nineteenth century was the colonial archive, although sometimes this remained an organizing principle and a source of motivation rather than resulting in the actual formation of a physical archive (Richards 1993). Elkington identified science as one of two possible reasons for Europeans to visit an area perceived as dangerous, and Roviana was subjected to a variety of small-scale surveys. The earliest was carried out by Guppy in 1881.

Guppy was a surgeon aboard HMS *Lark*, which was conducting a hydrographic survey for the Royal Navy in the western Solomon Islands, but he was also an amateur anthropologist and a Fellow of the Royal Geographical Society in London, so he carried out his own research while he was in the islands. It is not clear whether Guppy visited Roviana, although he makes many comments about the people and culture, but he did conduct anthropometric surveys of people on Makira, Santa Anna, Treasury Island, the Shortland Islands, and Choiseul and also smaller surveys on Malaita and Simbo. He measured cephalic indexes (head circumference), stature, weight, skin color, and hair color and read a paper on the physical characteristics of Solomon Islanders to the Anthropological Institute (later to become the Royal Anthropological Institute) in

July 1885 (Guppy 1887, 98). Referring to the systematization of skin color devised by Paul Broca and published in the Anthropological Institute of London's handbook for amateur anthropologists *Notes and Queries in Anthropology* of 1874, Guppy writes that the skin of a "typical islander" "would be a deep brown, corresponding with number 35 of the colour-types of M. Broca" and that "the prevailing darker hue of the western islands is represented by number 42" (102, 120). He also records four types of hair in his survey: "woolly," "mop-like," "partially bushy," and "completely bushy," including the thickness of the hair and the diameter of the spiral (116). His conclusion was that "it would appear that in this group, the qualities of treachery and ferocity are possessed in a greater degree by those communities in which hairy men prevail" (119). He measured the sight of people using a test developed for recruits in the British army, but found no differences that would support the view that "savages possess superior powers of vision as compared with civilized races" (Guppy 1887, 122). Guppy attempted to grasp hold of Solomon Islanders through a range of measurements and fix them on a physiognomic and evolutionary scale, reinforcing the connections between external appearances and savagery.

The photographs taken by Lieutenant Henry Somerville were made during another scientific survey of the coast of New Georgia in 1893–94 as part of the British Navy's Hydrographic Survey of the South Pacific. Some twenty-five years after his time in the Solomon Islands, Somerville commented that New Georgians were "for the most part complete savages still, and to a certain degree cannibals," but his photographs also reveal a relaxed and often humorous relation with local people (Somerville 1928, 33). In his lecture illustrated with lantern slides in 1928 to the Cork Literary and Scientific Society, "Surveying in the South Seas," Somerville said of a photograph of a New Georgian and a European sailor standing side by side (figure 1.7): "This slide shows you the contrast in physique between an ordinary young Englishman of 20 or so, and a New Georgian of about the same age. The contrast is scarcely a fair one really, for many of the natives were of better build than this specimen" (36).

The invocation of an anthropometric intention, interested in discerning specimens rather than individuals, reveals Somerville's concerns with science, and he took an extensive series of anthropometric measurements of people in Roviana and also Marovo Lagoon. His series of notebooks containing these are housed in the manu-

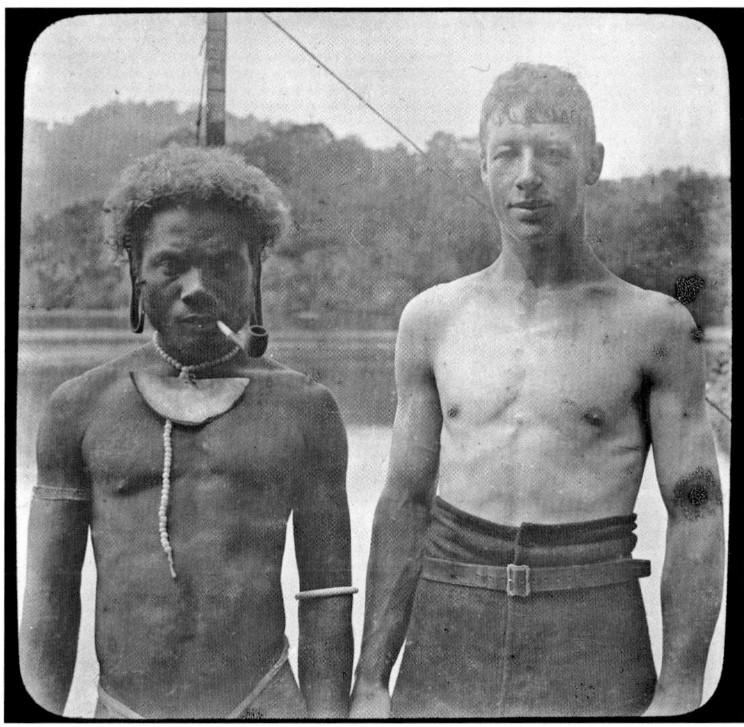

FIGURE 1.7 New Georgian man and European sailor. Photograph by Henry B. Somerville, 1893–94. Courtesy of Royal Anthropological Institute, London. Lantern slide 13563

script collection of the Royal Anthropological Institute in London and, although one notebook mentions the fear induced by the calipers for measuring cephalic indexes, Somerville managed to amass a large number of records despite local reluctance to the process. The notebooks contain hundreds of measurements, painted watercolor swatches to indicate skin color, translated commands, drawings of nose profiles, some small white envelopes of human hair samples, and the odd anthropological note about material culture as well as a series of particularly revealing translated commands (see figures 1.8, 1.9, and 1.10). Perhaps part of local reluctance to engage with these anthropometric measuring processes was their resemblance to Roviana ideas of contagious magic — getting power over others through access to their body parts — in addition to the echo of ideas of headhunting and displays of mana.

Somerville refers to one photograph, that of four smiling Marovo men (figure 1.11) in this way: "Here we have four young bloods of Munggeri, a village near one of our camps, all great friends of ours, four happy young cannibals" (1928, 37). In his lantern slide show of

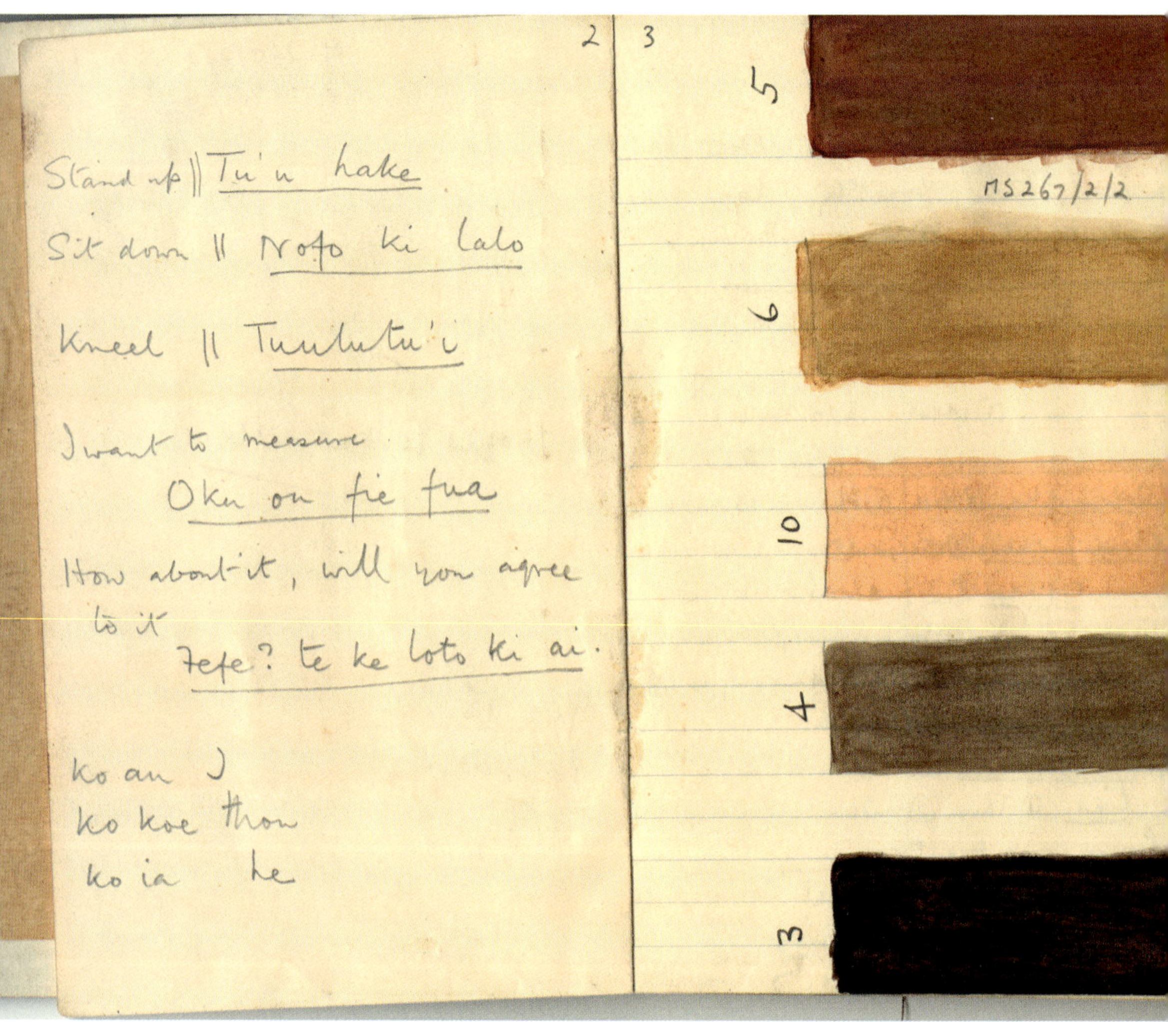

FIGURE 1.8 Watercolor swatches of skin color, from the notebooks of Henry B. Somerville, 1893–94. Courtesy of Royal Anthropological Institute, London. MS 267-2-2(2-3)3

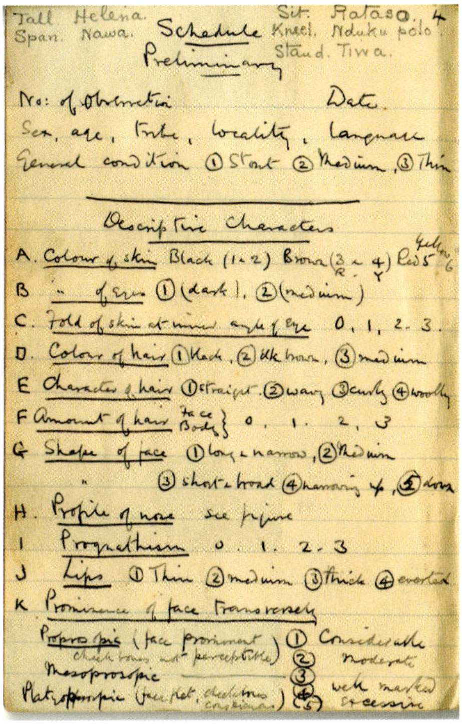

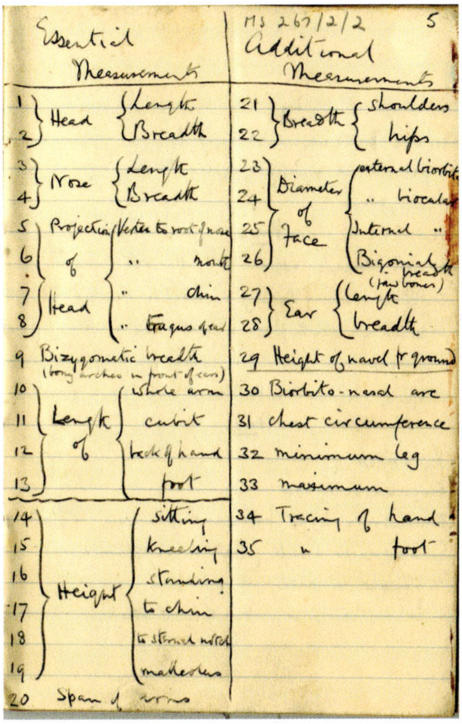

1928, he went on to recount a story of cannibalism involving those portrayed in the photograph. He discusses the fate of a white trader who was killed, after which

> his body was then cut up into small bits, and the bits had been taken round to every village of the lagoon . . . and had then been cooked and ceremoniously eaten by every young man in the place. By doing so they hoped to acquire, if possible, some share of the pluck of the deceased, and of his skill at cheating in trade. Reprisals had been taken for this murder by the British gunboat on patrol, and the traders' [*sic*] skull, and the bones of one foot had been recovered and suitably interred. And now here again were our friends of the year before[,] . . . wiping their lips, as it were, after the gruesome feast, and smilingly walking into our camp as if nothing had happened. (Somerville 1928, 38)

Somerville was undoubtedly playing to his Cork audience, and the extent to which he told exaggerated stories of cannibalism is unclear, although there were certainly occasions when he was deliberately

FIGURES 1.9–1.10 Plan for anthropometric measurements, from the notebooks of Henry B. Somerville, 1893–94. Courtesy of Royal Anthropological Institute, London. MS 267-2-2(4-5)3

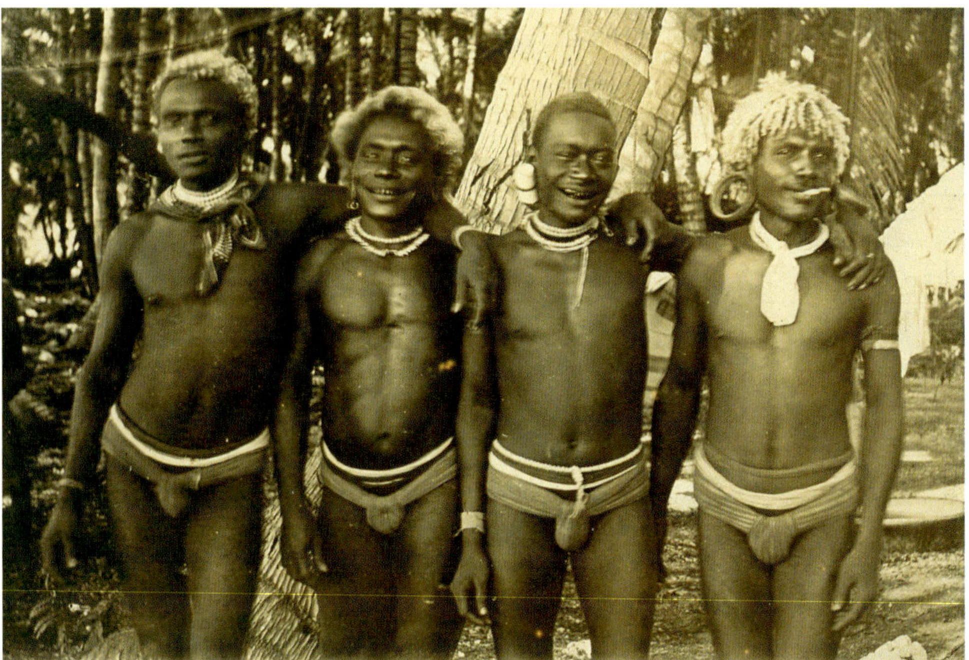

misinformed. Edvard Hviding, an anthropologist who has worked in Marovo Lagoon, has pointed out that the translation Somerville was given to one of the songs he recorded was perhaps intended as a joke — the translation was linked to local customs, but the correct translation of the Marovo reveals it as comment on the stupidity of the British. With his commentary, Somerville reveals a humorous image as another example of the duplicitousness of natives. Somerville and his men did establish reasonably good relations with local people and lived among them for weeks at a time as the crew split up into several small parties to survey the coastlines of Roviana and Marovo Lagoons.

Somerville pointed out in his ethnographical notes in the journal *Man*, published by the Royal Anthropological Institute in London, that he thought the New Georgians were "doomed to disappear" and that this was of no great loss to the world "except from a scientific point of view" (1897, 411). The notion that the people and culture were on the verge of disappearing was the motivating factor behind the salvage paradigm of surveys like Somerville's, and that paradigm left its trace in many photographs of Roviana from the late nineteenth and early twentieth centuries. Like Guppy, Somerville took with him a copy of *Notes and Queries in Anthropology*, published by the Royal Anthropological Institute and intended as a guide for amateur anthropologists to enable them to gather the kinds of information that anthropologists at home required. In 1882 William Henry Flower, curator of the British Museum and the president of the Anthropological Institute, argued for the archival value of photographs to ethnography: "With their histories carefully registered, [photographs] of any of the so-called aborigine races, now rapidly undergoing extermination or degeneration, will be hereafter of inestimable value. Drawings, descriptions and measurements are also useful, though in a far less degree" (1882, 184).

Photography promised a way of preserving that which was rapidly disappearing; it perfectly fitted the salvage paradigm of early anthropology. Somerville is an example of the amateur anthropologist collecting material for those at home, but, although his coastal charts of New Georgia were printed and regularly used by the Royal Navy, his notebooks full of precise anthropometric measurements were not consulted.

As early as 1832, Dumont d'Urville identified two distinct races: Polynesians or Micronesians and Melanesians, with the former racially, morally, and politically superior (Douglas 1999, 65). Douglas has discussed the ways in which scientists in the eighteenth and nineteenth centuries used artists' representations to differentiate Oceanic groups in terms of race and how "unpredictable exotic experience and the flow of empirical data back to the metropoles, especially from the Pacific, contributed significantly to the decline of neoclassical idealism in art and science — including a nascent anthropology — presaging the triumph of romantic sensibility in art and literature, the 'biologization' of the human sciences and, eventually, an evolutionist cosmology" (69).

Visual representations of Pacific Islanders helped instigate a shift in Victorian attitudes from a humanist view of race to a scientific one. By the time the photographers I am considering here were working, this view had long been the accepted one, and their work is explicitly informed by that biologization. When Williamson visited Roviana in 1910, he thought that the people of "Sychele" (Saikile) at the eastern end of Roviana Lagoon were "on a scale of culture somewhat lower than that of their western neighbours," this being mainly due to their physical appearance and the fact that their canoes were less heavily ornamented and they possessed fewer shell ornaments (Williamson 1914, 16). Although he also took photographs of religious sites and shrines (*hope*) and skull houses that contained the remains of ancestors (*oru*), and also a large series of taboo markers on Kolombangara Island, many of the images that Williamson produced were anthropometric in style.

In its adoption of a broadly anthropometric aesthetic and a profile pose, which is intended to reveal the local style of dress (*puke-pukete*), Williamson's photograph of two Roviana women (figure 1.12) conforms to an accepted way of representing racial and cultural types. Williamson was interested in types rather than individuals and, although he recorded the exact dates when photographs were taken, he did not record the names of any of the people he photographed. Although the Methodist mission had been established nearby at Kokeqolo for eight years, this photograph—and many other similar images taken by Williamson—reveals that missionaries' attitudes toward dress had not yet been adopted by the population as a whole. Williamson comments: "Their [Roviana people's] mode and ideas of life have been very little modified anywhere, and in most of the villages they still remain unchanged" (1914, 18).

Light

The arrival of the Methodist mission—known locally as *lotu*[9]—in Roviana in 1902 initiated a period that was concerned with producing "new persons": with fashioning Christian individuals and, importantly, Christian bodies. This was achieved in practice through disciplining bodies, but also visually through contrasting "savage" and converted "Christian" bodies—similar to Somerville's anthropometric endeavors—an effort to which photography contributed substantially. The mission was concerned with establishing a narrative of before and after that was necessary for the transformation of individuals through the salvation it offered. The mission required a savage past against which to contrast the saved individual (see Lattas 1996b). The *Australian Methodist Missionary Review* from March 4, 1902, published accounts of the arrival of the mission in Roviana and declared that "the inhabitants are known as the most inveterate head-hunters of the Pacific, and for many years the traders have earnestly pleaded with the Naval authorities to suppress this horrible

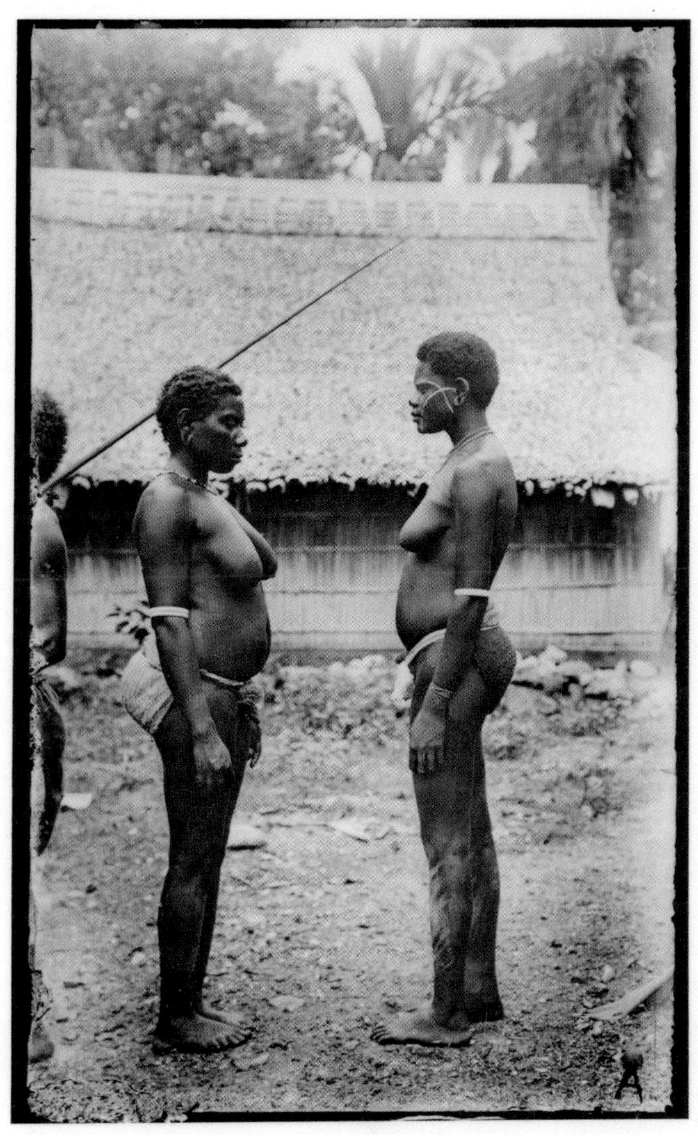

FIGURE 1.12 Two Roviana women. Photograph by Robert Ward Williamson, 1910. Courtesy of Royal Anthropological Institute, London. 78615

practice. . . . No men have ever needed the Gospel more than the much-dreaded natives of New Georgia" (4).

When Reverend George Brown visited Roviana in July and August 1901 aboard the ss *Titus*, he "found the people in a state of great excitement over a large feast which Igava [Inqava] was about to give to celebrate the opening of a new house which he had just built" (*Australian Methodist Missionary Review*, September 9, 1901, 3). The house was opened without the usual requirement of heads taken in raids to inaugurate it, which was remarked on as evidence of the influence of Charles Woodford and the success of pacification. Brown was in Roviana to further discuss the possibilities for starting a mission there, but Woodford had advised him not to mention the opening of a mission building as it was likely to be rejected outright by local people. Officially, the Methodists were responding to a call from Guadalcanal people who had worked as indentured laborers in Fiji for a mission to be established on Guadalcanal, "to go and save the people who are in spiritual darkness" (*Australian Methodist Missionary Review*, September 9, 1901, 6). But Roviana was eventually chosen as a base in the Solomons because it was a site that would not encroach on any of the territories already claimed by other missions: "Outside the dotted line which in the latest map issued by the Society [Melanesian Mission] 'shows the present sphere of work'" (*Australian Methodist Missionary Review*, September 9, 1901, 8). Brown was well aware of the power of visual images on native audiences, having made considerable use of them elsewhere in the Pacific (see Brown 1908), and one of his first actions was to give a lantern slide show to Roviana people:

> I did this with a set purpose, as I wished to show them what the Gospel had done for other people. We had a big crowd, and Igava [Inqava] stood quite close to me, and, as he understood English very well, I was able to address some of my remarks to him for his own special benefit. I showed them in the slides what the people of New Guinea and other places were before the introduction of Christianity and what they were afterwards. I showed them the missionary in Fiji with his school boys, and the missionary's wife with her school girls, and some other views which I thought would explain the object of our visit. (Brown 1908)

In deciding to use this kind of visual imagery, Brown was following in a long tradition of colonial attitudes that suggested that the "native mind" was more susceptible to images than abstract concepts. Brown used photographs to spread the "word of the Gospel," but also importantly to demonstrate the amazing power of the mission to make images and control them. Photography was one way of demonstrating a technological superiority; but it was also a way of magically dazzling others through the use of images and mimesis (Behrend 2003). But despite the favorable impression the lantern slide show apparently made, Inqava remained opposed to the mission. Brown decided not to directly ask Inqava for permission: "The people all know that we intend to come, and so far as I can learn, there will be no serious objection to our coming. It will be much better to come without having asked permission rather than to come in the face of a refusal" (*Australian Methodist Missionary Review*, October 8, 1901, 2). Brown was a keen photographer—many of his images appeared in the *Australian Methodist Missionary Review* and his own books (Brown 1908, 1910)—and he had already made a series of photographs on an earlier visit to Roviana in August 1899 (see figure 1.2). Commenting that "many of the villages in that part were destroyed some years ago by H.M.S. Royalist, for some outrages committed against white men and they do not yet appear to have recovered," Brown visited some local "tambu houses" only to find that "the best of these had been destroyed by the ship of war, some years ago" (*Australian Methodist Missionary Review*, November 6, 1899, 2, 3). On Nusa Roviana he saw "a large wooden idol or totem pole, at a place called Okarapa or Kokorapa. There was no house over this but the women could not go near it and the men living there did not appear at all comfortable when they were near it. The bush in which it stood seemed to be a kind of sacred grove. We managed to secure the goodwill of the few people about and were able to photograph it, and also get some other pictures of interest" (3).

Brown was concerned with documenting the savage, dark practices of the recent past because these were useful in developing narratives of conversion. To this end he took a series of photographs of religious sites in and around Roviana in 1899 (figure 1.13). Photographs of material culture, such as shrines and skull houses could visually stand for "heathen practices." The photograph of a religious carving (*beku*) on a shrine (figure 1.14) was reproduced in an article in the *Australian Methodist Missionary Review* that extolled the desperate need for the people of Roviana to emerge from the "darkness" of their former "savagery" and into the "light of Salvation," and in-

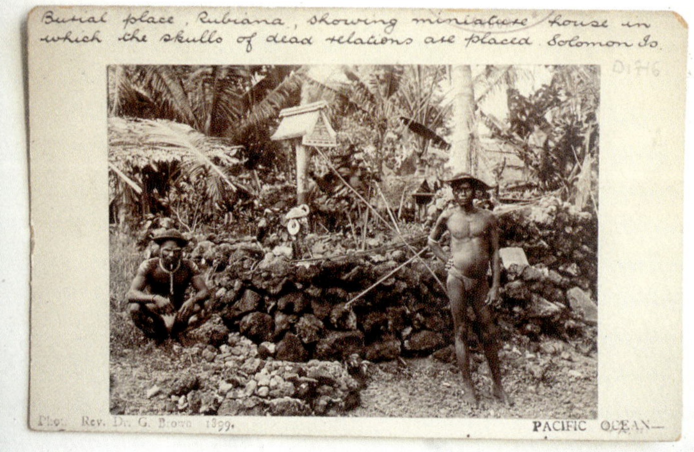

FIGURE 1.13 "Burial place, Rubiana, showing miniature house in which the skulls of dead relations are placed," Ancestral shrine, Munda. Photograph by Reverend George Brown, 1899. Courtesy of Royal Geographical Society, London. PR 056649

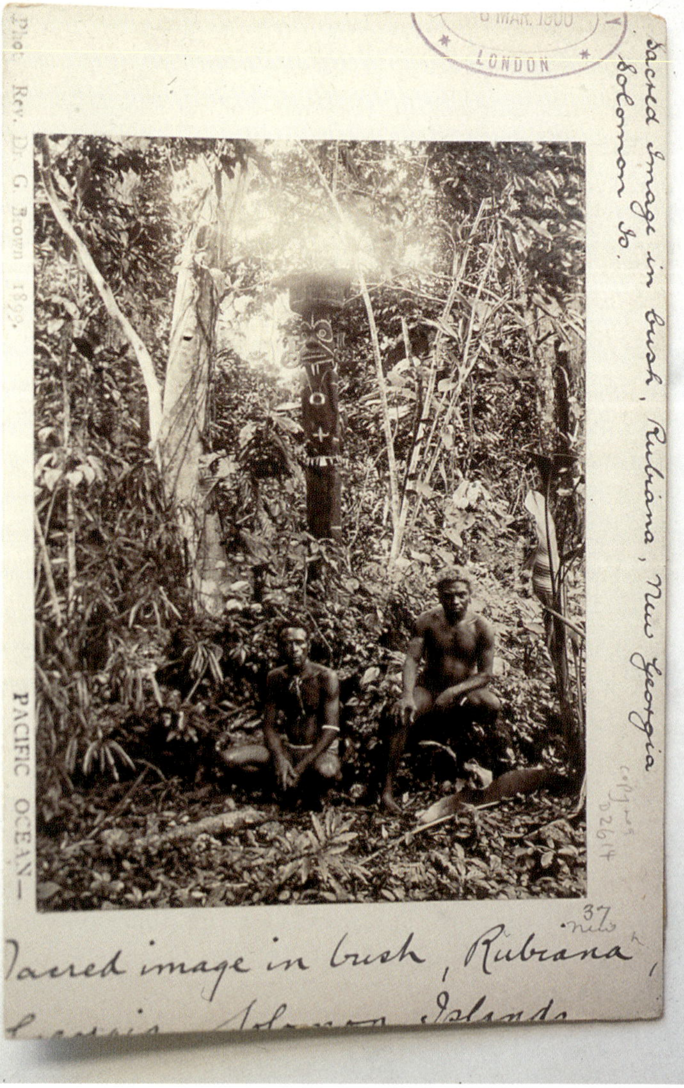

FIGURE 1.14 "Sacred image in bush," Munda. Photograph by Reverend George Brown, 1899. Courtesy of Royal Geographical Society, London. PR 056652

cluded a plea for funds to set up the mission in Roviana (*Australian Methodist Missionary Review*, December 8, 1900, 7). Missionaries required savagery in the recent past accompanied by a series of redeeming, or redeemable, features in order to justify conversion. The concern in Brown's photographs is not just with difference and the shock of savagery but with creating an interest in the work being done to abolish it. The photographs that Brown took elsewhere in the Pacific include many images of named individuals, some of which he included in his autobiography (see Brown 1908; Gardner 1999).

Figure 1.15 was reproduced as figure 2 in Brown's book *Melanesians and Polynesians*, but in this case the individuals remain unnamed in a book that otherwise features many portraits of named individuals. Another photograph (figure 1.16) reveals some sense of before and after, through the adoption of a European dress by the wife of a prominent local banara called Gumi, but, given the date, this was not a sign of any direct mission influence. There is another photograph of Gumi's wife standing alone in profile on a white sheet without a skirt and wearing only local dress—*pupukete*—and it was perhaps Brown's intention to contrast the two images to present a missionary discourse concerned with the fashioning of chaste Christian bodies. But Brown also took photographs that were intended to be humorous, although in a way that also underwrote ideas of savagery (figure 1.17). The distended pierced earlobes of Roviana men were visually emblematic of bodily difference, and Methodist missionary views encouraged a series of paternalistic metaphors around such differences. These were phrased in terms of adult and child bodies as well as light and dark. But there was an ambivalence to this discourse that justified itself on the grounds of difference—which legitimated the right to convert—but also seemed concerned with "the eventual erasure of difference in the name of a common humanity and modernity" (Eves 1996).

The Reverend John Francis Goldie, who was charged with actually setting up the Methodist mission in Roviana, and who ran it until the outbreak of World War II, was concerned with the "construction of order" and was a proponent of the "industrial mission" that was concerned with creating "productive" bodies. In a short article he asked whether the Christianity that the mission offered was "merely a creed, and the nominal membership of a human society called the Church, or is it a new vision, new aspirations, and

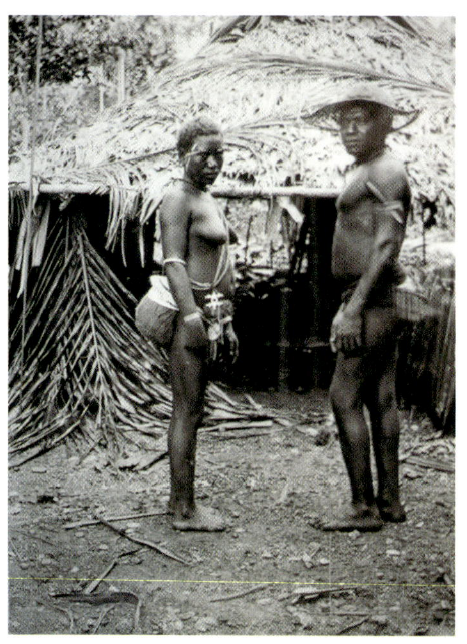

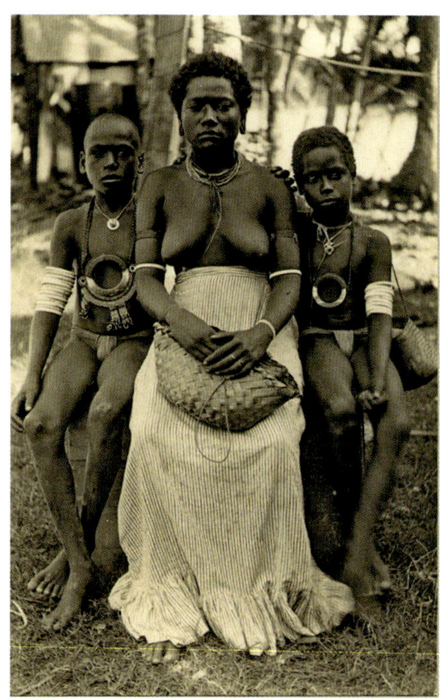

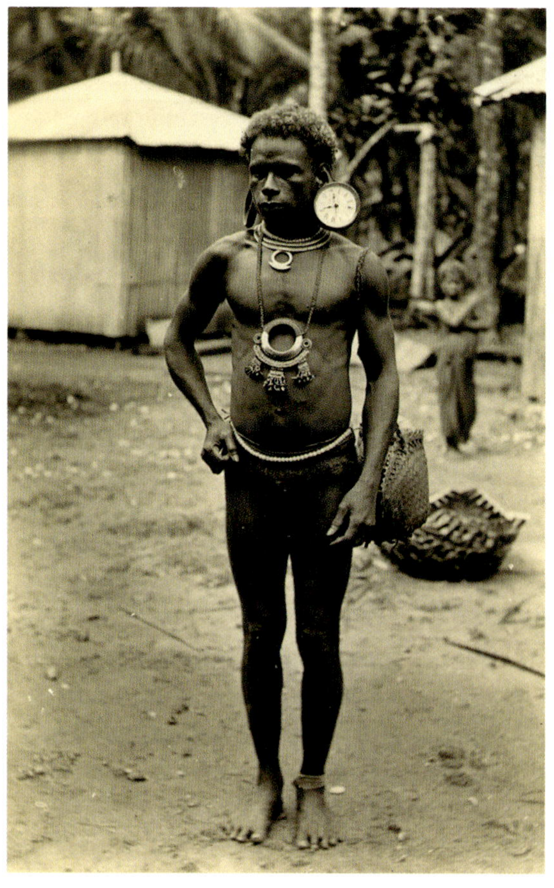

FIGURE 1.15 (*above*) Roviana man and woman. Photograph by Reverend George Brown, 1899. Courtesy of Royal Geographical Society, London. PR 056650

FIGURE 1.16 (*above right*) Wife of banara Gumi and her children. Photograph by Reverend George Brown, 1899. Courtesy of Rautenstrauch Joest Museum, Cologne. 9707_600

FIGURE 1.17 (*right*) Roviana man with a clock inserted in his earlobe. Photograph by Reverend George Brown, 1899. Courtesy of Rautenstrauch Joest Museum, Cologne. 9733_600 a new power to will and to do—in other words, a new life? . . . The chief business of the Missionary is not to make boats and plantations but to make men—Christian men. Not to build houses, but to build character" (Goldie 1916, 2–3).

The photographs that the mission produced were intended to reveal and help construct this "new life"—a phrase that continues to be used in the present to end all services of an offshoot of Methodism, the Christian Fellowship Church in Roviana. The photographs, which were either taken by Goldie—who remains an important and much-revered figure in contemporary Roviana—or his coworker Stephen Rooney, were intended for audiences in New Zealand and Australia and had a significant impact in raising funds for the mission as well as forming opinions. But some photographs were also distributed locally around Roviana to certain prominent individuals and families and had a considerable impact as material objects and signs of conversion. In many of the photographs, the bodies of Roviana people are the sites for the inscription of narratives of conversion.

Accompanied by captions that frame the images as conversion narratives, these photographs (figures 1.18 and 1.19) function as visual representations of the new life that the mission saw itself as initiating. There is a concern with portraying savagery—but it needs to be a savagery that can be effaced. If it is an irreducible savagery, then there is no hope of conversion. Goldie commented on Cheyne's account from 1844 of New Georgian cannibalism and the suggestion that "human flesh formed their [New Georgians] chief article of diet" (see Cheyne quoted in Shineberg 1971), and argued that "[T]he people of the New Georgia group were cannibals, but not in the same sense as the Fijians, who loved human flesh as an article of diet. Those who have taken part in these cannibal feasts tell me that in connection with human sacrifices and great religious festivals human flesh was partaken of, but few liked it; to many it was so obnoxious it made them ill. The New Georgians were crafty and cruel; but they were also remarkably clever and intelligent" (Goldie 1915, 563). Goldie wanted to differentiate Roviana people from "real savages" who were located elsewhere. This is the difference between the narratives of race in photographs produced by the Methodist mission and those in images produced by other photographers. As far as Goldie was concerned, some aspects of Roviana culture were to be condemned, headhunting and cannibalism foremost among them, but others were redeemable. The mission encouraged and ac-

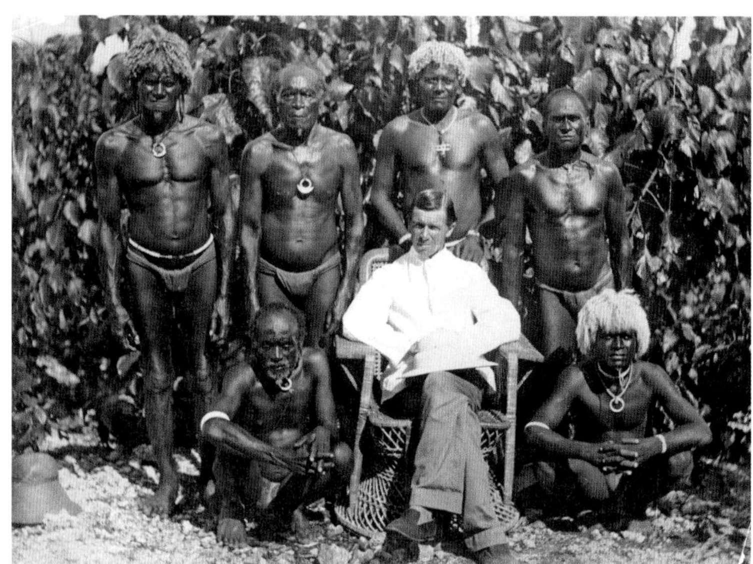

FIGURE 1.18 Reverend John Francis
Goldie and Roviana chiefs (Inqava
standing second from left),
ca. 1902–6. Courtesy of Methodist
Archives, Auckland. de B16d

FIGURE 1.19 George Videre,
Solomon Taveke, Tomothy Ototo,
Timothy Loe, Sakaia, and India
at Kokeqolo, ca. 1910 (from left
to right). Courtesy of Methodist
Archives, Auckland.

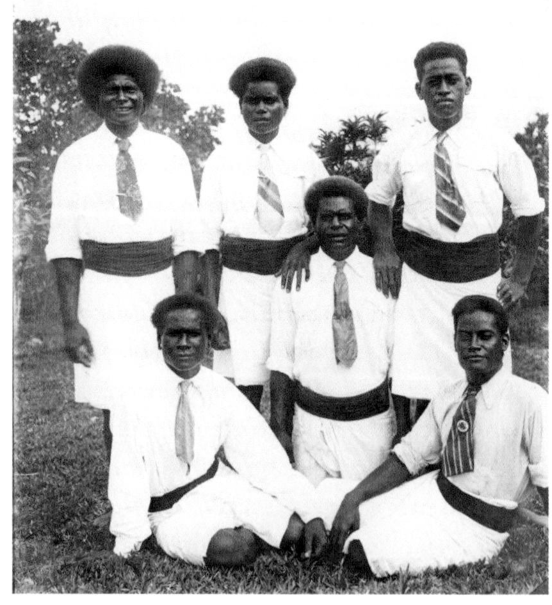

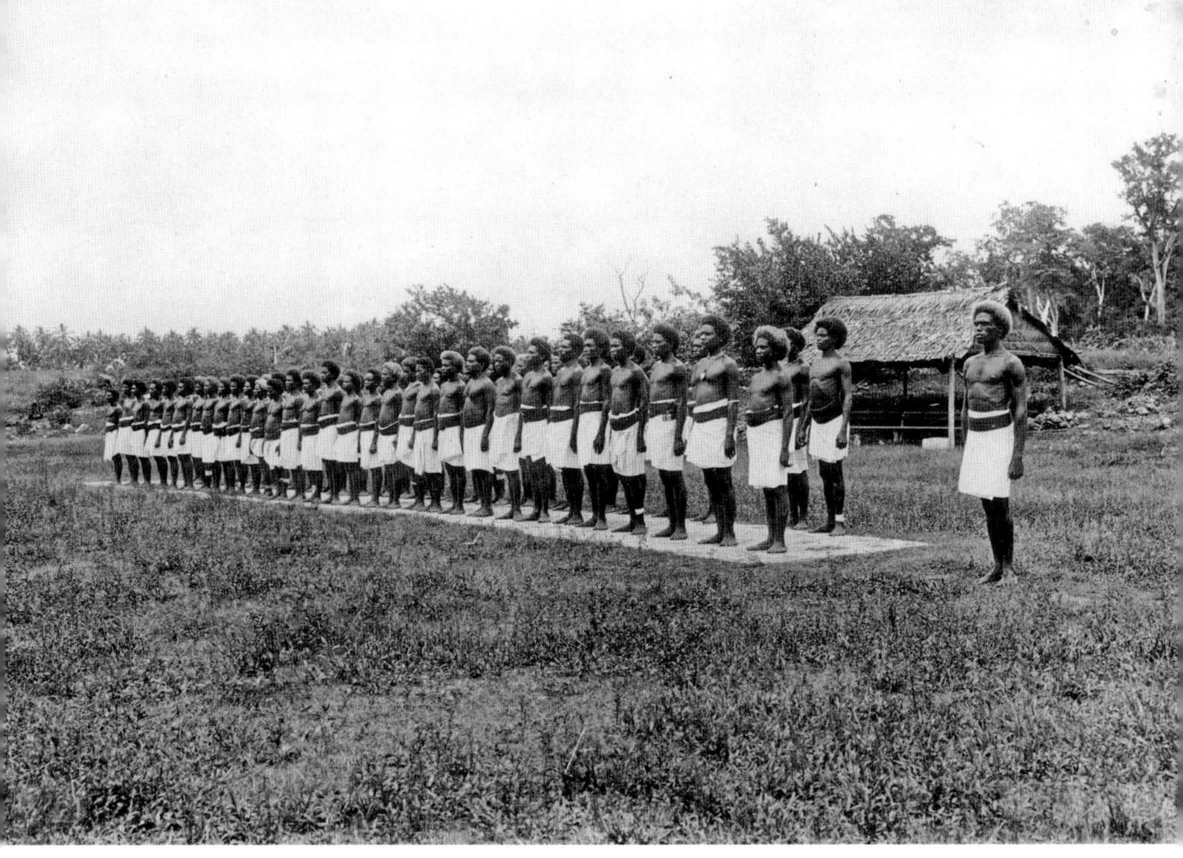

FIGURE 1.20 Mission-school students on cricket pitch, Kokeqolo, ca. 1910. Courtesy of Methodist Archives, Auckland. de B16c

tively maintained certain "traditional customs," such as the building of tomoko, despite the earlier attempts of the British colonial authorities to destroy them, and tomoko were raced at Christmas and other holidays, effectively appropriating some of their locally perceived mana for other ends.

There is also a generational framing to some of these photographs; although the members of the mission school are dressed in white European shirts and lap-lap, and wear ties, they are all "sons of headhunters" (figure 1.19). The photographs also involve a kind of infantilization, and Goldie refers to "new-caught sullen peoples / half devil and half child" (1908, 24). Roviana people are children who can be formed into adults. People are the victims of savage customs and not inherently evil (see Thomas 1994, 130–31). Goldie thought that Roviana people were industrious, and he divided earlier practices into positive and negative "customs and practices which can be selectively expunged and adapted as the people are assimilated to a Christian order" (Thomas 1993, 51).

The emphasis in a photograph (figure 1.20) of students lined up

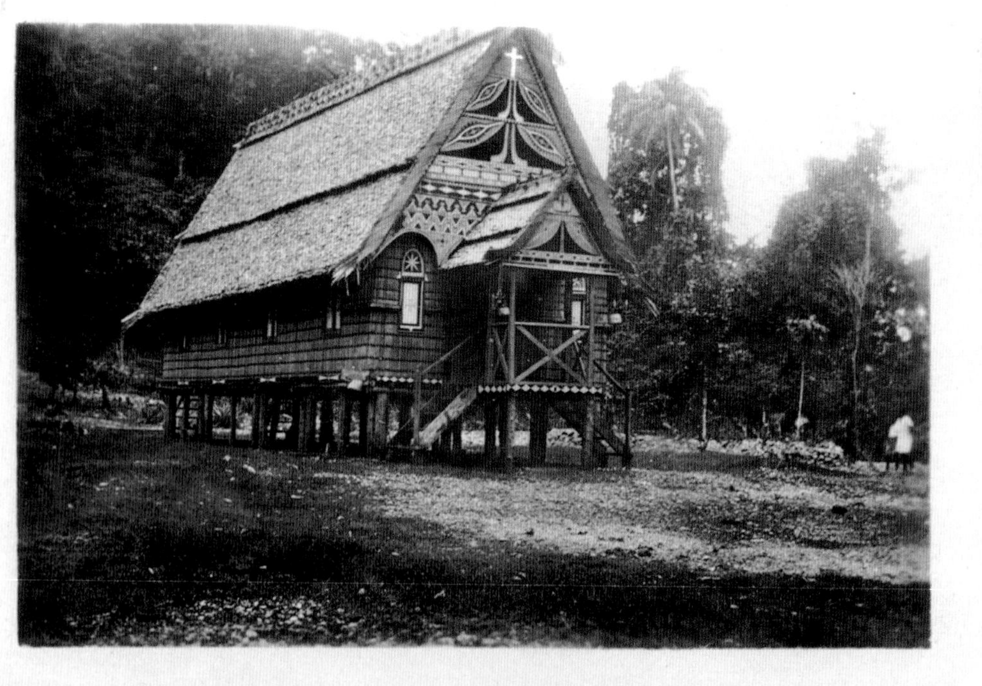

for inspection is the docile, mutable body capable of discipline and transformation. The performance is reminiscent of the lineup in front of Thurston's camera (figure 1.3) in its enactment of power. But the missionaries needed to preserve some of the material culture of heathen times in order to provide a contrast for before-and-after stories, as this was seen as a major narrative factor in raising funds. They also sought to appropriate some of the power associated with these material forms, and the mission not only encouraged the continued building of tomoko but also participated to some extent in distinctly Roviana notions of generosity and efficacy. In so doing, the mission perhaps allowed Goldie to take on some of the qualities of a banara like Inqava, and this is certainly how elderly Roviana people described Goldie to me. This interpenetration of forms, Christian and Roviana, resulted in some extraordinary hybrids.

In creating the new Methodist church on Nusa Roviana in the visual style of an ancestral Roviana skull shrine (figure 1.21; see also figure 3.16), complete with its representations of stylized eyes and a spirit door, the Methodist mission was effectively making a whole series of explicit connections between Christian and Roviana beliefs and practices. Through this appropriation of a local form, the mission was also actively maintaining certain continuities with the savage past. Andrew Lattas suggests: "The process of forgetting can never be complete or total, for Christianity requires a particular memory of the past . . . in order to objectify and mediate its conquest of subjects through conquering the sites and spaces which mediate and locate their identities" (1996b, 297). Photographs, such as those by Thurston (figure 1.3) and Goldie (figure 1.20), did not merely create representations that were secondary to practices and realities. They constituted political actualities in themselves. Colonial officials, anthropologists, missionaries, and other visitors to Roviana could regard the culture not as an array of practices and relations but as a thing depicted or described that was immediately subject to their gaze. As Thomas points out, "that other people and cultures could be subsumed in the form of a picture and seeing a thing first as a representation, and secondly as something beyond a representation created a particular sense of power on the side of the viewing colonist, which was of course not necessarily reflected in real control over populations" (Thomas 1994, 112; see also Heidegger 1977).

Gele Aranga

One of the photographs that Williamson took in Roviana in 1910 (figure 1.22) shows an encounter on one of the lagoon's beaches, between Williamson and a Roviana warrior (*tie varane*), who stares back at the camera and the photographer. This was perhaps Williamson's idea of authentic savagery. The image of a man with a shield and spear facing the camera like this appeared in many colonial depictions of Roviana. It underwrote some of the textual accounts of savagery, but photographs like this may have been the result of negotiations in which Roviana people both had their own expectations and also knew what was required of them.

Williamson's photograph from 1910 has a visual counterpart in one of the dozen or so photographs that Faletau Leve (see Prologue) had in his possession in 2001. It shows his wife, Daisy; their first son, Alpheus; and an old man, Boaz Sisilo, holding a wicker shield (*lave*) and a spear (figure 1.23). The photograph is housed in a wooden frame made by Faletau, signaling the importance of this image of Sisilo, an uncle of Daisy's and a paramount chief (*palabatu*). He is

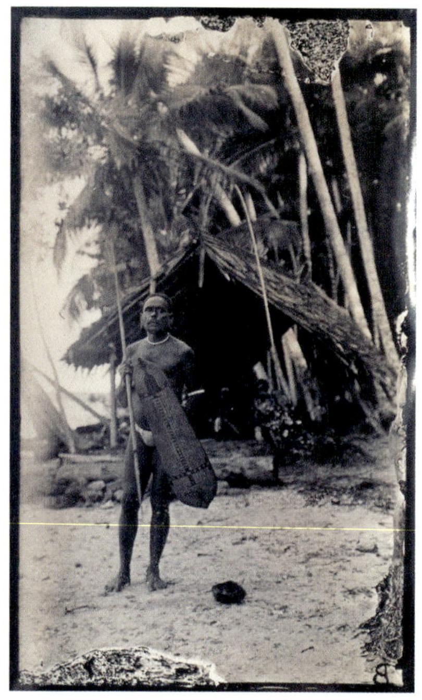

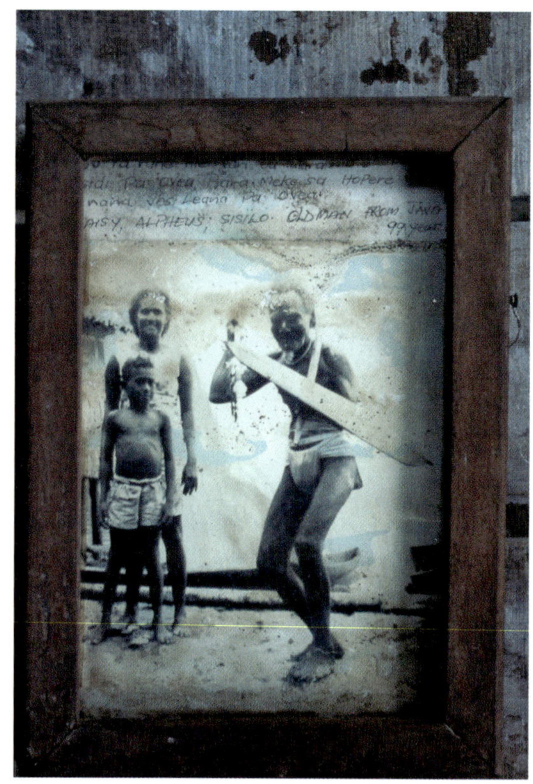

photographed standing in a pose that is locally called *gele aranga* (aiming) and was used in both fighting and dancing. This involves holding the spear in an overarm grip ready to throw, the shield in front of the body, while making small jumping movements back and forth, and distracting and fixing your opponents with what Faletau calls "savage [or fierce] eyes" (*mata-na pinomo*).[10] The aim of these savage eyes was not just to intimidate and scare those facing you but to look beside them, to look slightly to one side, then the other, to confuse them about your intentions. Faletau said that this movement helped you see "clearer." He also asserted that the eyes in the photograph of Sisilo could watch you — they were watching us as we spoke, and they could "bite."

The photograph was taken by Faletau on his Kodak Box Brownie sometime around 1970; he was vague on the exact date. He told me that he had asked Sisilo to adopt a pose of some kind when Faletau took the photograph in the village of Ovea on Vella Lavella. According to Faletau, Sisilo stood in the gele aranga pose to make him-

self "come out strong." The text on the photograph, handwritten by
Faletau, records: "Today me and the old man [Sisilo] talked about
the bush [uncleared land] between Ovea and the Pirara river. . . . He
gave me something." Today Faletau retains land rights around Ovea
village as a result of the transaction memorialized by this photograph.[11] The photograph, or photo–object (Batchen 2004b), acts as
mnemonic for the transaction, which was also commemorated with
other objects. Faletau gave Sisilo a knife, of foreign make, as well as
shell valuables and Solomon Island dollars, in return for access and
rights to the land. The old man had promised the shield—which
allegedly had bloodstains on it from headhunting raids on Choiseul in the early 1900s—to Faletau on his death. But Sisilo hid the
shield shortly before he died, and Faletau never received it. Faletau's account of his photograph of Sisilo suggests that Williamson's
photograph could be seen to involve a kind of double vision—both
a Roviana performance (gele aranga) and an image of authentic savagery. The rereading of Williamson's photograph that occurs by
juxtaposing it to Faletau's demonstrates the importance of considering not just Roviana understandings of visual performances such
as gele aranga but Roviana people's uses and expectations of photography itself.

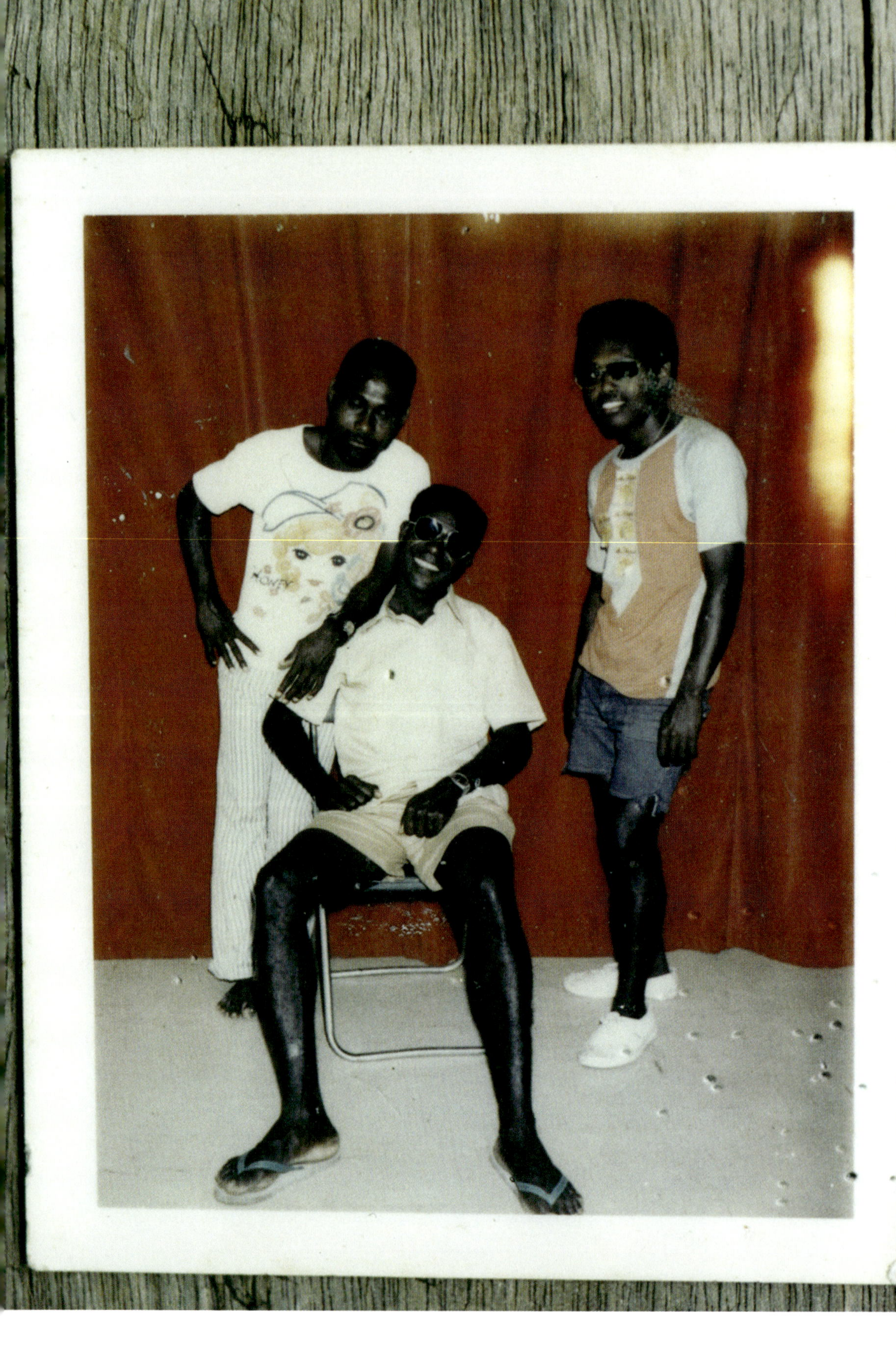

"A Devil's Engine"

An elderly Roviana woman provides an account of first contact with a photographic camera, given mostly in English, but with certain Pijin words thrown in for dramatic effect, as though this was what "they" (the people from before) would say: "The first time they saw a camera they thought it was a devil's engine [*enjin blong debil*]. [Laughing.] It was the white man's devil. They were scared. They thought it would take [*kasem*] them [raising her hand and then clenching her fist as though grabbing something out of the air], so they ran away. They were frightened and they ran away. They hid in the bush. Now we know these things [gesturing at my camera]."[1] The account contains the basic elements of a story repeated by those Roviana people who consider themselves to be, in some respects, more familiar with cameras. These stories, all of which figure some constellation formed from a basic set of elements — the scared native, the knowing white man, the mysterious capturing device — are often recounted with a sense of humor, although this is sometimes tinged with a certain nervousness. They are historically vague but all are set "before," as in "before *lotu*" (the mission), but generally meant in the sense of "people from before" rather than actually occurring before the arrival of the Methodist mission in 1902. In some ways the laughter attempts to establish a distance between the narrator and their incredulous, less-knowing, superstitious, and pagan ancestors. The narrator in this instance, Josephine Wheatley, recalls that her Roviana ancestors were afraid of the camera when they first encountered the strange object in the hands of missionaries, locally based expatriate traders, or other outsiders sometime in the late nineteenth or early twentieth century. Such stories, like other first-contact narratives, have an almost mythic quality and are part of local attempts to establish a temporal and cultural shift between now and before. They are stories that Roviana people tell each other. They also reveal a great deal about enduring attitudes toward photographic magic in Roviana.

I am concerned with the possibility of other understandings of photographs and photography and want to avoid presuming at the outset a unified universal phenomenon called photography, a nature that is the same across cultures. But I do not want to discount any similarities of practice. The previous chapter explored some of the ways in which Roviana was visually imagined through photographs and other images produced by outsiders. Now I want to look at Roviana photographic attitudes and practices. What are local expectations of the medium? What is at stake is the possibility of a range of vernacular practices — Roviana photographies — in relation to any presumed universal notion of photography.

Although the encounter that Josephine describes might have occurred after the arrival of the Methodist mission in Roviana in 1902, her memory of the term *debil* being used is not necessarily an indication of any direct mission influence. *Debil* is a Pijin word that is used to refer to what are known in Roviana as *tomate*, spirits of various kinds, and *debil* was already in common use before the mission arrived. However, the allusion to the camera as a "devil's *engine*" does reveal the use of a foreign word — *enjin* in Pijin — that is seemingly without any direct local equivalent. What engines previously existed in Roviana culture? Despite the fact that stories like Josephine's are in some ways anecdotal — they describe a generic type of encounter and not necessarily any one specific historical event — that she, and others, recall this particular phrase being used in the oral accounts that have been handed down of the "time before" is important. What is intended in describing the camera as an engine?

From the late eighteenth century onward, Roviana people would have gradually encountered or known about a range of European technologies: from trade goods such as iron tools, and particularly iron ax blades, to optical devices like telescopes and cameras. Judith Bennett (1986, 23) suggests that the first iron tools were seen by islanders as possessing mana (efficacy) — did the same apply to cameras? Perhaps the use of the term *engine* by Josephine in this context emphasizes the efficacious nature of the camera — an engine that produces affects and effects things. Or perhaps the use simply reveals the lack of other words, such as *technology*, as a way of describing it? Trachtenberg points out that the inception of daguerreotypes in the 1840s in Europe was referred to as the invention of a "great engine" (1992, 184). He suggests that "the camera does resemble a machine with moving parts, a polished glass eye, a mysterious chemical procedure[,] . . . but 'engine' resonates or rumbles with other senses. By the 1840s, the word had evolved from the simple sense of a product of ingenuity to the more complex modern sense of a self-powered machine, a self-contained mechanical entity requiring no external power" (Trachtenberg 1992, 184).

He goes on to argue that the figure of the camera as engine "hum[s] with wariness about what living energy may lie within the camera-made image, what latent magic the image might perform" (Trachtenberg 1992, 185). Roviana expectations of power in relation to the work of spirits and ancestors concern an ability to produce appearances and conversions, and the production of photographs is a process that, from its inception in Roviana, is directly entangled with local economies of power, particularly in relation to vision and representation. This productive efficacious capacity of the camera — its functioning as an *enjin* — coexists with its ability to take things; it is capable of "catching you." The types of camera used in the late nineteenth century with their luminous ground-glass screens inverting the scene before the lens, and the accompanying paraphernalia of the black hood and the strange malodorous chemical baths, may all have contributed to a Roviana understanding of cameras and photography as an essentially magical process. It was certainly popularly perceived as such during its infancy in Europe and North America, and the act of taking a photograph with the equipment used at the time had many elements of ritual about it (see Trachtenberg 1989a). This magical ability to catch you and to mediate between the seen and the unseen world, the world of the living and that of the ancestors and spirits, was, and remains, a prominent feature of Roviana reactions to photography, as it does with other cultures of photography. But the assumption that photography was treated as Euro-American magic because there was no local understanding of it, or no local equivalent for it, is entirely wrong. There were local contexts for understanding cameras, photographs, and the process of photography, and they were not feared because they were something new and modern — and therefore misunderstood — but were recognized as closely connected to existing Roviana "engines of visualization" and to local expectations of mediation, efficacy, and power in the visual realm (Maynard 1997). Josephine continues: "You were told to shut your mouth when you had your photograph taken. Otherwise your spirit would come out and be taken.[2] People did not want to look directly at the camera for the same reason. People wore perfume to have their photo taken [laughing]."[3]

Josephine's stories of first contact with the camera and with photography evoke differences and distances that are similar to those involved in European accounts of native fear and lack of understanding of photography. But they also reveal a persistent fascination with photographic magic. European accounts frequently seek to establish the native's primitive beliefs as inferior to modern knowledge. But, in the context of my questions to Roviana people about early attitudes toward photography, many of their narratives were intended to reveal the extent to which *they*, the Roviana people of today, are not like *them*, the Roviana people of before. Although this is perhaps also an appeal to certain notions of modernity and Christianity, Josephine's stories function as temporal and cultural markers of difference in terms of local historical narratives. Most Roviana people were far less ambivalent about the potential dangers of photography, and they were more serious in their narration of early encounters. Sesolo Makoni, in his seventies, insisted: "The photograph is a dangerous thing. Devils stop there [are in the photograph]. If you have a photograph, you have to try to come out good. When people first saw the camera [*kamera*] they were afraid it would take their shadow [*maqomaqo*]. This is what the camera does. It takes your shadow. You have to be careful."[4]

Many contemporary Roviana people continue to express uneasiness about certain aspects of photography. To be photographed involves a sense of exposure, of vulnerability to the attention and actions of predatory spirits. Eric Michaels points out in his discussion of photography in relation to contemporary Australian Aboriginal communities: "Traditional peoples' first encounters with photography sometimes lead them to conclude that the camera is a dangerous magical instrument capable of stealing some essential part of their being, causing illness or death. Generally such anecdotes are not explained but get filed away with other exotic superstitions held by curious primitives, leaving these people to sort out their own relationship to cameras, photographs, film, and now video" (Michaels 1994, 1).

In considering some of the historical and contemporary approaches to photography in Roviana, my concern here is precisely to consider this relationship to cameras and photographs, and to conceptions of photography as a network of processes and relations, and to trace the relationship's links to other local beliefs. Indigenous accounts of such historical encounters with photography are often a means of explaining present attitudes, as much as they form any commentary on the past, and they are a recurring feature of contemporary accounts of the magic of photography. For some Roviana residents, this continues to involve an avoidance of photographs of themselves. Joyce Kevisi, an elderly Roviana woman, remembered that:

> When we were young we wondered how they could make this thing [holding a photograph of her daughter]. How can it take [kasem] you? We said that the Europeans [*tie vaka*] were very clever. We called them shadows [maqomaqo], but now we also call them pictures [*pikisa*] because we just follow, just like we call a plate a *peleta*. I was very shy when they took my photograph. I am still shy today. My photograph is ugly [*dono hikare*]. I wanted to come out good. They asked me to relax but I could not do it. I do not know how to stand in front of a camera [kamera]. I do not want to be photographed [*kamkamera*—literally "camera-ed"].[5]

Joyce has never owned or used a camera and, although she does have photographs of her family, she has none of herself. Her reluctance to appear in front of the camera, while caught up with Roviana notions of female modesty (which is itself bound up with various kinds of visual propriety instigated through mission-school education), is typical of contemporary Roviana attitudes toward the potential dangers of being caught by the camera. Local concerns center around presenting your self to the camera in a particular way in order to "come out good," and many older Roviana residents remain uncertain of how to pose in front of a camera. It is assumed that there is a set of specific bodily techniques involved with posing for, and taking, photographs that many older people see themselves lacking. The only examples of snapshot-style photographs that exist in Roviana—the type of unposed shots that are ubiquitous in Euro-American traditions—are those taken by teenagers, many of whom either copied the style of popular music magazines and videos or adopted the styles of photography that they encountered in the photographic albums of other teenagers who have spent time in Australia. Even these unposed photographs of friends, when discussed with teenagers themselves, show a marked preference for making the whole-body visible in the same way that photographs taken by their parents and grandparents do.

With Roviana people's long history of dealing with a range of Others from across the sea, we should not assume that photography's initial reception in Roviana was conceptually overwhelming or bewildering. Although stories about first contact with photography often report the fear or suspicion induced by the strange machine, elements of that concern are bound up with local Roviana ideas about the visual and representations, this is not a lack of understanding of photography. Such stories also demonstrate some of the complexities involved in those early encounters in terms of relative power relations.

John Stockdale's compilation from 1789 of the British naval officer John Shortland's first encounter with Simbo people, as discussed by Christine Dureau (2001),[6] talks of how the islanders were the ones who initiated contact with the ship in order to trade. For a substantial period after first contact in the late eighteenth century and into the nineteenth century, European traders were to some extent co-opted into local standards of exchange and participated in local networks rather than exert any kind of economic dominance of their own (see Bennett 1986; Shineberg 1971). Europeans were quickly assimilated into the material world of trade rather than being treated as divine beings, and at this point New Georgians retained a relatively substantial degree of autonomy and control over exchanges. The white men—tie vaka (literally "men of the ship")—needed to resupply, which was one of the main reasons for ships stopping in the area. They required friendly trading relations in order to do so. As Dureau points out, "the pre-pacification period was characterized by accommodation rather than rupture, the shifts entailed in incorporation were gradual, the degree of dependence obscured" (Dureau 2001, 142).

The British anthropologist Arthur Hocart recorded a first-contact narrative in Simbo in 1908 that reflects the shift in power relations that had occurred by this point. In the account given to Hocart, the Simbo people are afraid and uneasy of tie vaka (Dureau 2001, 141). In both Stockdale's and Hocart's accounts, Simbo people want iron, but for Dureau, Hocart's account reflects the domination of local people that was achieved through "pacification" during the four years after the declaration of the Solomon Islands as a British protectorate in 1896. The passivity ascribed to Simbo people in their account to Hocart reflected their current state of domination and dependence rather than their position at first contact.

The account of first contact that Dureau herself recorded in 1990 concerned the arrival of the mission (lotu) and described how its arrival had brought about a period of peace, although this was not actually the case as violence and raiding continued for some time after the arrival of missionaries of the Methodist Church on Simbo in 1903. The narrative of lotu requires an image of a savage past, and the first-contact account reflects this, emphasizing the suspicion and aggression with which the first missionaries were met. Local history in the western Solomons is divided into before and after lotu and is not directly concerned with first contact. Dureau reports that Hocart's account was irrelevant to Simbo people in 1990 (2001, 144). The coming of the mission is "a contact story that acts as an origin story" (153), and the idea of a savage and hostile response to the arrival of the mission is in keeping with missionary discourses, which require a particular memory of the past (see Lattas 1996b).

Several popular travel books and anthropologists' accounts of the western Solomons from the late nineteenth and early twentieth centuries specifically refer to local people's initial reactions to photography. These stories about native encounters with cameras, gramophones, and radios form a subgenre of first-contact narratives, one in which the new technology is synonymous with the strange figure of the white man and the modern world. But, although they strive toward producing and clearly differentiating the modern and the primitive, such accounts are often full of inherent ambiguities (Moore 2000). Alongside their overt or covert narratives of technological superiority, they are perhaps also attempts to displace fears about technology onto others. Ostensibly concerned with the natives' shock of encountering the new technology — the primitive reactions of others — these narratives reveal an underlying Euro-American uneasiness about the medium of photography. They effectively play out the spectacle of shock in the space of the Other, and the intended amusement at the misunderstanding of others is perhaps an attempt to construct a distance from them and in so doing dispel some of that uneasiness.

Historical accounts of first contact between Europeans and western Solomon Islands peoples reveal that the latter did not think these outsiders possessed any particular supernatural status; they were not "spirit people" or "ghosts" (Scheiffelin and Crittenden 1991). There was a long history of dealing with outsiders of various kinds, and these light-skinned visitors were just one more "people" who could be engaged with through the normal relations of trading and headhunting. In Roviana the common term for European visitors was, and is, *tie vaka*. It implies that Europeans are outsiders in the sense that they come from elsewhere, but they are people (tie), not some kind of supernatural beings.

The anthropologist Williamson, who visited Roviana in May 1910, gave the following account of how local people reacted to his camera:

> The attitude of the simple Rubiana [Roviana] people towards the camera was variable. Very few indeed had ever seen such a thing before, or knew what it meant, and some of them were frightened, the women sometimes rushing with loud shrieks into the bush. But I rarely had difficulty in getting groups. I found it a good plan to direct the camera to some distinctive object, and persuade some brave souls to put their heads under the cloth and see the picture on the focussing plate. This was the cause of wild excitement; and these bolder spirits then aided me in adducing someone to stand before the camera. . . . I am sure the people often realised in a general way that I was making pictures of them, though I suspect their idea was that the picture which they saw was that which would remain. At times so popular has been the camera, that for the sake of justice and peace I have had solemnly to photograph everybody, and thus produce general contentment, unalloyed by knowledge of the fact that in many cases the operation was but a dummy one. (Williamson 1914, 31–32)

By the time Williamson is writing in 1910, Roviana people would certainly have had some knowledge of photography even if they had not all encountered it directly; visiting and resident Europeans had been taking photographs in and around Roviana for many years. In suggesting that "very few indeed had ever seen such a thing before," Williamson was possibly talking about the reactions of people from the eastern end of Roviana Lagoon who may have had less firsthand contact with photography. He might also have just assumed it. He certainly replicates the general assumptions that visiting Europeans had about the kinds of knowledge that so-called savages might possess, and there is an allied assumption that once they know what photography is, they will lose their fear. However, the implied contrast with a rational Europe is spurious. In mid-nineteenth-century Euro-American vernacular photographic practices and popular culture, a sense of unease was a general feature of attitudes toward the medium, often existing alongside more allegedly scientific approaches. Williamson's account suggests that local attitudes to the camera consisted of a mixture of fear and amusement, and this is true of contemporary Roviana attitudes toward photography. The trick that Williamson plays on the "unsuspecting natives" demonstrates the importance of the ritual of photography, but his suggestion that he had to photograph everybody seems to contradict his description of the fear that the apparatus induced. Ten years before Williamson, in 1900, Count Rudolphe Festetics von Tolna attempted to photograph people in Munda, but writes that while his wife was talking to "King Inqava," his attempts to take a photograph of people were thwarted because "all the natives are hiding in their houses because they are afraid of the camera apparatus (Festetics von Tolna 1903, 325).

The accounts of Williamson and Festetics von Tolna talk of the fear induced by the new technology of photography, and it is precisely photography's status as a new form that is at issue here. But it seems that although the camera was at times the subject of fear, at others it was a source of amusement and novelty—a response that resembles those of European and North American audiences. But, whereas Williamson asserts that most local people did not know what photography "meant," I would argue that photography *was* understood in local terms and allocated a place within the existing visual regimes of Roviana. This does not mean that it was not subject to a certain amount of fear, but that that fear was already an existing feature of various local representational practices and beliefs around the visual—not necessarily a reaction to new technology. Other accounts of reactions to photography suggest a more knowledgeable attitude by local people. Hocart recorded the attitudes of Simbo people to photography a few years before Williamson visited Roviana:

> Among photos they certainly preferred human subjects, but even this could not fix their attention for long; they noticed chiefly the arm-rings and such ornaments; naked savages provoked their mirth. They liked to recognize someone, and when the news spread of Njiruviri's picture in "The Discovery of the Solomons," people were continually coming to see it. For portraits they had little interest and liked full-length figures. They declared our half-plate camera was good but the quarter-plate was no good and it was with trouble that Njiruviri was induced to be photographed with the latter. In looking at pictures they turned them often upside down as the right way up, yet they always noticed that the image in the camera was upside down.[7]

Hocart is writing in 1908, so this is not a story of first contact, and he is also writing about the reactions of Simbo people, who might be said to have had a longer history of sustained contact with Europeans. But Hocart's account does seem to suggest that there was a lack of interest in photographs, that they could not hold people's attention for long. Despite ignoring their orientation by holding photographs upside down, and in so doing raising important questions about the assumption of a three-dimensional perspective space being universally recognized in photographs, Simbo people recognized what photographs are and what they meant on their own terms. Despite complex issues of realism and perspectivalism—the sense in which the photograph is recognized as representing a three-dimensional space—this is not a misrecognition but a fundamental grasp of some of the magical aspects of a photograph's ability to capture something of a person. As was the case with Euro-American reactions, a mixture of anxiety and fear, but also novelty and entertainment, were common features of initial Roviana responses to photography.

Cameras were only one in a range of optical devices that Roviana people would have encountered in their dealings with outsiders, as this passage from Williamson reveals: "A still greater joy to them [than Williamson's compass] was my pocket magnifying-glass. Under my instructions they looked through it at their hands, at hairs from their heads, at pieces of cloth, seeds, shells, everything they could get hold of: and indeed, so popular was this new wonder-toy that I began to fear that I should not be able to get it back again. These things would undoubtedly be regarded by the people as implements of magic, and would necessarily enhance the importance and presumable power of the man who possessed and manipulated them" (1914, 25). Like other optical technologies, such as binoculars, telescopes, microscopes,[8] and surveying instruments, that Roviana people may have encountered in their dealings with outsiders, photography reveals new worlds.[9] The Methodist missionary Reverend George Brown talked about the "powerful reactions" of Roviana people to the magic-lantern shows he gave them when he visited in 1901 (1908, 26). But Williamson's description of local reactions to his magnifying glass suggests not only the revelation of a new world for Roviana people but also the important connection made between such devices and magic.

These European accounts of early encounters with photography reveal much about the expectations of their authors as well as assumptions about local knowledge. But despite their colonial tone, the accounts also suggest that local reactions to photography did not involve a lack of comprehension of photography but a fundamental grasp of some of its properties as a medium, and I now want to consider contemporary Roviana understandings of photographic magic.

Snowfall

Large flakes of snow fall to the ground that has already been blanketed by a thin white layer (figure 2.1). Their slow, erratic movement has been suspended by the camera, yet it is seductively easy to visualize the snow continue to fall. It is also easy to describe this "paltry paper sign" as if it *were* the event rather than its mediation (Tagg 1988, 12). The photograph was taken by Clarinda Gasimata, a teenager from Ilangana (a hamlet of Munda), when she was a scholarship student studying medicine in New Zealand in 2000. That night in Christchurch was the first time she had experienced snow, and her mother, Voli, told me that Clarinda took the photograph because she wanted to share her excitement with her parents and family back home. Voli showed me handwritten letters from Clarinda in which she describes the photographs she sends back as a way of "keeping in touch."[10] The physical connotations are important. Before she left, her father, Isaac, had bought her a cheap 35 mm Japanese automatic camera from a Chinese store in Honiara with just that purpose in mind. Other photographs in the album (figure 2.2) sent home by Clarinda show moments recorded by her friends: sitting with a boyfriend playing computer games at a console in a Christchurch arcade, with her stuffed toys in her university dormitory room, in a café with friends, and so on.

I sat with Voli on the floor of her house, close to the lagoon's edge, while passing photographs back and forth to each other, asking questions, and telling stories. There seems to be something immediately recognizable and reassuring about these objects and this process. We were laughing about snow while sweating in the intense heat and humidity of early afternoon that had sent people searching for shade in which to sit and talk. The kinds of contact that are facilitated by these photographs, maqomaqo (shadow or soul), as Voli calls them, are clearly of great value to her. The photographs are rituals of family—a way of being connected. They provoke laughter and tears.

But what kinds of connections do the photographs establish? They connect Clarinda and Voli with wider worlds: with the modern world of photography and photographic consumption, a world that is elsewhere and yet also here. A great many of the photographs that contemporary Roviana people possess come from elsewhere. It has been argued that photography itself is a central feature of modernity, a technology that fosters a specific set of attitudes toward the world (Slater 1995). Given the relatively small Roviana population, and bearing in mind the way that Pierre Bourdieu has written about the inhabitants of a small French village who declared that they had no need to photograph each other because they've "seen each other too many times already" (1990, 34), what is it that compels Roviana people to photograph themselves?

Clarinda's photographs are in what Voli refers to as the "snapshot" style, something she learned while at college in New Zealand, and their seemingly ubiquitous nature—a student photographing themselves and their friends—is precisely the point here. What is the nature of this familiarity? The anthropologist Edmund Carpenter has argued that photography brought with it a new sense

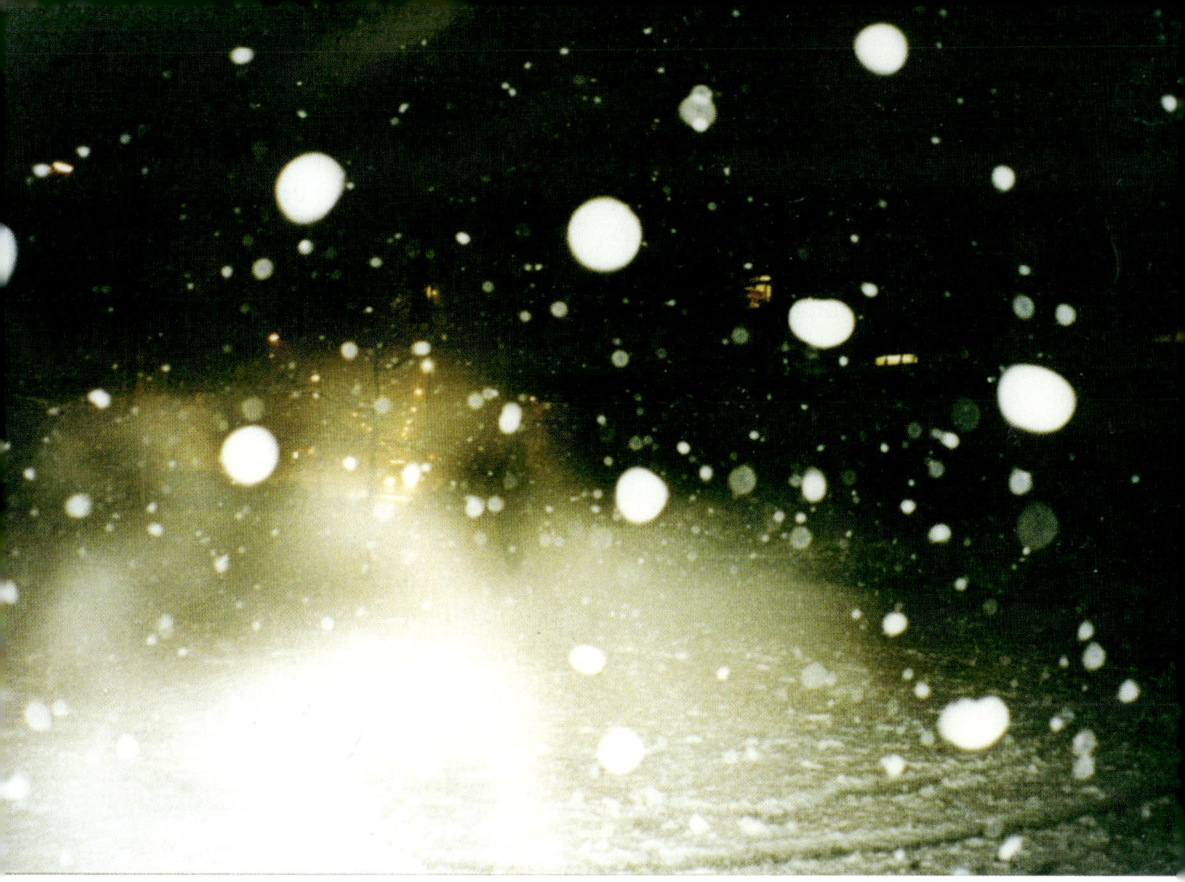

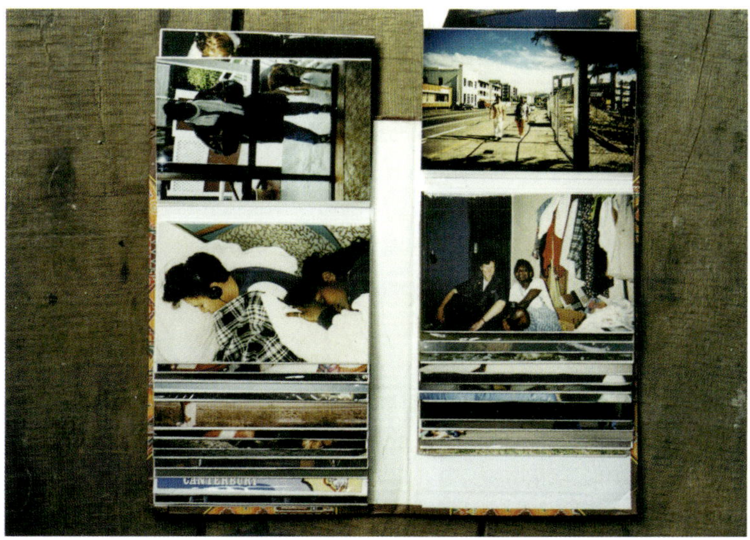

FIGURE 2.1 Snow in Christchurch. Photograph by Clarinda Gasimata, 2000.

FIGURE 2.2 Clarinda's photo album.

of individuality when it was first encountered by some Papua New Guinean cultures in the 1960s (Carpenter 1995). It created a sense of the detached individual separate from the "seamless web of kinship and responsibility" (488). Has it similarly atomized Roviana culture? Has photography induced what Carpenter refers to as the "tribal terror of self-awareness" in Roviana (488)? Photography is something that appears to so-called modern audiences as mundane, ubiquitous, everyday, and yet it is something on which so much depends.

Within accepted Euro-American understandings of photography, this image of snow falling is seemingly simple to comprehend; visually (we know what the photograph is of), processually (we know what the photograph is), and socially (a daughter in a foreign land staying in touch). This photograph falls easily within the genres of family, snapshot, or personal photography — the vast Euro-American project of photographic self-archiving. There is a sense in which photographs exert themselves over subjects, ask them to do their bidding, rather than the other way around. Photography asks subjects to define themselves in relation to itself — an extension of its body (see Batchen 2004a).

But any apparent legibility is deceptive here. There is a white fog in the photograph that obscures our vision. On closer inspection, a small shadowy figure is just visible in the distance, silhouetted against the streetlights — the form is hard to distinguish because of its blurred shape — although *shape* seems too concrete a term for something so indistinct. This nebulous apparition and the accompanying lack of visual clarity are particularly unsettling for Roviana people. Rather than being seen as the effect of light and optics, the indistinct white fog — along with blurring, double exposure, and many other photographic accidents — is the work of malevolent spirits (tomate). Voli tells me: "In this [the photograph] you can see the spirits [*debil-debil*]. They are there. That is why the photograph comes out like this."[11]

For Voli the white fog in the photograph is evidence of the presence of spirits — it relates to the world of the spirits in the same way that Rosalind Krauss suggests that the photograph itself is a trace, comparing it to a fingerprint or the rings of water left on tables by cold glasses, or the tracks of birds on beaches (Krauss 1985, 110). Clarinda was deeply unhappy during the period in which she took the photograph, and for Voli — and for many other Roviana people

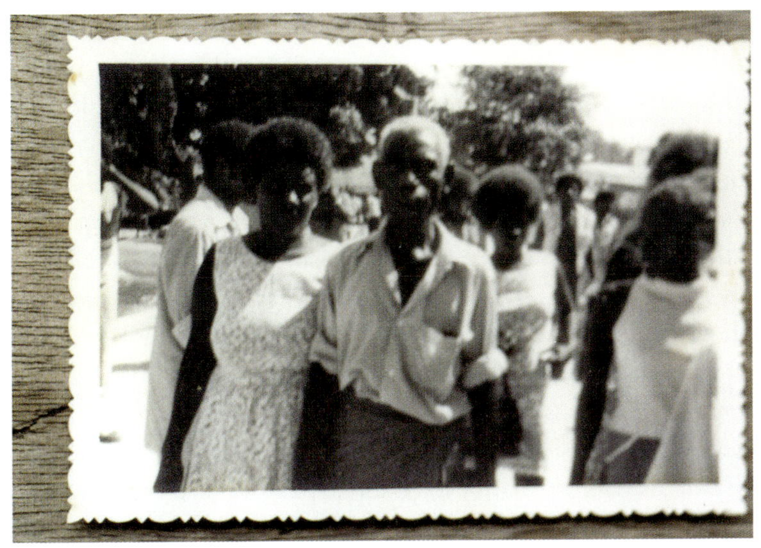

FIGURE 2.3 Philip Lomae (center) with Flori (right), and Voli (left). Photograph by Donald Maepio, 1979.

who talked about their own photographs that were blurred or indistinct in a similar way—there is a direct connection between this inner turmoil, the malevolent activity of spirits, and the physical manifestation of the photograph. They are inextricably and causally entangled. This Roviana understanding of photography—importantly, not a *mis*understanding—demonstrates both points of connection and differences with Euro-American models. What other explanations, technical or otherwise, could be provided for the white fog within the diversity of Euro-American photographic traditions? Voli's reactions to Clarinda's photograph demonstrates the importance of local expectations of photography as a medium to any understanding of the role of photographs in Roviana culture, and that Roviana concerns and fears around photography are not limited to the late nineteenth or early twentieth century.

Donald Maepio's photograph (figure 2.3) of his uncle Philip Lomae (center), with Donald's sister Flore on the right and Voli on the left, reveals that these anxieties persisted, certainly for older generations of Roviana people.[12] Philip had just been discharged from the hospital in Honiara after having just been diagnosed with terminal cancer. He died several weeks after this photograph was taken. Throughout his life Philip had not let anyone take his photograph, despite coming from an extended kin network that had, relatively speaking, considerable access to cameras, with two people owning them. Donald was the first and only person who was allowed to photograph Philip. He only relented because he wanted to "leave something behind him." Donald says that Philip did not let people take photographs because he was afraid of what they would do with the photograph, and "he did not want them to look at him" (note "at him," not "at a photograph of him"). According to Donald, this, and not the realization of his impending death, is why Philip looks unhappy in the photograph. Donald tells me that this is the only photograph of Philip, and although he is happy for me to copy the photograph now, at the time of Philip's death, the photograph—which only arrived back from Australia several weeks after Philip's funeral—was hidden away until his closest relatives signaled that they were able to look at it.

Understanding the role of photographs and of photography in Roviana means paying attention to what it means to be "written with light," in local terms. The use of the photograph as a monument in this way may seem an instantly recognizable practice, but the particular ways in which it intersects with Roviana biographies reveals local understandings of the medium that both overlap with and differ from Euro-American ones.

Josephine Wheatley continued her account of Roviana people's early reactions to photography by describing at some length the story of a relative named Punai Leve (Faletau Leve's father). Punai was born sometime around 1880 and died in the 1960s, so her story provides an insight into Roviana reactions to photography over a considerable period of change. It also comments on relations with the British anthropologist Hocart. Again, the story was recounted in English with the odd Pijin or Roviana term used for effect:

> Hocart wore a loincloth like local people. He also chewed betel nut. So whenever Punai went to visit him, he took betel. Punai thought Hocart's eyes were like a stingrays [implying a dangerous type of eye contact]. When I was young, he [Punai] told me that when he first saw Hocart's camera he thought that "a debil-debil comes out of that enjin, and all the souls are inside. It's where all the souls are kept. If you take a photograph, you take their spirit." Punai told me this. The photo can take your maqomaqo. He did not want his photograph taken. He was scared. . . .

> The British-born trader Norman Wheatley had a basic darkroom in his house. He showed people photographs and he took lots of photographs of people here. People learnt about photographs

from him. Sometimes he took photographs of old people, and if they died, people said he had taken their spirit. They did not like it and they were angry with Norman. Punai knew Hocart and worked for him while he was here in Roviana. One man on Nusa Roviana was photographed by Hocart, and he also took this man's genealogy. The man died and then people were worried about talking to Hocart. People liked Hocart's pens and glasses. Hocart's genealogy was used in the court case [about a particularly contentious local land rights issue; see Schneider 1996]. Hocart wrote a note for Punai to take to Norman's store. He told Punai that the paper could "talk." Punai was scared and held the note carefully. When he got to the store, Norman read the paper and told Punai what Hocart had said. Punai did not know how this happened. . . .

Punai used to listen to the radio at Kitchener's [Kitchener was Josephine's husband and Norman's son] and he heard them when they put monkeys in space. He did not believe it. When I was young, I was told to count to ten when I was having my photograph taken. We had to do things again and again for the camera. I was in lots of mission photographs. I like to have my photo taken. When I was young we were so proud of photos we would display them in the house. Now all I see here is photos of Tom Cruise. People do not make the family photos we grew up with. I often look through my old photos on my own, but sometime I show friends. . . .

I lived on the island [nearby Hopei] on my own, I used to look at my old photos. This made Kitchener's ghost appear. My wedding photo was taken by Bishop Wade. We did not get the photos until much later. I used to have a box Brownie. Daisy's father, Gasimata, brought a camera off Norman Wheatley. He wanted to take photographs of all his daughters. When the prints came back from Australia, all you could see were coconuts. He had pointed the camera in the wrong direction. "Take a photograph like Gasimata" was how we used to describe a bad photograph.[13]

It is uncertain when Roviana people started taking photographs themselves. Norman Wheatley, who had started out in Roviana in 1892 as an agent for the Williams, Woodhouse & Kelly trading partnership on Nusa Zonga Island, married a local woman, Nuatali, and acquired land at Lambete in Munda. He had planted coconuts and set up house there by 1900, and this is where he also set up a darkroom. Norman was an active participant in local networks of exchange, and it's possible that the first photographs taken by Roviana people were produced under his guidance in the first two decades of the twentieth century. Josephine recalls that Ellen, Norman's daughter, was trained by him to use the darkroom. Although European members of the Methodist mission took photographs of local people, they did not actively encourage Roviana people to pick up the camera themselves. Other than posing for the camera, and perhaps being given a print later, no one I spoke to could remember any of their relatives being involved with photography through the auspices of the mission. This does not mean to say that the effects of being exposed to photography's workings through the ritual of being photographed were not substantial. Josephine remembers that Norman used to take photographs of local *banara* (chiefs) and then give them prints as a way of extending his influence and local renown.

Josephine suggested that Roviana people were initially afraid of photography, that the devil the camera contained could capture some essential part of a person and store it inside. As we have seen, her account, as with many others in Roviana that are similar, constructs a division: those of the time before, like Punai, who were scared, and those that came after, like Josephine, who were happy to have their photograph taken. But she also expresses nostalgia for a time when people were proud of their photographs, when the few photographs people possessed would be displayed prominently in their houses. Prior to the advent of photo albums in Roviana in the 1960s, any photographs people possessed were roughly mounted in locally made wooden frames, usually without glass. Very occasionally, commercially produced frames from Australia or elsewhere were used. Josephine remembers that framed photographs were hung high on the wall of the main room of people's houses. The Methodist mission at Kokenqolo had its own rudimentary darkroom in the early 1900s and gave photographs to valued members of the congregation. Josephine said that if these were given to "people who did not know about photos," they would often be stored out of sight in woven baskets that contained *bakiha* (a particular class of bracelet or armband made of fossilized clam shell) and other locally produced shell valuables.

The number of Roviana people who actually practiced photography in 2001 remained relatively small, at least by comparison to urban centers like Honiara, and certainly by comparison to the vast scale of Euro-American production and consumption. Prior to the 1950s, there would have been hardly any local practitioners. Josephine had an interest in photography because her father, Lawrence MacMahon, was a European working for Burns Philp in Gizo and had a darkroom and his own plate camera in their house. She remembers that she used to watch the negatives and prints being developed. Josephine's exposure to photography is unusual for a Roviana person of that period, and most people I spoke to argued that before the 1950s no one had any desire to learn about photography — "it was a thing for the tie vaka" — and no one could remember any Roviana person other than Kitchener Wheatley who took photographs before World War II. Certainly, few could have afforded the expense of camera, film, and postal fees for the processing of the film via Australia. Josephine could not remember how long Norman operated his darkroom for, but it would certainly have disappeared, along with Norman's house and plantation at Lambete, as a result of the destruction of much of the Munda area during World War II. The great majority of any scant existing photographic record was also lost at this time, as people's belongings were destroyed or misplaced when they were forced to hide in the bush for a long time to avoid the occupying Japanese forces.

The earliest surviving body of photographs in Roviana dates from the late 1940s or early 1950s, and the numbers of these are very small. The only photograph that Josephine has that predates the war is one of her husband-to-be, Kitchener, which he had taken when he was studying in Fiji (figure 2.4). She refers to it as his passport photo, although this does not necessarily signal that that was its intended use, only that the style is similar to that required in official documentation and identity papers under British colonial rule. Head-and-shoulder portrait photographs in circulation in Roviana, whether made in a photo studio and intended for official use or simply framed that way are referred to as "passport style." The photograph of Kitchener arrived accompanied by a "love letter," and Josephine recalled that this sending of photographs as a token of love was a fashion that Kitchener had learned in Fiji: "After the war it was very fashionable to have your photo taken. Kitchener was ahead because his father was Norman [Wheatley — i.e., a European]."[14] Josephine and Kitchener were married just after the end of the war, and Kitchener bought their first Kodak Brownie in the late 1940s. She remembers that they took lots of "swap photos" to send to people.

Talking of a photograph from the 1950s (figure 2.5), Josephine remembers that the dress she is wearing was a new one that she had copied from passengers she had seen on the steamer—at that point some Australian-run cruise ships briefly stopped in Roviana. Formally, the photograph itself resembles prevalent styles of representing family that were the norm in Euro-American popular practices. The pose is typical of the two albums she has of photographs from the 1950s and 1960s that show individual family members and groups standing together. Kitchener sent the films away to Freemans Studio in Sydney, and it took six weeks to get the prints. The negatives were also sent back and, very unusually in terms of Roviana photographic practices, Kitchener had a special album for keeping them, although most have now been lost or have disintegrated.

Josephine also showed me an album of color photographs from the 1990s sent by her daughters, who now live in Australia. These show similar family groups to the 1960s photos, but the majority of the framing of individuals is not full-length. Josephine's disdain for the "rubbish" photographs, often torn from the pages of Australian magazines, that people now pin up in their houses, is typical of the first generation of Roviana people who practiced photography in any sustained way. The kind of formal, posed, family portraits that Josephine grew up with are certainly no longer the types of photograph that many younger Roviana people have, or take today, and the snapshot photography that has been adopted by those under thirty with access to a camera is disparaged by Josephine: "People do not come out good in these photos. We used to be proud of our photos. But now people do not care."[15] There has been a recent shift away from the kind of whole body, formally posed photographs of family that Josephine grew up with. Teenagers such as Voli are now conversant with other photographic styles and genres, but I witnessed teenagers being taught by their elders how to take a photograph that would make people "come out good"—a whole legible body facing the camera straight on.

But the majority of Roviana people do not have as many photographs as Josephine, with her relatively substantial record of her family, and the fact that Voli only has one photograph of herself

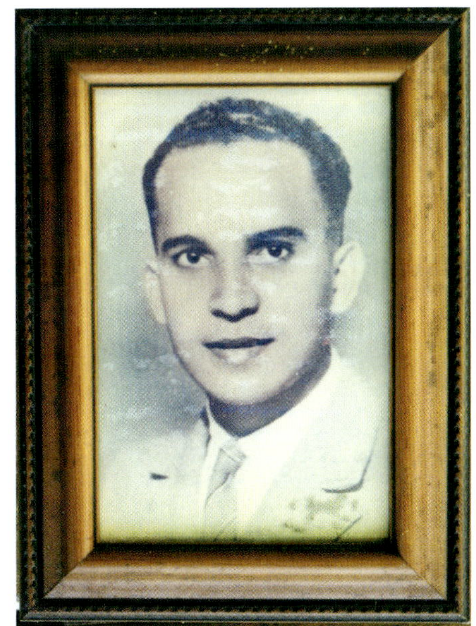

FIGURE 2.4 Framed and tinted photograph of Kitchener Wheatley, 1940.

FIGURE 2.5 Josephine Wheatley (right) and Florence Nose Tino (Faletau's sister). Photograph by Kitchener Wheatley, 1951.

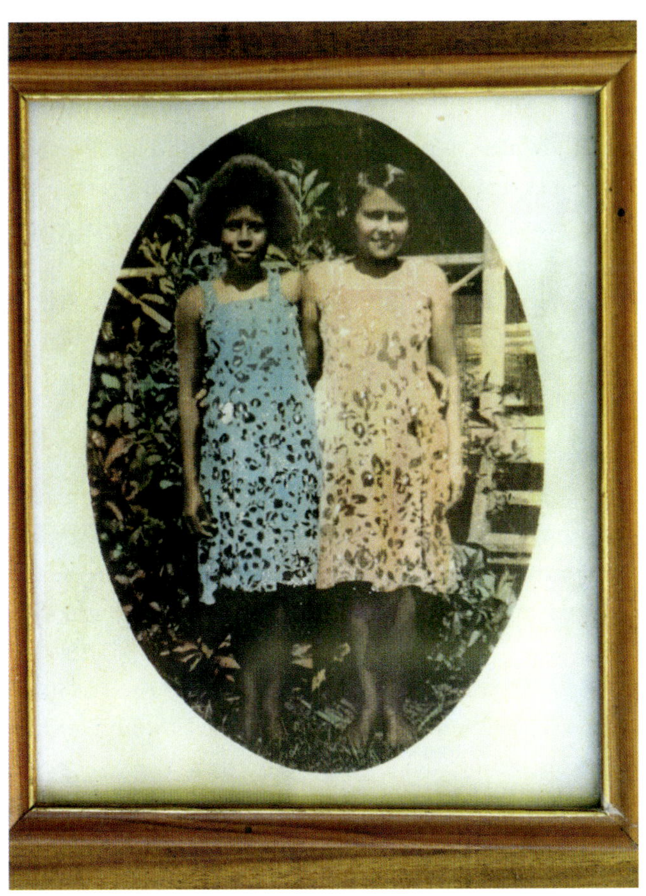

as a young child, taken in 1953 (figure 2.6), is a more common experience for most people. This faded image shows Voli as a three-year-old. She cannot remember who took the photograph, but it is one of her most treasured possessions. It was taken on her birthday, and she does recall that she had just eaten some bread—a novelty at the time. The photograph and its handwritten inscription, "J. Voli at Vivirua" (figure 2.7), are an affirmation of Voli's existence—"this is me"—an insistent statement of identity in the face of change. The nostalgia that Voli feels when delicately handling this fragile piece of paper is sufficient to move her to tears. How can this small faded object have so much identity invested in it? How can it bear that weight?

Such is its hold on notions of self that the thought of being without a photograph of oneself induces a particular kind of fear—the negative corollary of the kind of archiving that photography demands of us. Photographs are accompanied by the apprehension of their loss—they provide only a fragile reassurance. Many older Roviana people told me stories about particular photographs they had lost during the chaos that resulted from the Japanese occupation of Munda in 1942 and the subsequent large-scale battle with U.S. Marines in July and August of 1943. This was a time when many people in Munda fled to the bush, where they remained for many months, leaving belongings behind or losing them in the move. That individuals can remember specific photographs is a testament to their enduring hold over people, and the events of World War II had a profound effect on Roviana people and on their exposure to photography.

A photograph "made in a box" by a U.S. soldier in Munda (figure 2.8), was, according to Voli, the photograph's current owner, taken at the time "when everyone came back from the bush" (returned to Munda after hiding from the Japanese and the fighting). The grass skirts that the women are wearing are from Tonga, not Roviana, and are a staged costume that in many ways plays to colonial imaginaries. Some local people acquired them from Tongan missionaries working for the Methodists at Kokeqolo; others copied the style and wove their own. The soldiers wanted photographs of *susu* (breasts). Voli remembers her mother talking about how they "dressed up" for the soldiers and then sold them the skirts. The nudity is shocking for Voli. At a time when Roviana people had been Christian for decades and wore dresses, going topless was not acceptable, and certainly not

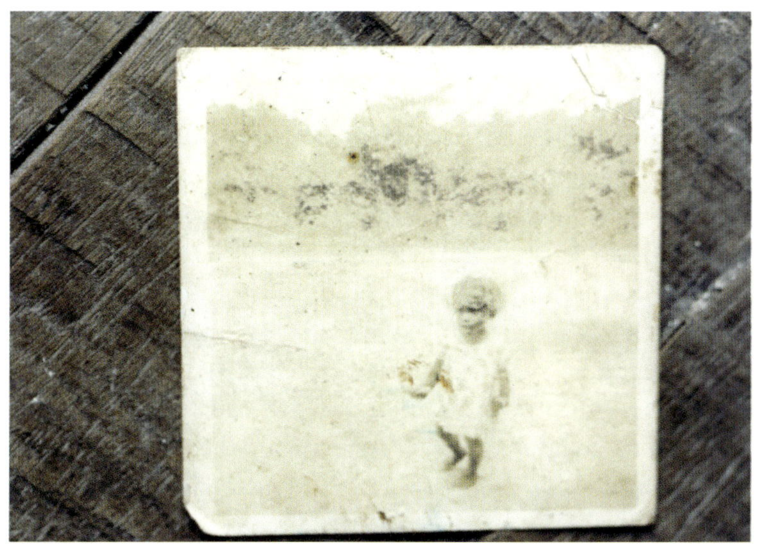

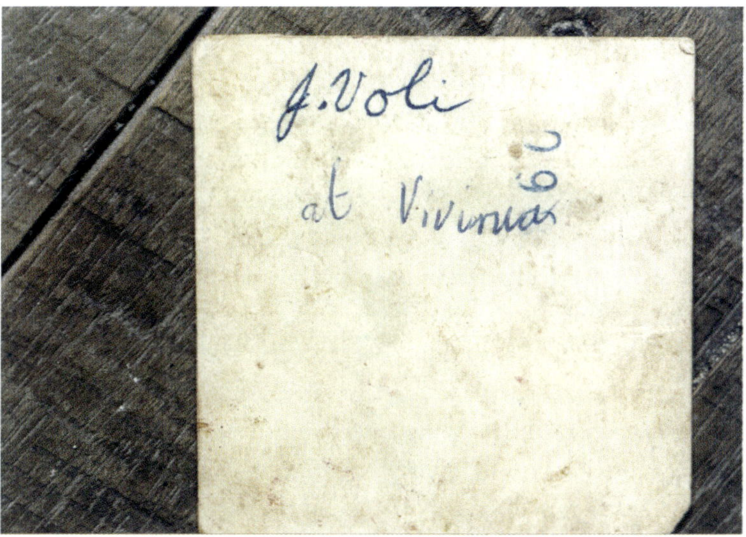

FIGURE 2.6 Voli Gasimata, 1953.

FIGURE 2.7 The back of the photograph of Voli Gasimata (figure 2.6).

for women of this age group. The names inscribed on the reverse of the print (figure 2.9) by Voli's mother, Florrie, reveal a kind of proximal or tactile desire in placing the names in the order they would appear if you could see through the photograph, an attempt to grasp the image more securely.

In addition to exposing Roviana people to unprecedented violence, World War II paradoxically ushered in a new period of "love" that changed local attitudes to photography. Prior to the influence of U.S. soldiers and the rise in popularity of "love photos," young Roviana couples would exchange elaborately carved immature coconuts. This was their way of "sending memory," and it involved the use of fingernails to press a geometric pattern into the soft casing of the nut. The man would incise one line of pattern — full of secret meanings arranged between the couple — and then send the nut to the woman in secret for her to inscribe the next line. The nut was passed back and forth in this manner until "it was full up" with patterns, and Voli asserts that it was both "a letter and a picture (pikisa)." Love photos took on some of the roles of these earlier forms.

Americans gave away a great deal of surplus goods and other material culture during their time in Munda (enterprising Roviana people sold the Americans specially produced local wooden carvings and other "traditional" objects in return) — the beginnings of the current trade in carvings made for the tourist market. But older people reassured me that the objects were not the personal property of the soldiers but "were only given to them for the war." Roviana people started drinking and smoking as a result of the war — something that had been strictly controlled under the British. Americans had nude pikisa, pornographic photographs, and also photographs of dead Japanese soldiers; older people still remember the shock of seeing these kinds of photographs. That one might possess a photograph of someone who had subsequently died was an acknowledged aspect of photography, but that anyone would photograph someone who was already dead was problematic. The Americans' enthusiastic distribution of material goods, including photographs, to Roviana people, made them think that the British were mean. It seems that, in the networks they entered into through this redistribution, the Americans approached local ideals of generosity and sharing that the British had consistently refused to participate in. The U.S. Army used a wooden box-like assembly that housed a camera, but could also process the negative and produce an instant print, much like the

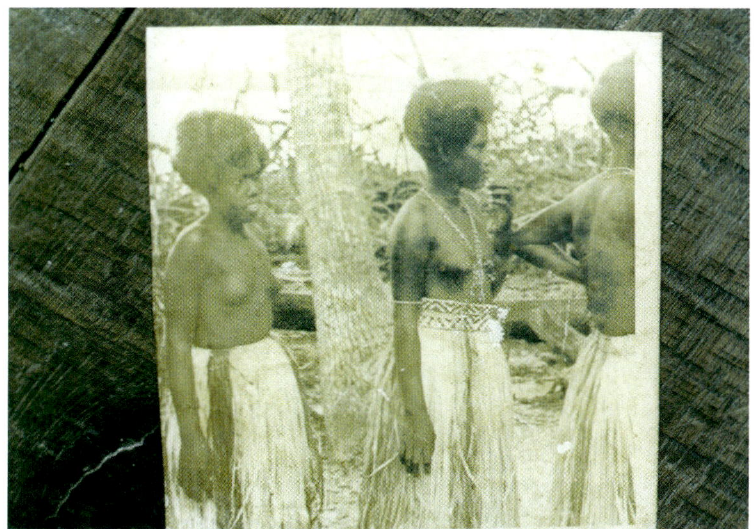

FIGURE 2.8 Salote (left), Florrie (Voli's mother, center), and Edina (right). Photograph taken by unidentified U.S. soldier, ca. 1944.

FIGURE 2.9 Back of the photograph of Salote, Florrie, and Edina (figure 2.8).

homemade street cameras still used in vernacular photographic traditions around the world. Faletau remembers that the soldiers took lots of photographs of local people and gave them to them.

Although the events of World War II were relatively short-lived, they had a powerful impact on the local desire for consumer goods manufactured elsewhere, and the war undoubtedly increased people's exposure to photography. But, for the majority of Roviana people, those who were not part of traders' families or working for the British administration, photography remained distant throughout the 1950s and early 1960s. Despite some knowledge and also firsthand experience as subjects in front of the camera, acquired from missionaries, colonial officials, or expatriate traders, the number of Roviana people who actively practiced photography remained few. Photographs arrived from elsewhere, either geographically or from outsiders based in and around the area. This changed in the mid-1960s with the gradual arrival of cheap instamatic Japanese cameras in the Chinese-owned stores in Gizo, Honiara, and other centers, and with the development of a small photographic studio in one of these stores, An Tuk's.

Studio Stael

During my visits to Honiara in 2000–2001, the Chinese-owned store An Tuk's was frequently shut because the owner had received threats that his business would be burned to the ground if he did not pay to have it "protected." This type of extortion was a regular feature of the "ethnic tension" and general lawlessness that was at the time a part of daily life in the capital. So I had to ask the owner's family for permission to see the photographic studio that I had been told formed part of the store (figure 2.10). After stepping into the boarded-up store after the intense light and heat of the street, my eyes took time to adjust to the gloom—the musty odor of damp—and my skin prickled with the sudden change in temperature. It was a strange space, empty yet retaining something—an accretion—of the presences that had passed through it.

An Tuk's has operated some kind of photographic service in Honiara since the 1950s. Even though there is now an intermittently working 35 mm processing and printing machine in a rival Chinese-owned store in Honiara, An Tuk's was for many years the main store in the Solomon Islands that catered to the photographic needs of local people. Sadly, An Tuk's has not preserved anything of this photographic record. Chinese-owned stores in Gizo and some other regional centers in the Solomons also sold cameras and accepted film for processing in Australia, but nearly all the studio photographs that I saw in Roviana were taken in An Tuk's. Various members of the Tuk family also took commissioned photographs for people and, when requested, occasionally traveled outside the capital to other islands in order to record major local events such as weddings and the installation of new banara. In the mid-1970s the chemist's shop in Honiara, which was run by an ex-pat Australian, also offered a processing service via Australia, but this was short-lived, and An Tuk's has remained until recently the main conduit for photography. Initially the service that An Tuk's offered in the 1950s involved selling Kodak Brownie cameras and film and then sending the exposed film to Australia to be processed and printed. You had to write, or dictate to the store owner, a detailed description of each photograph to send off with the film, but often film would get lost and prints would fail to be returned. Several weeks, or sometimes months, after the film was sent away, a set of contact prints was returned to the store for collection by the customer. It is unclear whether the negatives were also returned with the prints; the An Tuk family was vague about the issue. However, no one I spoke to in Honiara or Roviana could remember ever receiving any negatives with their prints, and apart from two people, nobody in Roviana possessed any.

Importantly, in Roviana photography is largely considered a way to produce an image—singular. It is not seen as a reproductive technology in the sense of allowing the creation of multiple copies. Even Roviana people who had owned Kodak Box Brownies, and could be expected to know something of film and processing, said that they never expected to get, or would have bothered to keep, negatives. This lack of concern for photography's reproductive potential—seen by many Euro-American commentators as central to its identity—reflects a similar focus on photographic prints in Euro-American traditions of what is frequently referred to as family photography. There are a multitude of albums and frames for safely keeping prints (figure 2.11), but far less emphasis is placed on the negative. People keep family albums full of prints but do not always have the corresponding negatives; the two become separated in the process of "archiving."

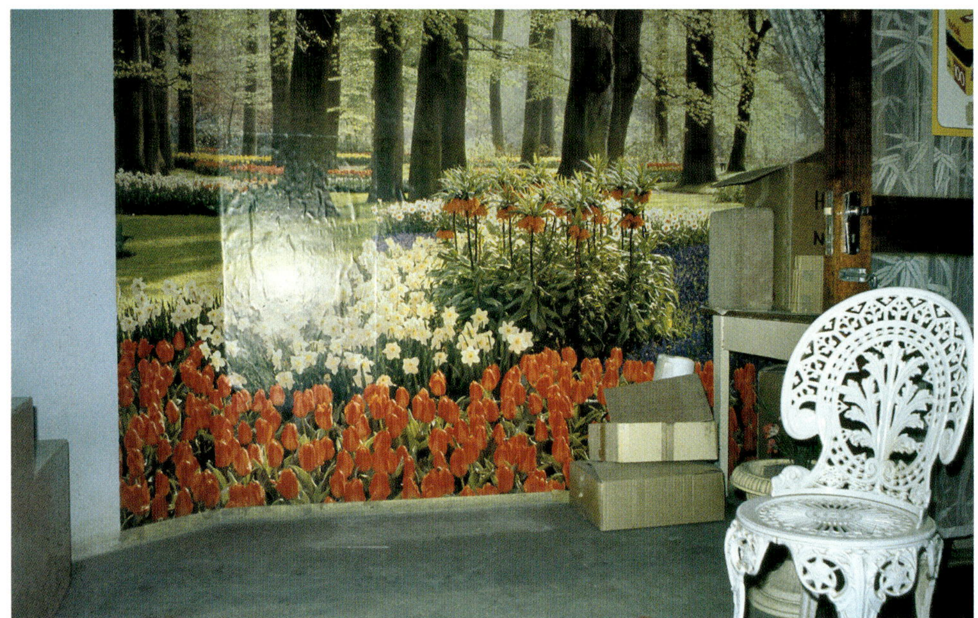

FIGURE 2.10 Studio backdrop in An Tuk's store, Honiara.

FIGURE 2.11 Frames and photo albums in An Tuk's store, Honiara.

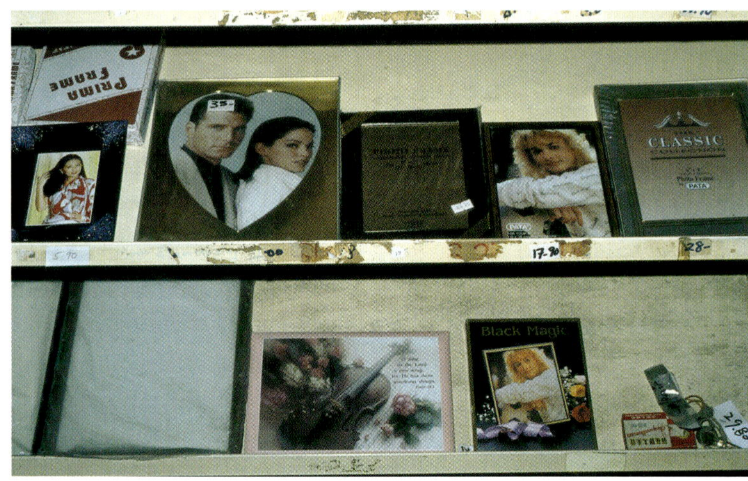

By the early 1970s An Tuk's had established a small studio on the premises that specialized in taking Polaroids—instant photographs that do not require any additional processing. A corner of the store was equipped with a simple folding chair and a variety of plain-colored curtains were used as backdrops. The studio quickly became popular and was busy on the weekends with people queuing to get Polaroid prints made to send to friends, particularly romantic pursuits. Throughout the 1950s and 1960s, the practice of sending love photos steadily increased in popularity, and the introduction of the Polaroid camera made this practice far more accessible as prints were comparatively inexpensive compared to the cost of buying a camera and film or commissioning a photograph. The prints were also instant and could be distributed to friends immediately. However, Polaroid prints cost $1.50 each in Solomon Island dollars throughout the 1970s, which still put them beyond the reach of many when you consider that at the time a yard of 'calico' (Pijin term for printed cotton) was forty-five cents. The *studio stael* (studio style) portrait was popular throughout the 1970s, and, regardless of their provenance, any photographs taken against plain backgrounds are still referred to by Roviana people as studio stael. Figure 2.12 shows a Polaroid from the late 1970s that is typical of the studio stael. There is no emphasis on particular poses or studio props of any kind, but there is a general preference for full-length portraits so that the photograph will make the person "come out good," in the sense of the requirements for a fully legible, whole body.

In terms of other traditions of photography that have adapted the medium to local concerns and expectations, and also responded to the demands made by the medium, Stephen Sprague has described the Nigerian Yoruba practice: older men are photographed in traditional dress sitting so that they face the camera with their hands on their knees, with the camera positioned at waist level so that the viewpoint is from the position of someone looking up or paying homage. Sprague identifies what he calls the "traditional formal portrait" style of Yoruba photography in which "*Ifarahon*, 'visibility,' implies clarity and definition of form and line, and a subsequent clarity of identity. This is emphasized in the photograph by the isolation of the subject against the neutral background, in the sculptural dimensions and symmetry of the figure, and in the inclusion of objects symbolizing the subject's position in Yoruba society" (1978, 55). Although there is no comparable emphasis on a formal pose or on

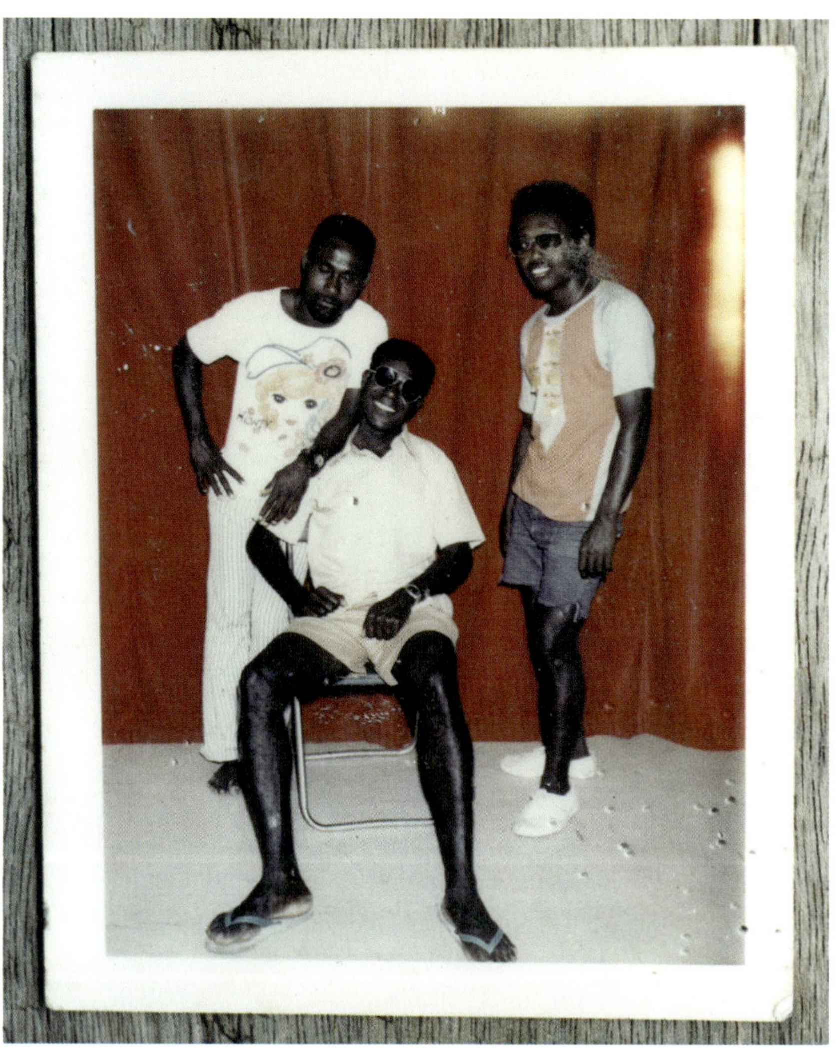

studio props in studio stael photographs taken by Roviana people, the practice of photographing whole bodies that are fully legible is concerned with the desire for a similar kind of visibility and clarity. Individuals are thought to stand out better when seen against a neutral backdrop: "It makes you come out good and be strong. You want to have a good picture. If you have rubbish [*rabis*] behind [a visually complex, or distracting background], you cannot come out good."[16]

Studio stael makes you "come out" from the flatness of the background. It reveals or discloses you, a process that Roviana people refer to as *va vura ia*. A complex background, or a figure that is not full-length, interrupts the ability of the individual to be revealed or come out good. Successful portraits are those that effectively isolate whole figures. There are formal conventions of seating in Roviana that position older senior men both physically and metaphorically in front of those who come behind, but these conventions have not been translated into any formalized practices of posing for photographs. The correlation between visual clarity and identity has as its opposite the fears and anxieties that are associated with any lack of visibility. Together they form a sliding scale, with blurred or indistinct photographs at one end and legible whole bodies at the other. Among older people in particular, there is a feeling that photographs that show parts of bodies are not quite right; they have not come out good, and this can have a potentially negative effect on their subjects. This figures a similitude or direct equivalence between photograph and subject. To have a photograph of oneself that has not come out good is to risk a similar dissolution of one's own body.

Voli remembers that when the Polaroid shown in figure 2.13 was taken, she was several months pregnant and had just bought the dress she is wearing. She recalls that An Tuk's had different backgrounds, all plain colors, dark blue, red, and this brown. She had the Polaroid taken to send to Isaac Molia, to whom she had just become engaged: "Lots of young people wanted their photographs taken in the studio to send to girlfriends and boyfriends. It was modern. We exchanged photos before we were married — it was the normal thing to do. An Tuk used to come out to the islands to take photographs of weddings, but we had a friend with a camera."[17] Polaroids significantly added to the idea that each photograph is a unique object in Roviana. They were also one of the key features, along with fashion and music, of appearing modern. Roviana people of Voli's generation — she was born in the early 1950s — remember that from the 1960s onward "people married for love" and often ignored parental wishes and any concerns for the extended kin group (*butubutu*), which had previously been the arbiter of marriage and lineage alliances. There is a strong connection made here between photography and a newly acquired sense of individual choice in terms of marriage.

Liam Buckley has described the shift in Gambian studio photography from the ability and desirability of photographs to portray "*jikko* — the character, mood, or personality of a person" — up to the time of independence in 1965 to a contemporary focus on "the number of props (*juuntuwaay*) that clients (*kiliyaan*) use during

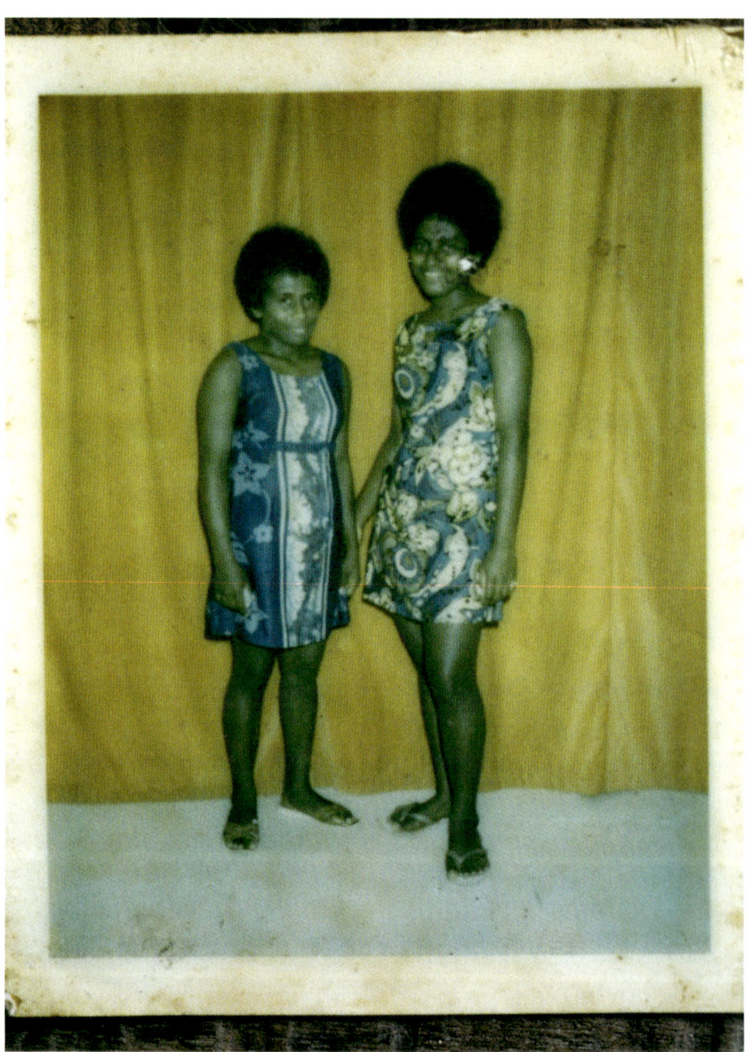

sittings. These accessories belong to a category of imported goods closely associated with fashionable living, and older photographers hold them chiefly responsible for driving *jikko* out of the studios" (2000, 72). The clients of Gambian studios use these props to "complete" themselves and a person's photographic clarity is "proportional to the number of things amassed and displayed within one's vicinity" (72). Although there is sometimes a similar concern with fashion and imported goods among Roviana people, there is no overt emphasis on the display of props in studio stael photographs.

This is not simply the result of the fact that studios like An Tuk's are Chinese owned rather than run by Solomon Islanders. The kinds of imported goods that Buckley discusses — cassette players, radios, watches, and so on — are all easily available in stores like An Tuk's, and also in people's homes and other locations where studio stael photographs are often replicated. The central focus for Roviana people is instead on whole, legible bodies. They may be wearing a new pair of sunglasses, or a new dress, but these are seen as incidental to the ability to come out good as a whole body — this is what makes a photograph strong.

Figure 2.14 shows Donald Maepio's sister-in-law, Savi Leve, and demonstrates the way in which studio stael was absorbed into other photographic practices. It was taken by Donald on his Brownie when Savi was fourteen years old and was staying in Donald's house in Honiara in 1979. An expatriate agent at the pharmacy in Honiara sent the film to Australia to be developed on Donald's behalf. Donald's wife, Rosemary, remembers that her sister was wearing her new dress that she had copied from tourist styles. The black-and-white Polaroid of Oso (a friend of Donald's from Baraulu, Roviana) (figure 2.15), taken by someone from An Tuk's in the lobby of the Mendana Hotel — the first big modern hotel in Honiara — in 1972, shows how "modern" spaces, wherever they were located, could be effectively turned into opportunities for studio stael photographs.

But, unlike the Indian clients of photographic studios discussed by Christopher Pinney, there is no desire in Roviana photography to make yourself "come out *better*" (Pinney 1997, 179; my emphasis). People do not borrow props or put on other styles of clothing. Roviana people would not consider impersonating a particular identity. Neither are there any strong traditions of assuming the dress or style of someone from another part of the Solomon Islands, despite this having happened briefly during the fighting in Munda in the mid-1940s (MacDougall 1992; Pinney 1997). My discussion of this dressing up in other photographic traditions provoked much laughter. Young people want to wear their new dresses, and to appear "fashionable"; older men wear their best white shirts and a lap-lap. They want to come out good, but there is no desire to play with the kinds of representational spaces potentially opened up by the photograph. Roviana people do not assume that the body is a fluid site capable of conjuring up different interior identities (Pin-

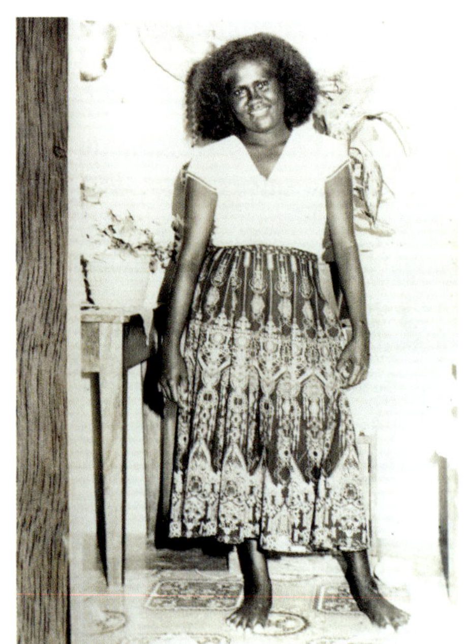

FIGURE 2.14 Savi Leve. Photograph by Donald Maepio, 1979.

FIGURE 2.15 Oso, in the lobby of Mendana Hotel, photo by An Tuk's studio, 1972.

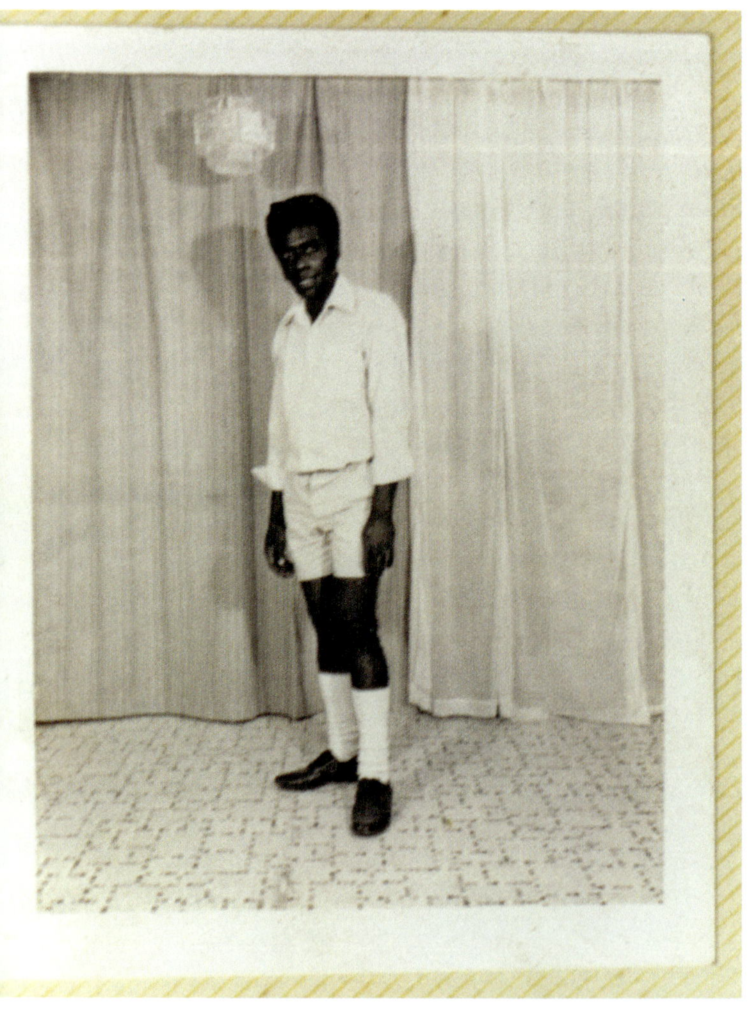

ney 1997, 209). Photography for Roviana people is about the fully legible disclosure of a whole body, whereas Indian clients of photo studios express an active dislike for "realistic" photographs (Pinney 1997, 180). The studio practices that Buckley writes about suggest that for contemporary Gambians, "the magic of the camera has nothing to do with the capacity to conjure up some imagined interior" (2000, 71). For Roviana people, studio *stael*, like other forms of photography, is very much concerned with photography's ability to reveal a whole body that is concerned with character and being strong, but we should be wary of making presumptions about the way it might be connected to any imagined interior.

Although the magic of photography for Roviana people is about its ability to capture character, we need to remember that studio *stael* is not indigenous in the sense that Indian or Gambian photographic studio practices are (see Buckley 2000; Houlberg 1992; Pinney 1997). The images produced in this style are part of a service offered to local people by Chinese traders that has only responded in a very minimal way to any local aesthetic concerns. There is no history of commercially run photographic studios operated by the British that might then have been taken over by local entrepreneurs—unlike the situation in Fiji where British-run studios were gradually taken over by Indian photographers (see Chandra 2000). Solomon Islanders do sometimes operate the cameras set up in, or owned by, Chinese stores for taking passport photographs, but no Roviana person has ever run a photographic studio.

Unlike other studio photographic traditions, in Roviana there is no interest in directly manipulating the spaces of the photograph. Some Roviana people drew analogies between photographs and X-ray images, suggesting that both made the "inside come out," and others commented that they had seen photographs of people "doubled," but that this was the work of malevolent spirits rather than any desired outcome of the photographer. There is equally no playing with the actual surface of the image in Roviana; the one example I saw of hand tinting was commissioned in Australia. There is no overpainting or any other kind of visual augmentation as there is in other vernacular traditions elsewhere in the world (see Pinney 1997). What matters is the link between photography and character (*hahanana*)—the physical dimensions of this connection—and the possibility of coming out good, along with the potential dangers of not doing so. Roviana people assert that photographs that make you come out good, ones that depict fully legible, frontal, whole bodies, are capable of making hahanana present in the image. There is a certain flatness that is thought advantageous; people are photographed straight on, not in profile. The aim is not to come out in any three-dimensional sense, but in the sense of being present in the photographic object. Haitians use images of people superimposed on sealed bottles and the like to show that they are safe, or that they have captured someone (Houlberg 1992). This resonates with local concerns but is achieved in Roviana through retaining the photograph's surface as a site for the construction of a presence that stares back, rather than through any processes of collage or montage.

In the late 1980s the Solomon Islands government made it illegal to own a Polaroid camera without a government-issued certificate because of a public scandal in the newspapers over their use in taking "lady pikisa" (pornography). Although photographic pornography is as old as the medium itself, there is a sense that new visual technology, such as Polaroid cameras and video, which dispense with the need for any processing by an external source, have enabled the production of homemade pornography on a large scale. Lady pikisa were circulated in Roviana in the 1970s and 1980s alongside pornographic magazines of Euro-American and Japanese origin, and in 2000–2001 groups of men would occasionally gather in people's houses to watch pornographic videos that they had bought from Japanese and Korean tuna fishers working on factory ships in the area and at the tuna-canning plant at Noro. Even in small villages within Roviana Lagoon that are nominally affiliated with the Christian Fellowship Church, which are generally recognized locally as being places of order where all alcohol is banned, people would occasionally connect a TV and VCR to a generator and watch a range of pornographic videos alongside action movies until the early hours of the morning. During the disorder of the ethnic tensions in Honiara, the only public cinema in Honiara, the Super Cinema, was screening semipornographic videos from the United States to an eager audience of young men (figure 2.16).

Contrary to a thriving local film industry and a huge popular visual culture, which is the source of many of the poses assumed by clients of Indian photographic studios (Houlberg 1992), Roviana people and other Solomon Islanders in 2001 had relatively few imported videos and magazines. However, in the capital, Honiara,

some people had access to satellite TV, and India's Star TV service
was very popular. The photographic mural that in 2001 formed the
backdrop for the studio of An Tuk's (figure 2.10) does not represent
some fantasy of modernity. Despite showing a decidedly European-
looking scene, with its formal display of tulips, the space created is
not concerned with any locally conceived "experiment with modernity" (Appadurai 1997, 6), or with visualizing any aspirations toward
Euro-American lifestyles. The mural that predated the current one
in An Tuk's was of a tropical — in this case Caribbean — beach with
white sand and coconut trees (seen in figure 2.17). Having a photograph taken, sending photographs to others, and having them to
display are all ways of being modern, but there is no sense that the
photograph itself is a space within which to experiment.

People use An Tuk's studio because it is the only one available,
other than one or two Chinese-owned stores in Honiara, that use
Polaroid cameras to take passport or other official photographs
against plain white backgrounds. There is no sense of any desirability
for a particular backdrop; the only issue is whether the photograph
is full-length or from the shoulders up. The latter has a dual role: as
the option for official images and as personal portraits in the context
of people's albums and piecemeal collections.

Studio stael reached the height of its popularity in the 1970s
and 1980s. It is not considered modern by the teenagers of today.
With the increasing availability, and relatively decreasing cost, of
cameras, photography has now come directly within the reach of
many more affluent Honiara residents. To some degree this democ-
ratization of photography has filtered down to Roviana. Young
people there sometimes have snapshot photographs that they have
been given by visiting cousins or relatives who have gone to school
in Honiara. Some even have the kinds of albums of photographs
that Clarinda sent home to her parents (figure 2.18). These young
people watch imported videos — Stanley Kubrick's *Eyes Wide Shut*
with Tom Cruise and Nicole Kidman, referred to locally as a "lady
film," proved a particularly perplexing film for teenagers while I was
in Roviana in 2000–2001. They occasionally look at a copy of a well-
thumbed Australian teenage music magazine, and one family in Roviana has access to satellite TV. The flow of images is increasing, but
access remains very polarized. Some people have very little exposure
to modern visual media of any kind.

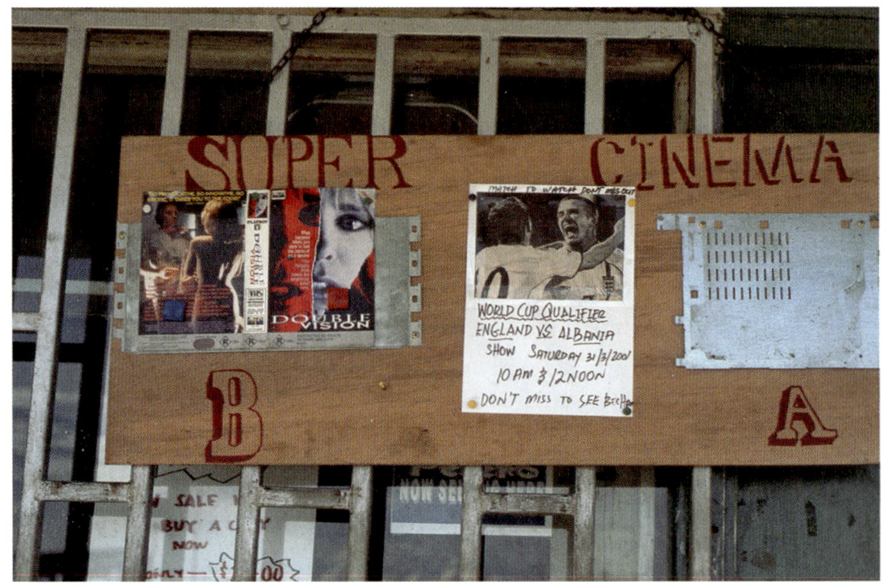

FIGURE 2.16 Entrance to Super Cinema, Honiara.

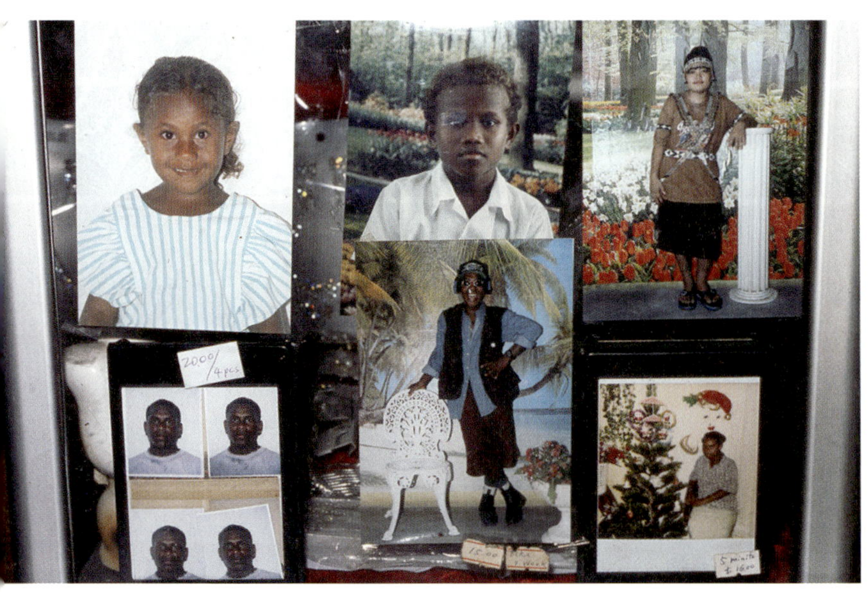

FIGURE 2.17 Photographs on display, An Tuk's store.

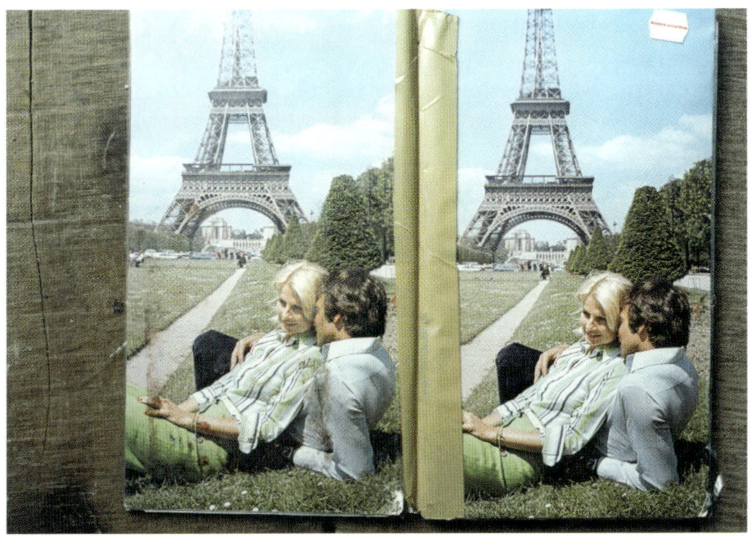

Albums

Outside of traders' families, like Josephine Wheatley's, the use of photographic albums was not popular in Roviana until the mid-1960s and, though a lot of families might aspire to owning an album, most still do not possess one. The few photographs that families do have are often kept in a far more haphazard way, although particularly important photographs are stored in small woven baskets inside larger baskets along with other objects, such as valuable shell rings and other ancestral heirlooms. Photographs are sometimes kept in creased and torn envelopes or housed in homemade wooden frames. There is a difference between the narratives that can be created by the juxtaposition and rejuxtaposition of photographs in these kinds of ad hoc collections and the desire to construct some kind of more fixed narrative in an album, even though, as we will see, the latter is seldom achieved. When looking through albums with Roviana people, individual photographs were often removed from their plastic sleeves and passed back and forth. Sometimes they were placed back where they came from, sometimes not. There is a fluidity to the kinds of personal and family narratives that these albums are intended to tell.

The albums that are kept by Roviana families range from the small, plastic books capable of taking only one print per page to those with multiple pockets and foldout pages, or large pages on which individual photographs can be positioned on a sticky background and then covered with a single sheet of acetate. The albums mostly date from the 1960s or 1970s, although some people reported that these were new albums that had been bought to replace earlier ones that had rotted away.

As was the case with love photos, the fashion for creating family albums was a product of exposure to the photographic practices of outsiders. In this case the outsiders were the British colonial officials working in the Solomons in the 1960s. Most owners of albums that date back to the 1960s worked for the British administration and said they got the idea of a family album from their employees. Donald Maepio has three family albums, two of which have plastic sleeves and, unusually, many of the photographs have been given a small caption and a number.

Although Donald told me that he has long since lost the list that the numbers refer to, this is the most overt example of family archiving that I came across in Roviana. Most albums reflected a far more haphazard mixture of photographs than Donald's roughly chronological sequence — influenced, he told me, by his bookkeeping when he was employed by the British administration. Donald took the majority of the photographs in this album with his Kodak 110 Instamatic camera, which he bought in the 1970s.[18] The labels show the names, places, and dates, and he wrote them because he wanted "a record": "Lots of friends come to look at these photos. The children like to look at them to see how they have changed. An album is a good thing for keeping. I want to have an album that is full up. When I first got the album in the 1970s very few people had one. They were very jealous. I got the idea for the album from the British people I worked for. I wanted to make a history album so that people could see it when they come."

Roviana people who own family albums like this often include images cut from magazines and photographs acquired from relatives, friends, and tourists. The aim is to have a full album, something that is difficult for families with little or no access to photography. There is a desire to show others your album — to ask someone to sit in your house and look at an album is a sign of being modern, but there is also an associated anxiety. Asking Roviana visitors, particularly any extended kin, to the house to look at an album admits the possibility of them asking for individual photographs, something that would be hard for a generous host to flatly decline.

As a result of this process, many families' albums are actually composed of photographs of other people's families and their extended kin groups. Talking of family photographic albums in the Gambia, Buckley reports that "it is common for people to write a 'welcome' in the inside cover of a photograph album. The invitation to view a collection of snaps is usually administrative and legislative in tone, and written in upper case: 'Attention! Attention! For your information, look at the card or picture to your satisfaction. But do not remove any card please. By Order. Thanks,' 'Please do not remove any picture from this album until you are told. By Order,' and 'Visit the pages but never pull out any card without permission. By Order.' A signature always accompanies the instructions, lending the authority of ownership that belongs to the individuated and named resident" (2000, 26).

The photograph of Frida Wheatley from another of Donald's albums reveals the circuitous route by which some photographs end up in family albums (figures 2.19 and 2.20). Taken in 1964 by a friend of Frida's (Frida is the cousin of Donald's wife, Rosemary), the photograph was sent to Frida's parents, Josephine and Kitchener Wheatley, in Munda. Rosemary told me: "When Frida came to stay back in Roviana in her holidays her cousins would stay with her. That was when Frida gave the photo to Virginia [Rosemary's sister] and then Virginia gave the photo to me because I had an album to keep it safe, and because Frida was away at school in Sydney. People send other people photos to look after. When someone dies we look back at all their old photos. Some we can give back."[19]

The photographs in Roviana albums reveal the contours of the family and, additionally, through the exchanges in which they are entangled, the wider network of relations with the extended kin group. This circulation of photographs among families and individuals works against the equation of family album with the nuclear family, which has been discussed as a central feature of contemporary Euro-American vernacular traditions (see Holland 1997). But Roviana photographic albums do resemble early photographic albums in Europe, which were often composed of a whole range of commercially purchased cartes de visite of royalty and famous figures of the day alongside photographs of members of a large extended family (see Holland 1997, 117). The process of viewing these kinds of Roviana albums reveals and effectively pictures the efficacy of the family's links with wider networks; Bourdieu has talked of

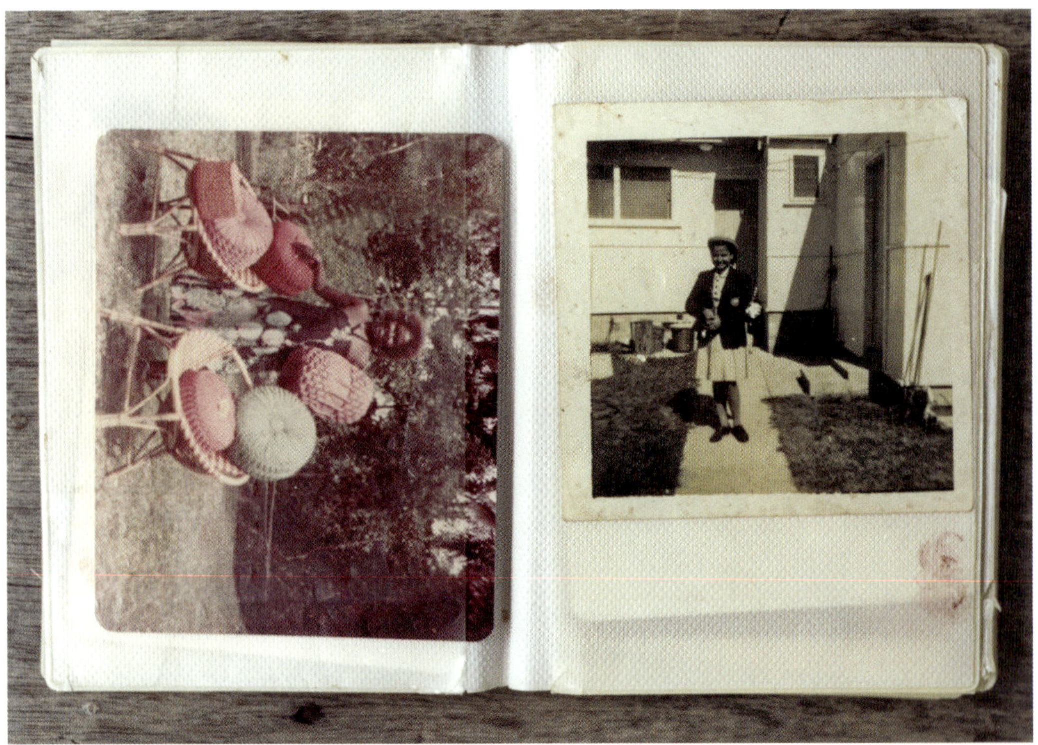

FIGURE 2.19 Pages from Donald Maepio's photo album. On right, Frida Wheatley outside a house in Sydney, 1964.

FIGURE 2.20 Back of the photograph of Frida Wheatley (figure 2.19).

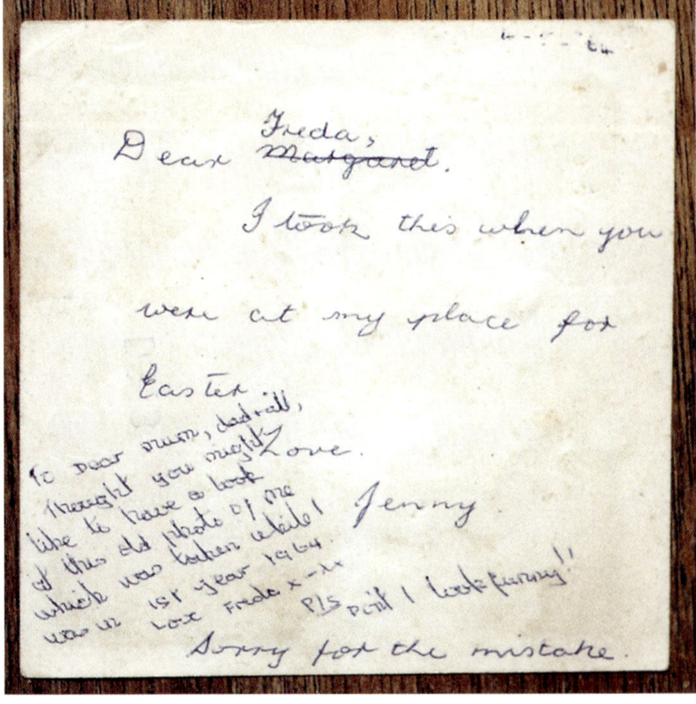

European wedding photographs as "sociograms," figural representations of social relationships (Bourdieu 1990, 23). Visitors and friends are invited to sit and look at the album and, as the pages are turned one by one and individual photographs are taken out to be passed back and forth, stories are told and connections slowly accumulate until they form a map of the family's position within the butubutu and relevant issues or bits of news are raised.

Donald is proud that he had one of the first wedding albums in Roviana—"even now it is rare," he said—and it reveals a range of links beyond the butubutu that are typical of those prominently displayed in some albums. The photograph on the top left of Donald's wedding album (figure 2.21; Donald and Rosemary are the couple on the left) was taken by Bruce Palmer, an Australian expatriate working on Vella Lavella, where the marriage took place on "Dec. 8th '73," as the handwritten note on the photograph records. The photograph of Rosemary (bottom right) was taken by another visiting Australian. Through their material biographies, photographs such as this reveal connections to expatriates and others in influential political and social positions. Donald explained:

> If you have photos you are very lucky. It is not a custom thing. An Australian lady took the photo of Rosemary and sent the print back to her. If the Australians had not taken photos I would not have any. I wanted new things. I wanted things to give to my wife. A photo is very special. It is something very different from our culture. We also exchanged handkerchiefs. Sending photos makes people happy so that their love can continue unbroken. Photos are even more important when you are not in the same place together. I also sent her plastic flowers from the Chinese shop. There used to be a song from Isabel [Island] in the 1950s about sending watches, dresses, and handkerchiefs to your girlfriend. It went, "every something from the ship is for you." But in the end the boy loses the girl. Sometimes there would be a suicide over love.

Photograph albums demonstrate connections with a wider world and the efficacy of the owner in mobilizing those connections. They were also concerned with the modern world of love—which, as Donald points out, "was a new thing for us." Donald bought his first camera, a Kodak Brownie, in 1963 from a British employer. Several people bought cameras from this man, who worked develop-

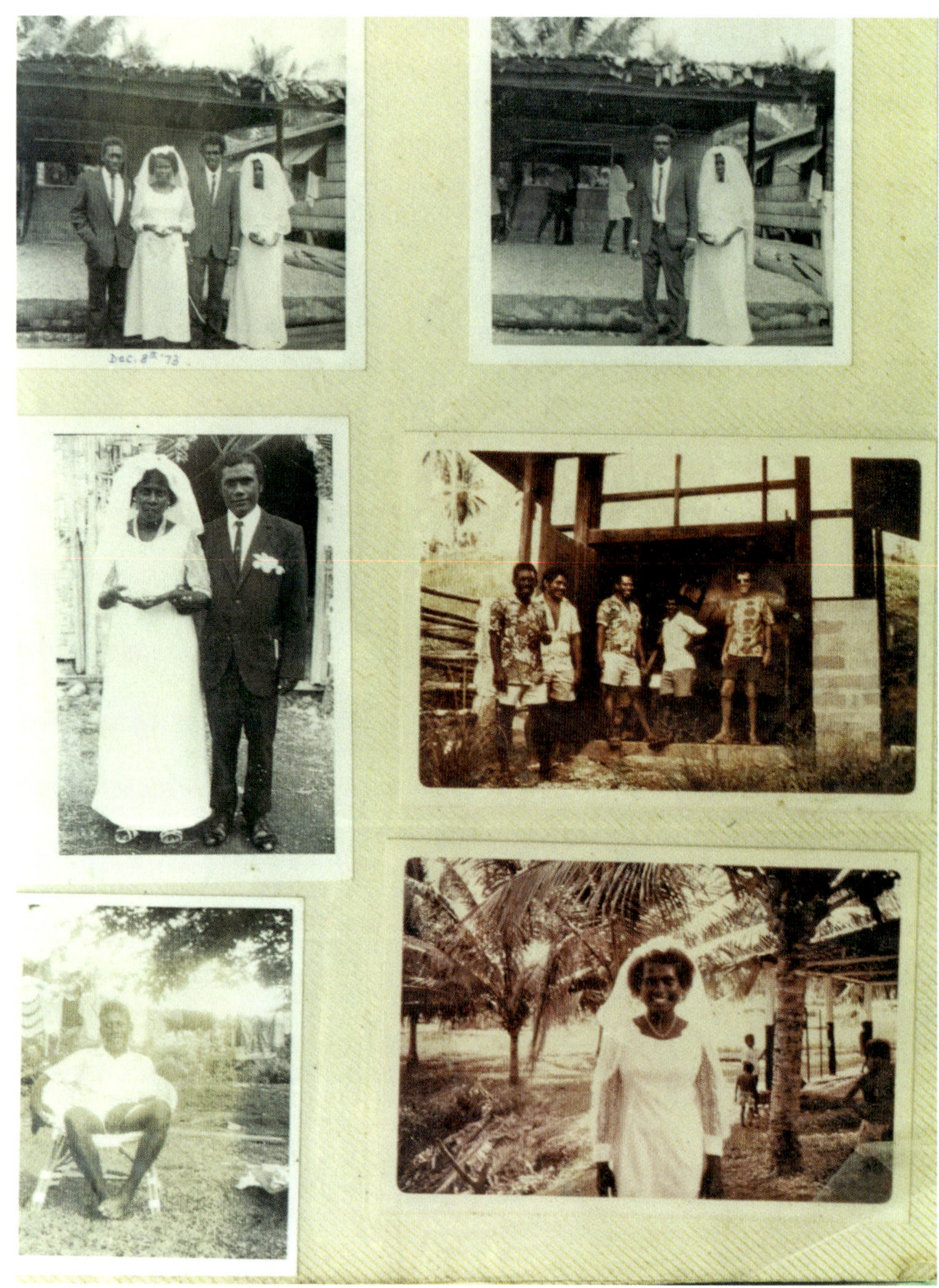

FIGURE 2.21 Donald Maepio's wedding album.

ing photographs in a laboratory in Yandina (Russell Islands) that carried out research on coconuts. It cost twelve Australian dollars to have a film developed by mail in Australia. Lots of film never came back, as a popular local myth has it, the film was stolen in Australia "to make postcards" for commercial sale, or the prints were stolen when they arrived back in the Solomons. When he could make prints in Yandina, Donald gave photographs to "every friend": Anytime that someone came to the house they could say they wanted a photo and I would give it." But when he was in Honiara he made an album and did not give anything away. Lots of people, both within and outside his own butubutu, asked him to take photographs. He made them buy their own film: "People wanted photos of their picnic." When he left Yandina, Donald only took photographs for very close friends.

The problem of having photograph albums, which was often reiterated to me by their owners, was that people could ask for images from them. One of the complaints often leveled against Roviana people who have lived abroad, or even for a protracted length of time in Honiara, is that "they do not want to share any more." Roviana conceptions of generosity mean that an album's owner is always having to devise ways of retaining the photographs that have been so painstakingly collected.

Roviana people have appropriated the Euro-American format of the family album, but the form is often more important than the content. Any photograph will do, even an image of Tom Cruise torn from a magazine. The narratives that these albums develop are fluid and not always coherent. Owners frequently had photographs in their albums of people they could no longer recognize—photographs that they could no longer remember how they acquired or who they were of. Catherine Keenan has suggested that "we do not . . . simply remember with the aid of photographs; we remember in terms of them, even . . . in the absence of an actual camera" (1998, 60). One of Voli's albums consists mostly of blank spaces where friends and relatives have requested photographs, and she is concerned that she "no longer has these memories" (figure 2.22).

Taking photographs from an album deprives the owner of those memories as though there were no way to "keep them" or retain them without the images. Voli expresses a similar anxiety about the gradual fading of photographs. The decay of the photographic object is a matter of grave concern for Roviana people. Donald took a

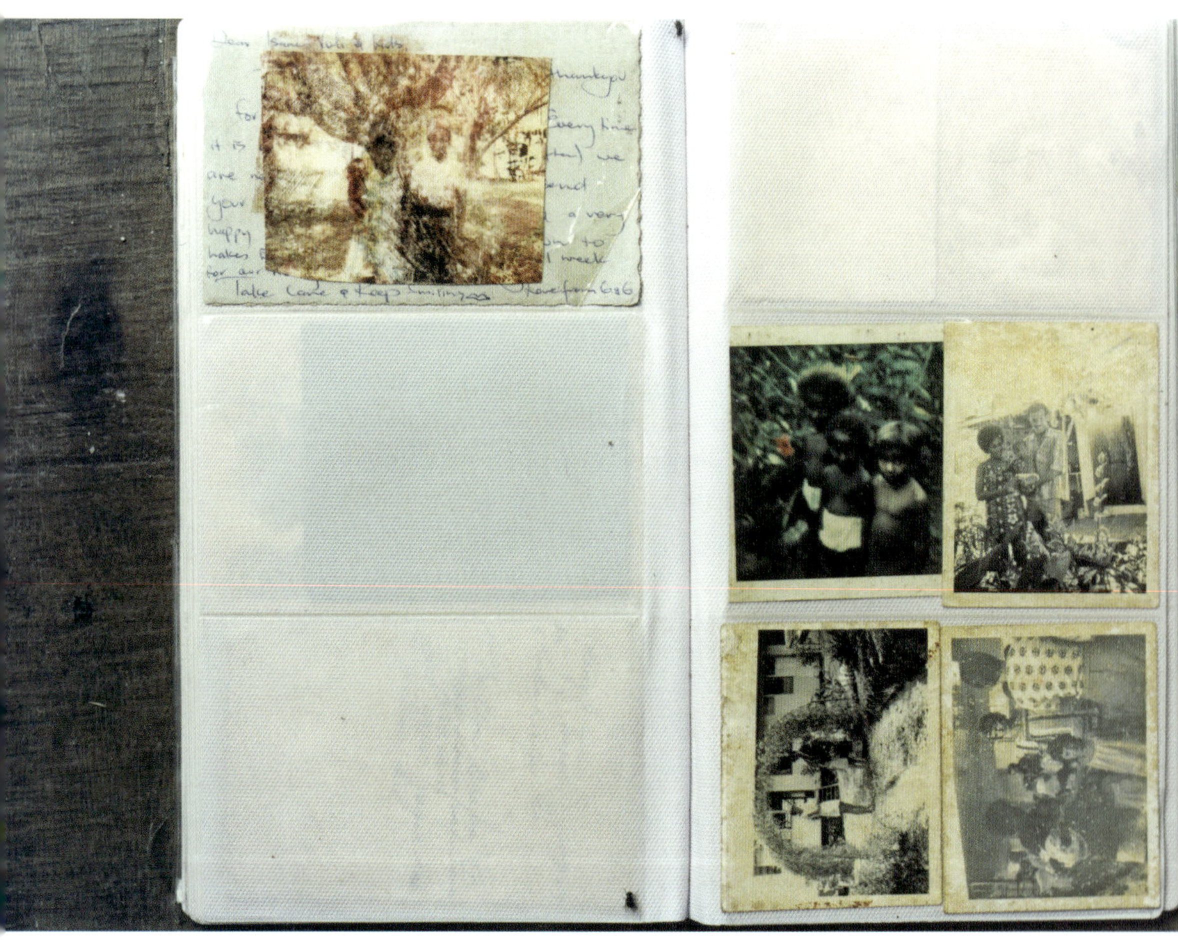

FIGURE 2.22 One of Voli's photo albums.

photograph of his father, Obed Bisili, in January 1982, six months before he died (figures 2.23 and 2.24): "It would be hard to remember him without the photo. I took two photos. One on his own so he would come out good. One with family. I am very lucky to have a photo of him before he died [these are the only two photographs of his father that Donald has]. Now I can remember. When I look at the photo I can remember him. I can hear his voice. Before we could only remember people by thinking of who they looked like [among the living]. Now we have this."[20]

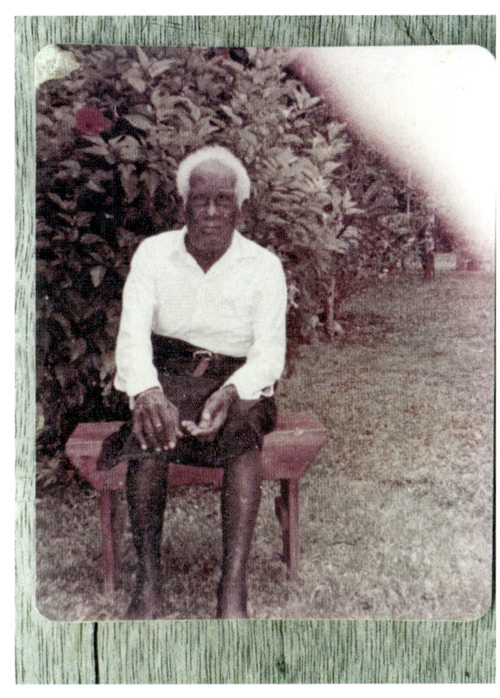

FIGURE 2.23 Obed Bisili. Photograph by Donald Maepio, 1982.

FIGURE 2.24 Donald Maepio holding a photograph of his father.

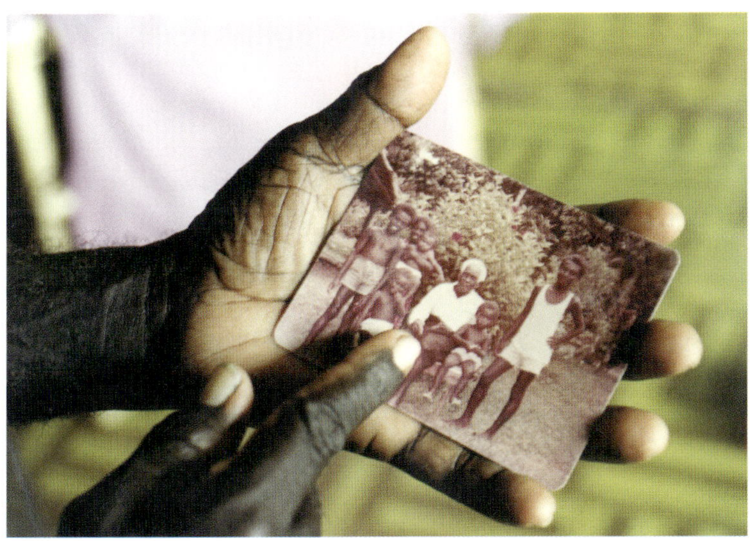

The photograph of snow taken by Clarinda is usefully seen in relation to another print included in the album that she sent home to her parents (figure 2.25). Clarinda first went to New Zealand in 1995 on a scholarship to study medicine in Christchurch. She was there for two years before returning to Munda after encountering "problems," although after spending time back at home she returned to Christchurch in early 2000 to complete her diploma. She graduated in September 2000 then went to Auckland, where she disappeared. Her mother, Voli, told me: "We did not know where she was living—we tried to find her." She wrote a letter to say that she did not want to come back to Munda. Voli said: "Her lifestyle is Western now. She is in-between." This is Voli's way of explaining Clarinda's decision not to return. For Voli this particular photograph evokes an almost unbearable sense of loss, but it is also an object that holds out a vital sense of connection. The memory work that the image is required to do seems familiar—a history shaped by longings and emotions, as much as remembered facts.

Clarinda's photographs were taken to be exchanged, to be given or sent to someone else—they circulate and connect. This is a primary feature of photography in Roviana, as it is elsewhere (see Chandra 2000). The particular scope of the exchanges, voluntary or not, is indicative of Roviana sociality. Clarinda's photographs resemble Euro-American vernacular traditions. But, importantly, as we have seen with the photograph of snow, the photographs also reveal Roviana notions of animism. How are we to understand Voli's concern for the presence of spirits in the photograph of snow falling? They are not posed in the way many Roviana photographs are. They are snapshots—they signal a change in attitude toward photography among younger people. The ritual of being in front of the camera has changed. For many Roviana people, the game of identity played out through photography is one that can have serious consequences. To be photographed entails both the promise of coming out good and the risk of not doing so. To remain unphotographed means you might not endure in the memory of others.

As I sat with Voli as she carefully handled the photographs that Clarinda sent, there was an obvious sense of physical connection. Keenan suggests that photography is a permanent feature of our memory, but is also antithetical to it, and follows Roland Barthes's

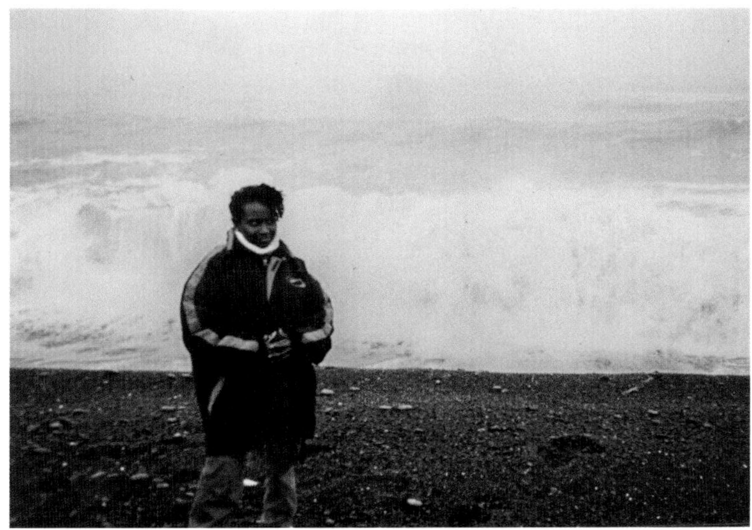

FIGURE 2.25 Clarinda on a beach in New Zealand, 2000.

argument that "photography is never, in essence, a memory.... It actually blocks memory, quickly becomes a counter-memory" (Keenan 1998; Barthes 1984, 91). According to Geoffrey Batchen, "Barthes based his claim on the presumed capacity of the photograph to replace the immediate, physically embracing experience of involuntary memory (the sort of emotional responses often stirred by smells and sounds) with frozen illustrations set in the past; photography, Barthes implies, replaces the unpredictable thrill of memory with the dull certainties of history" (2004, 15; see Keenan 1998, 63). Batchen goes on to suggest that the challenge for photography is to become something more physical, closer to touch, smell, or sound. As Voli recounts a series of stories about Clarinda that have been provoked by the photograph of her on the beach (stories that connect that beach with those in Roviana), the photograph involves a sense of physical connection. Or rather this physical dimension—which was always present—becomes of central importance. The photograph retains something of Clarinda; it is in effect a haunting (see Smith and Vokes 2008). Roviana attitudes toward photography suggest not so much a memory-image but a memory-object.

Presence

During one of the visits I made to Honiara in 2001, I stayed with Ronald Talasassa, a friend from Roviana. Ronald is a magistrate and, with the recent troubles in the capital, he had been mostly staying

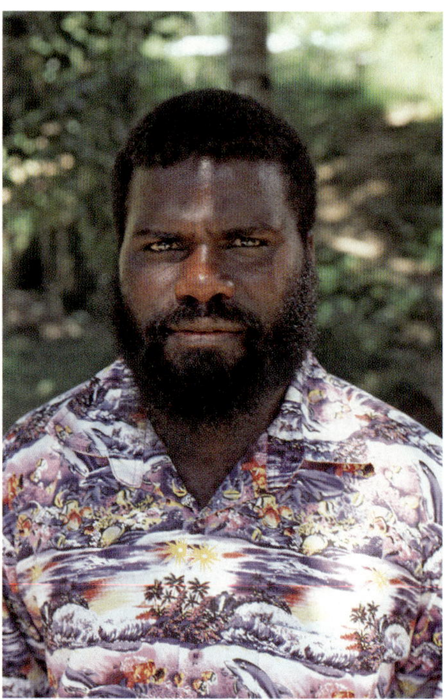

in a new house he had built on his parents' land in Munda. While
back in the capital to preside over an important court case, he kept
two armed bodyguards with him day and night. At his request, I
took a photograph (figure 2.26) of him early one morning. He wore
a favorite shirt and decided that the tree in his garden would form
a background from which he could successfully stand out. When I
showed him the print several weeks later, he had this to say about it:
"The eyes are strong [*ninira*] — you can see that I am strong inside; I
have a strong character [*hahanana*]. You can see that I can do things.
I will make things come out good."

For me the photograph is a portrait of Ronald. It is an image I
have on my wall at home. It is a coming together of likeness and
identity. When I asked him if he was worried about the fact that
the photograph does not show his whole body, he said that this was
not ideal, but, since the photograph was for me (I had taken other
full-length photographs for Ronald), he was not too concerned.
The visibility and clarity of whole bodies is an important expectation of photographs in Roviana. As one elderly woman pointed
out, "photographs [maqomaqo][21] are true because they show our
body [*tinina*]."[22] In a discussion of Euro-American daguerreotypes,

Trachtenberg suggests that the way they recorded any motion or duration as a blur prompts this question: "Is the picture of a person with a blur in place of a head, or the head cropped away, any less a picture 'of' that person, no matter how little a likeness it projects?" (1992, 188). However, photography quickly became an armature for a modern notion of the self: "[By] making the conventional idea of the continuous, coherent 'self' plausible . . . in its most primitive moments[,] . . . it displayed dangerous tendencies to subvert that same idea" (188). Trachtenberg suggests that the blurring that occurred demonstrated "the original strangeness and difference of daguerreotypy. Such images defined exactly what had to be overcome" (188).

Similar concerns haunt Roviana attitudes toward photography and photographs, such as Clarinda's picture of snow falling in Christchurch. Any lack of visual clarity in the photograph is seen to be potentially damaging to the self; it must be avoided if one is to come out good. If being photographed raises the possibility of this kind of dangerous exposure, why do Roviana people feel the need to represent themselves in this way? André Disdéri, the inventor of the cartes de visites, suggested that the photographer "must do more than photograph, he must *biographe*" (quoted in McCauley 1985, 41), and the photographer Marcus Aurelius Root commented in 1864 that "a portrait . . . however splendidly coloured, and however skilfully finished its manifold accessories, is worse than worthless if the pictured face does not show the soul of the original — that individuality or selfhood, which differentiates him from all beings, past, present, or future" (Root 1864, 161).

Photographs in Roviana are intended to display the character and efficacy of the person. As Eric Hirsch has argued for the Fuyuge of Papua New Guinea, "photographs show persons in a manner that is intended to persuade others of the appropriateness of their appearance and of the capacities thereby displayed" (2004, 23). The photograph of Ronald achieves this in the sense that it is an object that partakes of his presence, and in the way that it demonstrates his ability to come out good. This visual efficacy is mirrored by an ability to act in the world; this is the work of mimesis. Hirsch continues, "For the Fuyuge power is the capacity to appear efficacious: to be efficacious is to possess the ability to effect conversions" (2004, 33). But Ronald's approach to the photograph is grounded in Roviana attitudes toward likeness and identity that have a longer history than that belonging to the devil's engine.

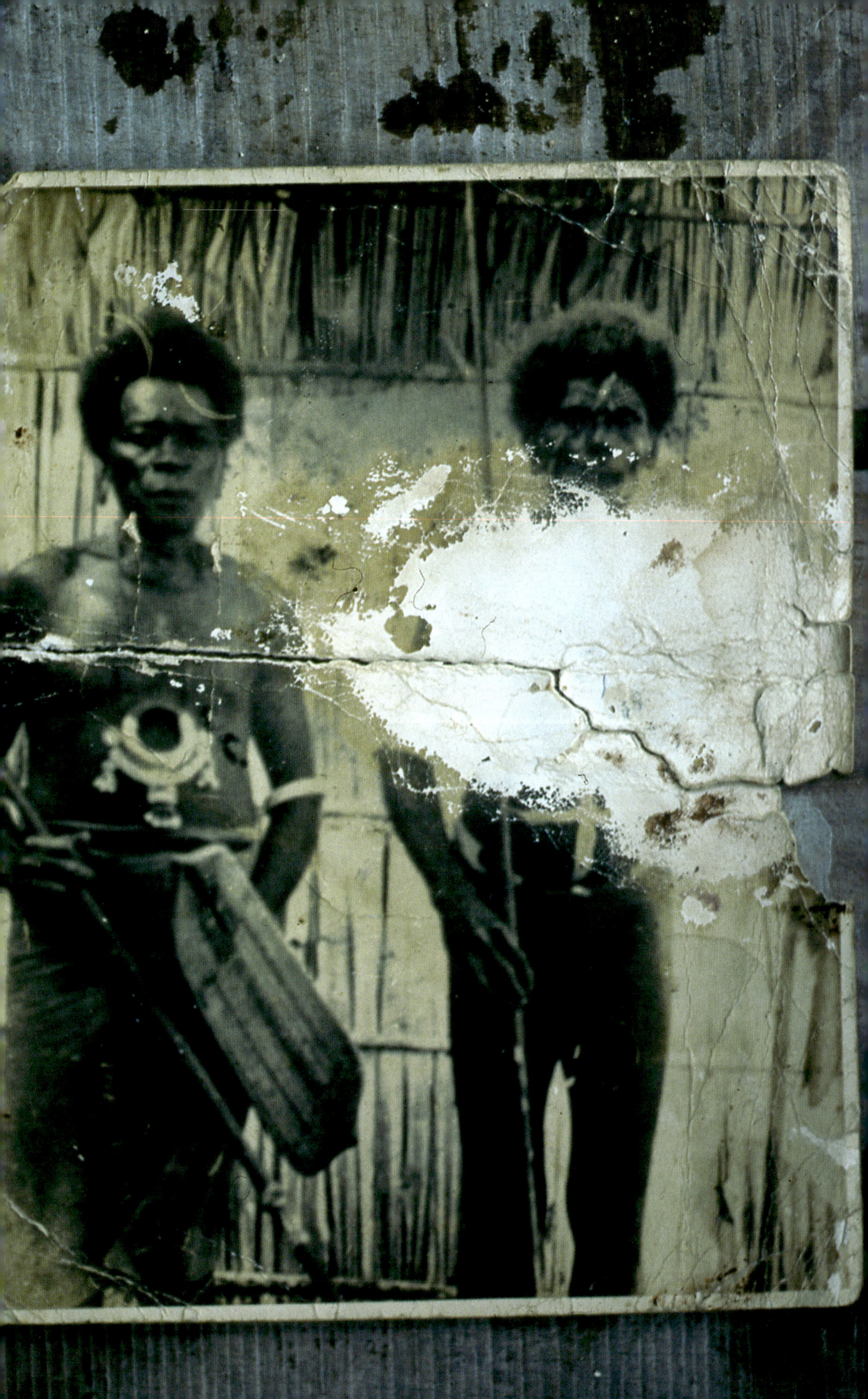

3

Photographic Resurrection

Who is like what? Resemblance is a conformity, but to what? To an identity. Now this identity is imprecise, even imaginary. Can one continue to speak of "likeness" without ever having seen the model?

—**Roland Barthes**, *Roland Barthes: Selected Writings*

First Resurrection

WHEN I VISITED JONI KIA HE WAS TEMPORARILY STAY-ing on Nusa Gele, a small, uninhabited island at the eastern end of Vona Vona Lagoon. With him were members of his extended family processing small amounts of copra while he made *buka* baskets to sell to tourists in Gizo. After arriving by canoe in the late afternoon, I found him sitting on the beach playing with his grandchildren under the shade of a large tree. Joni is in his late seventies, and, as we sat together and began sifting through the large pile of copy prints of nineteenth-century photographs I had taken to show him, he talked excitedly, pointing out people, places, and artifacts that he remembered. He showed some of the photographs to the children who had gathered noisily around him and recounted stories about the images—sometimes serious, sometimes with much laughter and shouting. Some of the photographs made him feel sad because he could not remember some of the details of the objects pictured. Some he dismissed as irrelevant. But one photograph brought him to an abrupt halt (figure 3.1). He gazed at it in silence before slowly raising it to his forehead, holding it there for several minutes as he

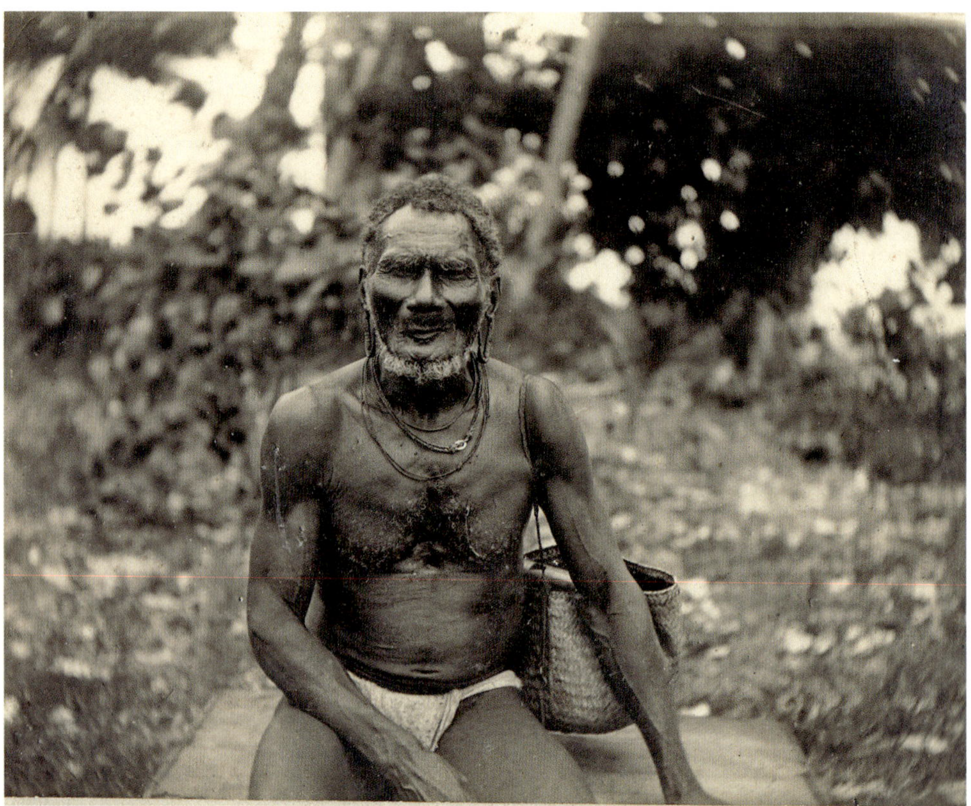

cried. This was the first time that he had seen the face of his grandfather Wonge, identified in the original caption for the photograph,
who died sometime around 1910. He sat there repeatedly running
his fingers over the image and murmuring his grandfather's name.
For Joni this photograph effected a sort of "resurrection" (Barthes
1984, 64).

When he recovered his composure, Joni held the photograph at
eye level in front of him and spoke to it quietly and then, still holding
it in his hands, told me about his grandfather. Wonge was a prominent Roviana *banara* in the late nineteenth and early twentieth centuries, a contemporary and relative of banara Inqava. Joni went on
to tell me stories of Wonge's exploits and to explain at length his
genealogy. Although Joni thought that when he was young he might
have seen one or two photographs of his grandfather, these were in
the possession of missionaries and he would only have been allowed
brief glimpses of them. After he had finished the stories, he showed
me a small shrine (*hope*)[1] dedicated to his grandfather located amid

the coconut trees close to the beach. Typical of such shrines in Roviana, it consisted of a roughly assembled mound of coral cobbles with broken shell valuables, called *bakiha* and *poata* in Roviana, strewn on top. But also, sitting upright in the center of the shrine, were several late nineteenth-century thick-glassed *gorogo* (*grog* in Pijin) bottles that had been given to Wonge by the European trader Norman Wheatley. Joni said he came to the shrine whenever he wanted to remember his grandfather. He could "talk to him" there. Joni described the experience of seeing his grandfather in the photograph: "He is here. When I look at it [*maqomaqo*], I see him. I can speak to him and he hears me. He can see me and give me blessing [*tinamanai*]. I can hold him and remember him.[2]

"He is here": the phrase seems simple enough but, like Allan Sekula's example of someone taking a photograph out of his or her pocket and saying, "this is my dog" (Sekula 1982, 86), it reveals a series of assumptions about the mimetic nature of photography and its ability to achieve a presence. The photograph, as an object that can be held, fingered, and caressed but also passed around and exchanged, is a material embodiment of memories and presences. It can make the dead present. But its very tangibility is simultaneously a source of comfort and distress. Joni's encounter with the photograph of his grandfather was described by him in terms of receiving *tinamanai* (blessing)—from the root word *mana* (power or efficacy).[3] This blessing was manifested through the photograph, which enabled Joni to establish a direct physical connection with his grandfather. Many other Roviana people similarly asserted that photographs put them into direct contact with the maqomaqo, variously the "shadow," "reflection," "spirit," or "soul" of dead relatives.[4] For Joni, holding the photograph to his forehead was a way of "honoring" his grandfather, and the gesture was repeated many times by Roviana people with other photographs. Joni's reaction to the photograph of his grandfather resembles a famous encounter that remains central to Euro-American photographic theory—the encounter between Roland Barthes and a photograph of his mother.[5]

Shortly after his mother's death, Barthes was looking through photographs of her, searching for the truth of the face he had loved. After sorting through a pile of photographs, which took him back through her history but nonetheless remained for him "ordinary objects," merely analogical images "provoking her identity," he came across one photograph of her that achieved for him the "impossible science of the unique being" (Barthes 1984, 71). Although he decided to take this photograph as the starting point for his understanding of photography as a whole, Barthes would not reproduce it for his readers because it existed only for him: "For you it would be nothing but an indifferent picture, one of the thousand manifestations of the 'ordinary'; it cannot in any way constitute the visible object of a science; it cannot establish an objectivity, in the positive sense of the term; at most it would interest your studium: period, clothes, photogeny; but in it, for you, no wound" (73).

Is this likely to be the reaction of contemporary Euro-American audiences to this photograph of Wonge? The material culture in the image is commonplace, as Joni himself pointed out: a small basket (*poroporo*), of a type that is still in use in Roviana; a loincloth made of calico acquired through trade with Europeans rather than a barkcloth *kabilato* or *kolekole*;[6] around Wonge's neck a *vusala*, a string and shell charm for protection from spirits (*tomate*); and distended ears from wearing large wooden plugs (*vikulu*). The photograph was taken by the Methodist missionary Reverend George Brown when he visited Roviana in 1899 to talk to influential local banara about setting up a mission.[7] It could have been taken near where I had been sitting talking to Joni, the only landing point on Nusa Gele because, according to Joni, Wonge had a small coconut plantation on the island and was often on the island to work on his trees in the early 1900s.

If the photograph does little to fulfill any ethnographic expectations in terms of material culture, it might then be consigned to the often residual category of "portrait."[8] Either way, the task involved with the photograph is one of identification, filling in the blanks; once the individual or the material culture has been named, and the importance to local culture, politics, or history assessed, the photograph can have an appropriate caption attached. Within this kind of context, the photograph has exhausted its usefulness. If this is the case, then Barthes is right, for Euro-American, or simply nonkin audiences, the photograph of Wonge does not exist. Only by reconnecting it with Joni is it reanimated, moved beyond the anonymity of the museum archive where an early print of it is housed. But does the photograph wound in the same way in Roviana? The answers to these questions have significant implications for any notion of a photographic nature — a photographic identity that transcends cultural boundaries—as well as for any understanding of photography in Roviana.

In his account of missionary life in Roviana from 1955, Clarence Luxton noted a particular local postmortem practice: "When a child died it was placed in an elevated position near its parents' house and a length of bush vine connected the corpse to the house to prevent it [from] being lonely" (1955, 94). This seems to provide a willing analogy for photography. As Jacques Derrida points out, "when Barthes grants such importance to touch in the photographic experience, it is insofar as the very thing one is deprived of, as much as spectrality as in the gaze which looks at images[,] . . . is indeed tactile sensitivity" (Derrida 2002, 115).

Within the context of cross-cultural encounters, the issue of whether expectations of photography are either a product of specific cultural contexts or inherent in the medium itself is of vital importance. How can the personal affects, and impacts, of the photograph be connected to broader culturally salient features, and vice versa? Judith Binney and Gillian Chaplin have discussed their project of taking early photographs back to Maori communities: "Few of them had ever seen any of the photographs before. Bringing the photographs was as if we were bringing the ancestors, the *tipuna,* to visit. Some of the oldest people talked directly to the photos. . . . Our visits [similarly] became a reunion between the living and the dead" (1991, 431–32). Binney and Chaplin also report that for many Maori people, photographs can possess *mauri* (life force), and the ways in which photographs are animated are clearly key to understanding the ways in which they are used (432). The power of photographs as material objects cannot be denied; why else the need to hold, finger, and caress them? There is an undeniable need for a physical connection to the photograph in Roviana—it has a corporeal power—as its ability to wound people such as Joni demonstrates. But how are these aspects of photography linked to other elements of local culture and to its identity as a medium?

Photo Objects

The existence of photographs as objects—their materiality—has until recently been largely written out of the history of photography. When it is acknowledged, it is usually only in accounts of technical processes, with no concern for the role that materiality plays in the way such photo objects exert a hold over people. Photography's history has largely conformed instead to an art-historical model in which accepted masters are responsible for advancing the development of the medium, and vernacular or popular photographies, such as the widespread Victorian obsession with "spirit photography," are confined to the margins. A number of recent studies, particularly the work of Geoffrey Batchen, have now started to address this imbalance, and there has been a move toward accepting the existence of a multitude of photographies (see Batchen 2001; Jeffrey 1999). Early Euro-American popular accounts of reactions to the medium often precisely stressed the materiality of photographs as objects, and vernacular photographies in other cultural settings often celebrate the tactility and physical connections held out by the photograph (see Pinney 1997; Sprague 1978). So it seems all the more strange that, particularly within the context of its encounter with other cultures, photography has been effectively dematerialized—all the emphasis is placed on what the photograph is of, not what it is as a medium.

In terms of popular accounts of photography's introduction into other cultural settings provided by travelers and explorers, the emphasis is on the shock effected by photography's sudden introduction. It is seen as signaling the arrival of the modern world, and it is seen as a medium that often displaces earlier representational forms and strategies (Slater 1995). But as Christopher Pinney has demonstrated in his study of photography in India, photography is often inflected by previously existing forms and is made to conform to the requirements of existing agendas, providing new opportunities to extend representational strategies rather than marking a rupture with previous forms (Pinney 1997). In order to understand how photography functions in New Georgia—what expectations are brought to it, how it is used—I need to consider the ways in which it is, or is not, connected with a network of local representational forms and strategies. As Batchen has argued, photographs have a "morphology" that needs to be taken into account when considering the history and uses of the medium (Batchen 2001, 59). The illusionary nature of photography as a unitary whole needs to be recognized, and what is required in its place is an ethnography of photographies in practice.

Beginning in the 1840s in Europe and North America, but also elsewhere in the world, early daguerreotypes, each one the unique result of the action of light and chemicals on a metal plate, were often treated as relics. Their lack of negatives, and resulting unreproduceability, enhanced their treatment within an animist trope. Encased in small, velvet or silk-lined boxes, daguerreotypes demand to be touched, but they also play on denying that touch — the daguerreotype image was fragile and had to be protected from actual touch by a thin sheet of glass. To view a daguerreotype one has to hold it by hand and turn it so that the light is reflected off its surface at a particular angle to make the image legible. Daguerreotypes were experienced in a tactile way, as much as they were looked at. In these early images there is a "comforting solidity" that is a key component of their memorial function (Batchen 2001, 60). However, Alan Trachtenberg has pointed out that turning a daguerreotype portrait to catch the light also revealed the image's capacity to transform itself into a negative: "When the eyes go black and the eye cavity appears a blank socket, how startling it is to find in your hands the visage of a skull" (Trachtenberg 1992, 176).

It is the combination of touch and sight that makes daguerreotypes, and indeed some photographs, so compelling. The act of handling a photograph is analogous to the process of photography itself — the camera is touched by the world, by light. The small size of daguerreotypes made them jewel-like, and they were usually surrounded by oval or round, ornately patterned and textured, gold-colored metal frames. They are a direct development of the tradition of preserving actual bodily relics, like the lock of hair, and many early cases for daguerreotypes and ambrotypes also contained a space for human hair, or used hair in constructing photo jewelry (see figure 3.2) (see Hallam and Hockey 2001). Batchen suggests, "A talismanic piece of the body thus adds a sort of sympathetic magic to the photograph, insurance against separation" (2004b, 76). Some cases for daguerreotypes were designed to be worn as jewelry, reinforcing this sense of physical connection, and perhaps, as Batchen and Elizabeth Edwards suggest, *photo objects* is a better term here than *photographs* (Batchen 2004b; Edwards and Hart 2004). From their inception, photographs have had an important physical connection to the person depicted.[9] This is the primitive practice that is still part of contemporary photographic practices.

There is a notion of proximal empowerment, of a magic enabled through physical contact, that is at work with photographs in Roviana too — and there is a sense in which these attitudes are part of

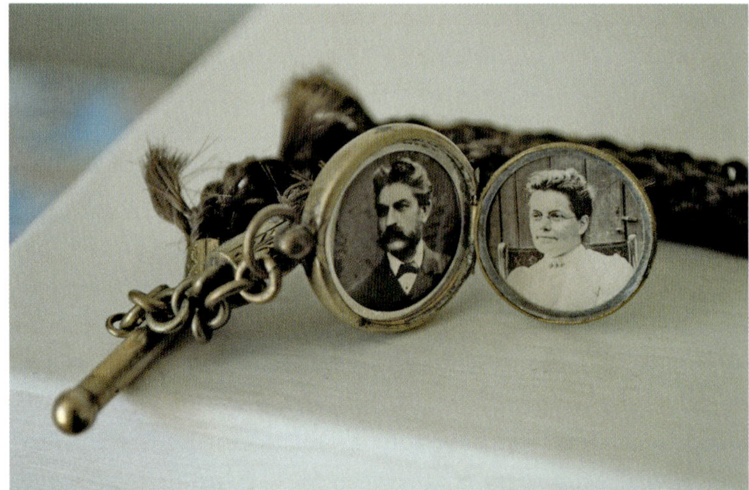

broader mimetic strategies that are a feature of earlier Roviana beliefs and practices. Ernest Elkington and Norman Hardy, in their account of Roviana from 1907, comment on Guppy, the British surgeon who conducted an anthropometric survey in Roviana in 1854: "He says that when the natives cut off locks of their hair for him, which he desired for scientific purposes, they told him that if any sickness or calamity befell them they would put it down to him" (Elkington 1907, 138).

Similar animist concerns are a feature of contemporary Roviana approaches to photography. The materiality of the photograph, the physical connections it allows, and its ability to be animated, are bound up with ideas of mimetic magic that are concerned with partible bodies. Is Joni's response to the photograph of his grandfather a sign that he has the same expectations of photography as Euro-American audiences? The act of touching photographs and the profound emotional responses they elicited were a frequent feature of looking at photographs with people in Roviana. The practice of holding the photograph to the forehead was most pronounced among members of the Christian Fellowship Church. The church was founded in 1960 by the charismatic Roviana leader Silas Eto, a student of the founder of the Methodist mission, Reverend John Goldie, and it is widespread throughout contemporary Roviana (see Harwood 1971). Its syncretic blend of Methodism and Roviana beliefs retains many ideas about objects that are animated in one way or another, and this reinforces an attitude toward photography as a material relic.

Photography is one way of materializing the past, of somehow maintaining a physical connection to it. But in Roviana it is an externally introduced technique of recent origins in a cultural context with a long history of techniques for achieving similar connections. There is a relation between the photograph of Wonge and Wonge's shrine that needs to be understood, and I want to explore the relation of photography to a range of other Roviana techniques for making the past present and for maintaining various kinds of contact with ancestors. These practices inflect and resonate with the contemporary uses of photography, and in order to understand photography in Roviana we need to look at the ways in which memory is materialized through other objects, such as shell valuables and religious shrines. Contemporary attitudes toward memorialization are influenced by the complex of beliefs associated with these objects. There are many difficulties involved in any attempt to reconstruct earlier practices—as Nicholas Thomas says how can we represent "some imaginary time that is at once pre-colonial yet accessible to our vision?" (1995, 286)[10]—but they need to be considered in order to understand what photography is in Roviana today.

Faletau Leve's wife, Daisy, has a photograph that vividly demonstrates the importance of photo objects in Roviana. The photograph (figure 3.3), has broken into two pieces, which are kept in a stained and tattered envelope that is itself stored inside a small woven basket with other valuable family possessions, including shell rings (poata). The basket, made by Daisy, is kept out of sight at the back of a shelf inside a bedroom. The photograph was taken in Pejuru village (in the Java area of Vella Lavella island) by a Methodist missionary, Reginald Nicholson, sometime around 1920, although the print itself may well have been made sometime after that. Nicholson was resident in Vella Lavella from 1907 to 1916 and from 1919 to 1921, and the print was certainly made before the evacuation of missionaries that occurred during World War II. Although the photograph was taken by missionaries—perhaps to show the unconverted state of Vella Lavella warriors—Daisy's use of the photograph, and the family narratives within which it is suspended, had a local application. Faletau refers to the photograph as taken "taem lotu himi stap" (at the time the mission was being established) and points out

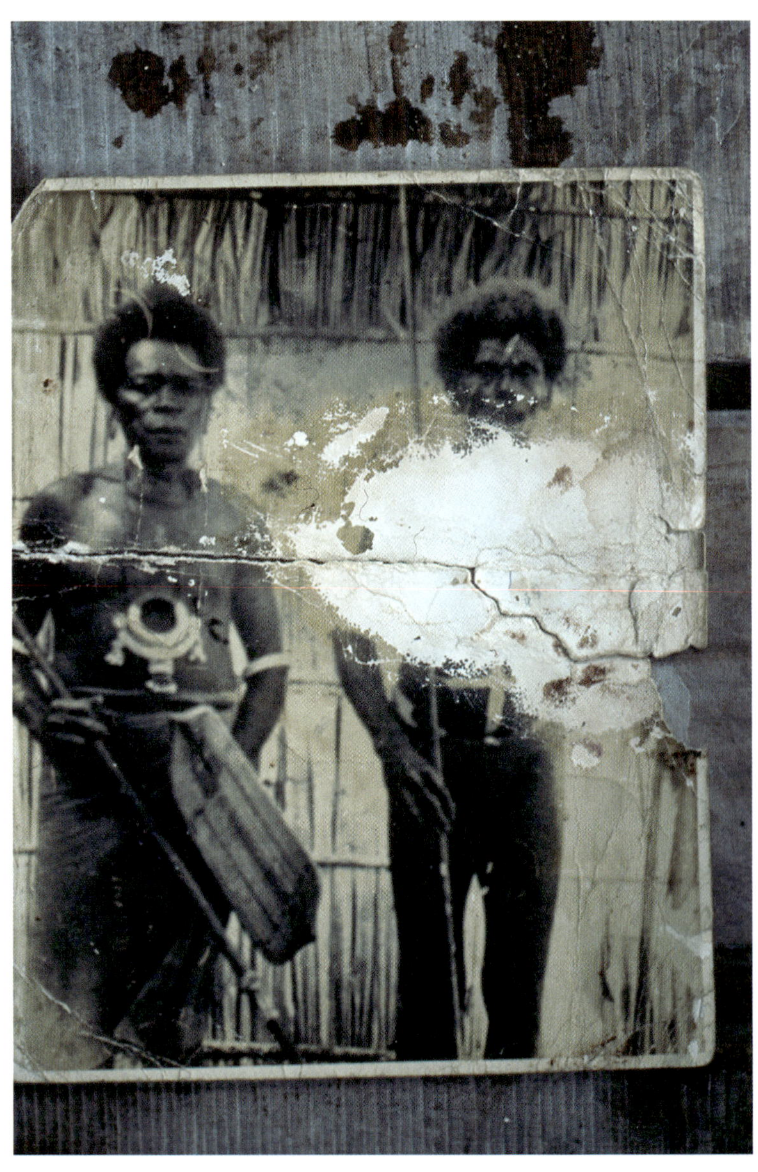

FIGURE 3.3 David Rike and George Sisu. Photograph taken
by Reverend Reginald Nicholson ca. 1920.

that the man on the right is wearing calico (European trade cloth) as another way of giving a general sense of the photograph's age. Faletau considered my attempts to work out the exact date irrelevant, and for once he did not recount a lengthy genealogy in connection to a photograph. This is because the photograph is from Daisy's *saed* (side), and therefore the genealogy was her story to tell. He did think it important to name the individuals in the photograph. The man on the left of the picture is David Rike, and on the right is George "Geosi" Tokuilo Sisu, an uncle of Daisy's from her father's side.

When Faletau, with Daisy's permission, showed me the photograph, it was with a palpable air of reverence. The envelope was removed from the basket and then the two halves of the photograph were taken out one by one and the photograph assembled on the table. Other photographs had been passed to me to look at, but Faletau made it obvious that this was not acceptable in the case of this object. This is the oldest photograph that Faletau and his family possess; it survived the rigors of World War II when many people hid in the bush to avoid the conflict. It is treated as a relic, an object with a tangible physical connection to the past. The large white patch on the right of the photograph is where the image has been worn away by Daisy repeatedly touching the print. Sisu was wearing a large shell valuable called a *bakiha rapoto*, suspended by a plaited string (*medaka*), similar to that worn by David Rike on the left, and Faletau told me that Daisy touches this part of the photograph "to remember, to talk to him, to get a blessing." When I spoke to Daisy, she said that the repeated stroking of the, now disappeared, photographic image of the bakiha was so that "I can be with him." She reiterated the notion that the physical contact provided by the photograph was a way of being blessed. I asked her if she touched the face, and she answered: "I do not touch it often. It is respect [for her uncle]. The eyes are strong. They can catch you." Once the image of the bakiha had worn away, and the photograph had become separated into two pieces, she stopped rubbing it. But she still takes the photograph out and holds it whenever she wants to talk to her uncle. Photographs display the residues of their handling — their material biographies — and this example reveals a powerful Roviana photo object. Both the photograph and the bakiha are efficacious objects, and the doubling that the photograph effects — binding image and object together — retains the opportunity for contact with what has been lost.

Although some aspects of the existing Roviana religious system fell out of practice under the influence of widespread conversion to Christianity, many of the concepts, such as the veneration of ancestors and concerns with spirits, continued to have relevance and meaning. They are still of real significance for Roviana people today. Some taboos concerning religious sites are remembered and acknowledged, even if the practices are not engaged in and the sites themselves are not maintained or fully understood. Rather than signaling a decisive end to previously existing beliefs and practices, the arrival of the Methodist mission in Roviana in 1902 ushered in a period of gradual change and modification of some Roviana beliefs (Sheppard, Walter, and Nagaoka 2000). Practices such as headhunting were significantly curtailed, but others such as the building of *tomoko* (large trading and raiding canoes) were actively encouraged by the mission. Importantly, there was a continuity of belief about material objects and their efficacy. Earlier practices also continued in tandem with Christian ones — Roviana people told me how people went to church but still worshipped their own spirits as well — and there remains an often ambivalent and sometimes contradictory mixture of the two traditions.

A diverse range of religious sites existed when the Methodist mission arrived in Roviana Lagoon, and some of these were mapped and studied by the New Georgia Archaeological Survey that was carried out by Peter Sheppard and others from the University of Auckland in the late 1990s and early 2000s (New Georgia Archaeological Survey 1996, 1997, 1998). Many religious sites in Roviana are still recognized, and many are used on a personal basis by individuals, at least in the sense of being appealed to or acknowledged in hopes and wishes, if not necessarily used in a physical sense. This is particularly the case with those shrines associated with garden or fishing magic. Some shrines, such as the one associated with Inqava at "Skull Island" (Kudu Hite) in Vona Vona Lagoon, have become tourist attractions, but many, even if unmaintained and overgrown, remain vital to issues surrounding competing land claims, and knowledge about the shrines is both carefully guarded and disputed (Schneider 1996).[11] A range of shell valuables continue to be associated with these religious sites and the ancestors connected with them, and these form part of a history of political and religious power in Roviana, as well as having various kinds of relevance in the present. In relation to the situation in Roviana from the seventeenth century until the supposed cessation of headhunting after the so-called British pacification in the 1890s, Peter Sheppard, Richard Walter, and Takuya Nagaoka point out: "Power or efficacy derived from ancestors is materialised, channelled and circulated through an interconnected set of cultural media. . . . The archaeologically visible component of the Roviana chiefdom system, the shrines and shell valuables, form[s] part of a set of power relationships in which head-hunting plays a fundamental role. We contend that head-hunting developed in concert with the other elements, which can serve as a proxy for this cultural practice" (Sheppard, Walter, and Nagaoka 2000, 13).

Along with other shell valuables, large shell rings, with their plaited string support, were sometimes placed in shrines, and the skulls of ancestors sat on bakiha in skull houses (*oru*).[12] Bakiha were made from fossilized tridacna shell and required many hours of labor to be ground into shape. A "true" bakiha, a bakiha rapoto, had an orange stain and was a sign of a leader's authority (see figure 3.4). Arthur Hocart recorded that in Simbo shell valuables live; after their owner's death they are broken: "They made the rings 'no good' to be like rotting, their shadow (*galagala*) goes to Sonto" (Hocart 1922, part 1, 81).[13] Sonto, or Sondo, is a small island within the Shortland group to the west of New Georgia and is the residence of ancestral spirits. Among Roviana people whom I spoke to, opinion was divided as to whether their ancestors broke bakiha after their owners' deaths or not, and certainly whole bakiha are visible today on shrines and in skull houses. But they agreed with the assertion that bakiha possess souls or shadows (maqomaqo) in the same way that people do. Religious offerings of food and specific plants made at shrines were burned so that the smoke would take the shadow to Sondo, and breaking shell valuables performed a similar function. Hocart also recorded: "Currency rings . . . are frequently presented to the spirits and also seem to be haunted by them."[14]

Some bakiha were inalienable and represented particular histories, and Roviana people in possession of this kind of heirloom bakiha today could recount long histories associated with the valuables. They produced bakiha from their woven storage baskets, which often contained the families' few photographs as well and, while holding the bakiha, related a series of genealogies and events in which the objects and their ancestors were implicated. In this sense, bakiha are important mnemonic objects for the telling of oral

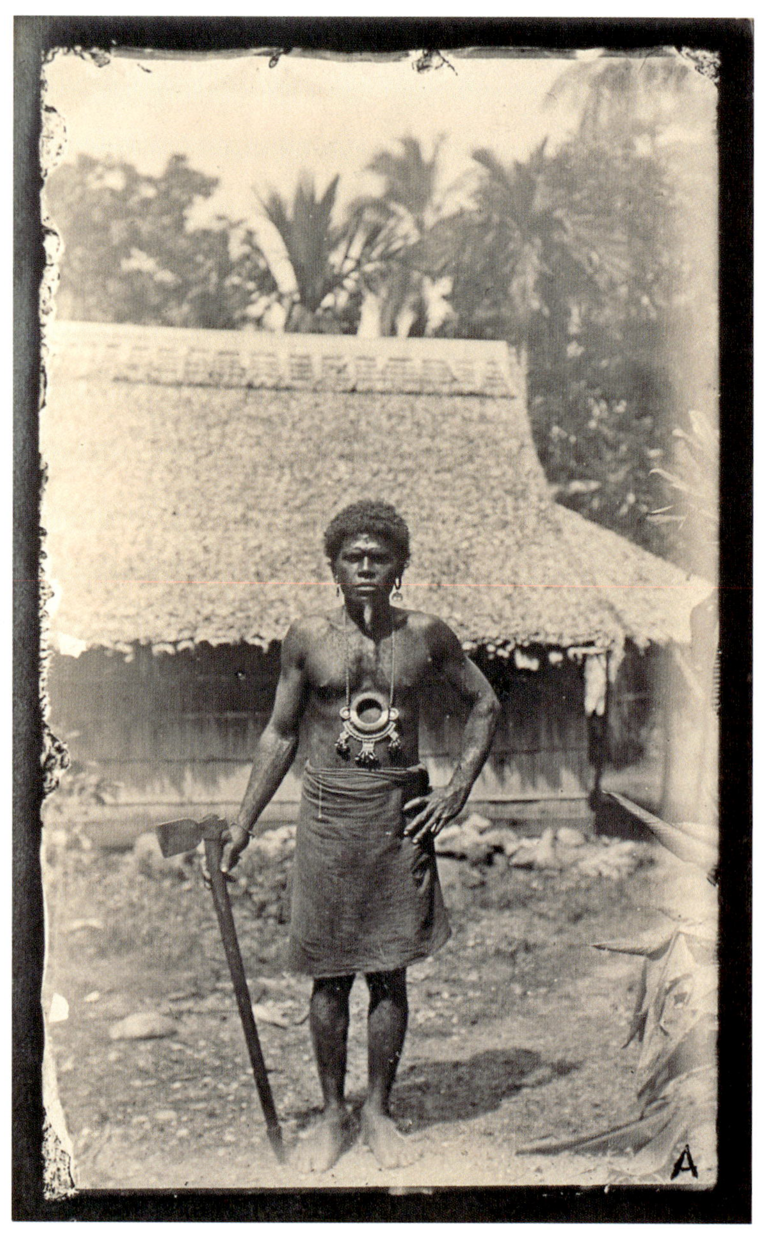

FIGURE 3.4 Roviana chief (*banara*) wearing a shell valuable
(*bakiha* rapoto). Photograph by Robert Ward Williamson, 1910.
Courtesy of Royal Anthropological Institute, London. 11364

histories in the same way that photographs are. Bakiha were also used to mark social transactions, such as the transfer of access to land, bride price, compensation payments, and establishing peace among hostile polities. Bakiha were also a means of financing large headhunting raids and paying for assassins to carry out particular killings (see Sheppard, Walter, and Nagaoka 2000, 12). Bakiha were a new media of leadership authority that was developed when previously inland populations moved to the coastal areas of New Georgia in the mid-sixteenth to early seventeenth centuries, as Shankar Aswani points out: "Consecrated bakiha emerged as divine signifiers and visible manifestations of chiefly authority. They embodied the actively manifest higher powers of the *mateana* [a class of divine beings] ancestors. . . . By authenticating the authority of chiefs, these sacred objects legitimised their control over the flow of ceremonial and commodity exchange networks" (2000, 45).

In addition to authorizing the power of leaders, some bakiha are objects that activate kin group (*butubutu*) and wider networks, and they embody histories through the stories that are attached to them, and these were kept as heirlooms (*merumeru*). Roviana people repeatedly told me that bakiha were like photographs: "They are the same as photographs. When you see one you can remember the person [the owner or the ancestor associated with a particular bakiha]. You can see them." They assured me that both bakiha and photographs had maqomaqo. The notion that photographs, like some other objects, have souls, is of key importance for contemporary Roviana understandings of photography.

Maqomaqo

Hocart recorded attitudes toward the soul on Simbo island in 1908:

> The soul is called *galagala*, which also means a shadow, a reflection; it is caught in a camera. A Shortland man says "it stop all over a man": by taking a looking glass you can see it. When a man dies, his soul (*galagala*) comes out at the mouth: some men can see it by the use of charms. . . . Rakoto says it is just like a man and big or small according as it belongs to an adult or a child. A certain shadowiness seems associated with departing spirits, for one man asked us whether a vague figure in an advertisement of Odol was a ghost. (Hocart 1922, part 1, 81)

Hocart's account, although reminiscent of that genre of often apocryphal stories about so-called natives' incredulous first encounters with photographic technology, actually reveals the way in which Simbo people *could* make sense of the camera. They understood aspects of this new technology within their own terms. Although there were, and are, fears associated with photography in Roviana, these are part of indigenous discourses, such as beliefs about spirits (tomate), and not simply the product of a failure to comprehend photographic technology. Roviana people understood the magic of photography.

The Roviana word most commonly used today to describe the soul is *maqomaqo*, and this is also the word used for a photograph. A photograph *is* a maqomaqo, and the term is a ubiquitous feature of contemporary descriptions of photography and photographs. Variously glossed as "shadow," "shade," "reflection," "spirit" — *Maqomaqo Hope* is used in translations of the Bible for the Holy Spirit — or "soul," maqomaqo is used to refer to the photograph as an object, and it also figures prominently in descriptions of photography as a process.[15] Roviana people told me how their ancestors had put mirrors, acquired from trade with Europeans, on shrines. They also repeated stories of souls being caught in mirrors: "After someone died you watched the mirror [*tiroana* — from *tiro*, "read"; the mirror was owned by the deceased] for three or four days. After this smoke would show up there. Then you could see their face clear and bright in the mirror like a baby. The body rose up in the mirror and then went up after the smoke. The body was smaller in the mirror. After the spirit [maqomaqo] left the mirror, they could take it back to the house."[16] The practice described here is within living memory and was prevalent in Roviana in the first decades of the twentieth century. It reveals the adoption of European media into local schemes of transubstantiation, and in 2001 Sesolo Makoni described his encounter with his photograph of his father in the following way: "When I saw it, he was alive. I kept that photograph [maqomaqo], and after he had died I looked at that photograph again and I thought that my father was still alive. When I look at that photograph, I say, 'that is my father.' Photography is the shadow [maqomaqo] on the paper [*pepa*]. They caught the shadow and it became a statue [*beku*[17]] in the picture [*pikisa*]."[18]

The photograph is an image that is alive, but how is this embodiment achieved? Makoni's account reveals the adoption of the Pijin terms *pikisa* and *pepa* in descriptions of photographs, and these terms are sometimes used as qualifiers in distinguishing the photograph from other manifestations of maqomaqo.[19] However, maqomaqo is commonly used on its own to describe a photograph, only being qualified on some occasions when being used in conjunction with maqomaqo in the sense of "spirit" or "soul." It is a ubiquitous feature of Roviana discussions of photographs, a term that people use in talking about photographs to each other. It was also a key term in responses to my questions about the copy prints of late nineteenth- and early twentieth-century prints that I had taken to Roviana with me. When I produced photographs to show people, they would sometimes shout excitedly, "maqomaqo, maqomaqo," as they called others to come and look. The language of contemporary Roviana discourse on photography frequently bears a striking resemblance to Hocart's early account. Simon Sasae told me: "The photograph [pikisa] is the spirit [maqomaqo] of your body. When I look at the photograph [maqomaqo pikisa] of my father, his spirit comes to me; he looks at me. This is because I have a history with the photograph. When I talk to the maqomaqo pikisa, the spirit sees me, and hears me too."[20]

The reciprocity of vision referred to here is an important feature of the use of photographs in Roviana that brings the photograph, the shadow picture, to life. To be in the presence of the photograph is to be seen by the spirit of the dead ancestor and to be able to communicate with that spirit. This communicative efficacy is a key element in attitudes toward a wide range of material relics of ancestors, including photographs, and is an important component of contemporary Roviana attitudes toward ancestors and spirits. Although knowledge of spirits and souls is sometimes fragmentary and contradictory, and also an often uneasy combination of indigenous and Christian notions, it is necessary to an understanding of Roviana notions of photographic presence, and of how the camera might be seen to capture the soul.

In Roviana, souls, spirits, shadows, ghosts, and photographs are all subsumed under the term maqomaqo. The anthropologist Lucien Levy-Bruhl argued in the 1920s: "Very often . . . the vital principle or 'life' of the individual is not to be distinguished from his shadow, similitude, or reflection . . . 'soul,' 'shadow,'" and he also pointed out that "these are words fraught with ambiguity, inexhaustible sources of error" (Levy-Bruhl 1928, 18). There are issues around what this soul might consist of, but, although people do sometimes use qualifying terms, Roviana people are generally unconcerned with precise definitions of maqomaqo. That commentators such as Hocart reported local schemes in which objects have souls suggests that, although "soul," "shadow," and the like may be Eurocentric translations, people and various objects possess maqomaqo in Roviana. It is a necessary, but partible, element of their existence. In one sense, Roviana people did not have souls before contact with Europeans (particularly the Methodist mission)—they had maqomaqo. The translated terms taken to be equivalents of maqomaqo are also caught up with Euro-American understandings of photographic presence—of what photography is, and how it works—and such concerns date from photography's inception. In 1843 Elizabeth Barrett wrote about daguerreotypes: "The Mesmeric disembodiment of spirits strikes one as a degree less marvellous. And several of these wonderful portraits, like engravings—only exquisite and delicate beyond the work of graver—have I seen lately longing to have such a memorial of every Being dear to me in the world. It is not merely the likeness which is precious in such cases—but the association, and the sense of nearness involved in the thing, the fact of the very shadow of the person lying there fixed for ever. It is the very sanctification of portraits I think" (quoted in Henisch 1994, 166). This is a clear statement of photography's magic, and it is as relevant for Roviana ideas about maqomaqo and conceptions of photography, as it is to Euro-American attitudes toward the medium. Photographs, or photo objects, are articulated with aspects of Roviana material culture and are connected to a morphology of other forms for materializing memory. Roviana materiality is intimately entangled with connections between the seen and the unseen worlds, and with maintaining links with the spirits of dead ancestors. For many Roviana people, it is maqomaqo that enables the efficacy and power of certain objects and relics, and that also animates photographs.

Embodiment

In 1908 Hocart recorded the Simbo postmortem practice of catching or transferring the soul, and contemporary Roviana people attested to similar practices being performed by their own ancestors, although they were often unsure of all the details. After death the belongings of the deceased are broken and the body is "hidden" by transporting it to an unfrequented spot on the coast. The soul, which has until now remained in the house of the deceased, is then transferred by a ritual specialist to a leaf that has been inserted in the hole of a small shell ring (*ovala*). Both of these are then placed in the thatch of the roof and "are henceforth spoken of as 'the soul'" (Hocart 1922, 84).[21] A series of prayers and rituals are performed by mourners and relatives, and after several weeks the skull is retrieved from the corpse and left to bleach. On the eighteenth day after death, the leaf and soul ring are reunited with the skull, which has further shell valuables attached to it, and both are then placed in the ancestral skull house in a ritual called "*vatome tomate* or 'putting in the dead'" (Henisch 1994, 90).[22] According to Hocart, if a man's head is not available, it is represented by a tall, angular upright stone, which is not worked in any way, but left as it was found, and is placed on a shrine or by a skull house. Alternatively, carved wooden or stone heads — the latter referred to as *tomate patu* (stone ghosts) — are used, and Hocart recalled: "One man was represented by a figure-head of that familiar prognathous type which in Eddystone [Simbo] is called *nunjununju* [*nguzunguzu*]." After thirty-six nights a ritual called "*londu*, which means 'to sink' or 'to set,'" is performed for the soul's departure. Puddings are prepared, and the baskets used to carry them are burned so that their shadows (galagala) can go to Sonto (or Sondo), the home of ancestral spirits. The spirits then come from Sonto to fetch the soul of the deceased.

This summarized version of Hocart's detailed account reveals several important instances of the mutability of persons and objects in which souls, spirits, and ghosts can be seated (*habotuana*), contained, or embodied in various material forms.[23] The soul passes to the material object through the mediations and performance of the ritual specialist. The ability of a tall upright stone to represent a man's head, as well as carved anthropomorphic heads, suggests the coexistence of several different approaches to representation, from concerns with presence to issues of visual mimesis. Contemporary Roviana stories about carved wooden or stone figures, which were associated with shrines of various kinds, reveal them as objects that are similarly thought to be the seat of spirits. *Beku* is the Roviana term commonly used to refer to the kinds of anthropomorphic carved figures associated with shrines, but the other word used in relation to these figures is *tigono*, or *tigono-na*, which Waterhouse records as "a fetish, an idol, or image. Supplication is made through this visible representative of an invisible *tomate* for *mana*. *Vina tigonona* now used for statue, memorial etc" (1928, 111). The figures can represent both named ancestors and spirits and *debildebil* (devils), as Roviana people now frequently refer to them. One well-known story that is frequently recounted today, often to children and outsiders, concerns the encounter between Reverend Goldie and a beku at the Kesoko shrine on Nusa Roviana in the early 1900s and is recounted by James Pitu:

> I know the story about the beku at Sidevele. It comes from what my ancestors told me. Sidevele is a chiefly village and that is where the shrine [hope] is. When the mission came to Roviana, Minister Goldie came here with his family to see this place at Kokorapa.[24] Minister Goldie came here with his son. Yes, it was with his son. His son was young and still had to be carried by his mother. Before our people were converted, none of them came to his place [the mission]. The missionaries came from Samoa, Tonga, Fiji. But they never came here and neither did Minister Goldie. He only came here after the mission and when our people at Kokorapa had been converted. Then Goldie came to see the place here at Kokorapa. He also came to see this shrine. The shrine had lots of stories, so they wanted to come and see it. He came to Sidevele where the shrine is. When he came our people welcomed him and he was taken to the places around the coast. . . . He asked about the shrine and they went to Sidevele, and when they came to this place they showed him the monument [*vina tigono*[25]]. "What do you do with this monument?" Minister Goldie asked. He asked this question of our people and of my father. My father said, "If we want power we go to him and ask for it." "Okay let me go and try that with my son," said Goldie. He walked up to the beku and he took his child with him. It was like a sacrifice [*vukivukihi*[26]]. Goldie said to the beku, "This is my child, try and take him." But nothing happened, so Goldie said the beku could not take him. Our people said, "That is okay, that is not a human being; it is only a beku." It was only carved for those people before (*tie pukerane*[27]) to worship. Goldie left Sidevele; they got in their canoe and left. When they were in Munda, Goldie's son died. This was at their house in Kokeqolo. Goldie did not come back to Nusa Roviana, but he called for my father. He told my father, "It is true; the things that were made

and carved *did* have power." . . . I think he must have also said that the Lord Jehovah must have given power to these things so that the people before could use them.[28]

Beku are objects that embody ancestral spirits and channel their power—beku possess agency; they do things. Ideas about the efficacy and power of objects like beku are a regular feature of contemporary accounts of earlier practices, in particular those stories recounted by the older generation.[29] These ideas are an integral component of such stories and are used in constructing or ascribing some kind of coherence to earlier practices. This particular example also highlights the ambivalences involved in the process; on the one hand ideas about the power of beku are "heathen" beliefs from "before" (i.e., before the adoption of Christian practices), and on the other, they are entangled with claims of ancestral continuity and are therefore also potential sources of pride (see Dureau 1998). The popularity of the previous story, which I was told in slightly different forms on many occasions, is due in part to its suggestion of resistance to Christianization and its assertion of the power of beku, albeit within an account that in some sense finally reaffirms Christian beliefs. Like stories about headhunting, this story demonstrates how strong Roviana people were. Despite being Christian, older people repeatedly stated to me that shrines and artifacts associated with them still retained their power, although on occasions they explained that their ancestors had mistaken the work of "Jehovah" for that of their own spirits. Although shrines are not necessarily actively maintained, they are still treated with respect, particularly by the older generation, and have occasionally been desecrated by contemporary Christian groups, an action that demonstrates shrines' continuing importance as symbols of the "time before" (before the mission).[30]

The founding of the indigenous Christian Fellowship Church in Roviana involves another story of embodiment and of power seated or inherent in material objects. The story is well known to members of the church throughout Roviana and concerns events that occurred when Goldie returned there to celebrate the Methodist mission's diamond jubilee in 1952. The way that Goldie passed on his mana to Silas Eto, the founder of the Christian Fellowship Church, is recounted by Davita Agobe: "Minister Goldie said take this box in your hands Silas. It is the box of the Holy Spirit. I give it to you now.

When I am gone open it and begin your work in the Holy Spirit. . . .
Goldie placed the black shining box in Eto's hands. . . . This is how
Silas received the black box, which is not a real box but rather a sign
of the Holy Spirit, the black box is now the body of the Holy Mama"
(Davita Agobe in Harwood 1971, 80).[31]

In addition to concerning notions of embodiment, both these
stories also importantly serve to maintain a connection of some
kind between Christian and indigenous beliefs through a discourse
of materialized spirit. Such stories suggest a continuity of indigenous ideas of embodiment, and, as Sheppard, Walter, and Nagaoka
argue, "the notion that engagement with the West resulted in the
demise of an indigenous political and religious expression, seriously
distorts a complex and creative resortment of Roviana ritual, idea-
tional and politico-economic practices" (2000, 11). In the story
about the shrine at Sidevele, *representation is subsumed by presence.*
What is at stake here is the way that certain objects become the
living embodiment of what they represent, and in so doing manifest a power to affect people and events. Older people often recognized particular beku in photographs that I showed them, and
their stories about beku stressed the efficacy and power of these objects while simultaneously providing occasions for recounting the
process of Christianization. In this sense, photographs of beku are
themselves objects that, performed in this way, can articulate those
changes through the subtle interplay of difference and continuity.
So, when Makoni recognized a particular beku (figure 3.5) in one of
the prints I showed him, he responded with a mixture of pride and
concern to acknowledge or establish a distance from earlier beliefs:

He is the seat [*hambotuana*] of the chief. It is a place called Ade
in Munda. The people before put up that beku. He is a monument [vina tigono] for the chiefly tribe in Munda. That is where
they get [*vina ria*[32]] their power [mana] before they could go and
fight or make a feast. They would come and pray to this beku.
They would see him and he answered them. No one could go
near him or spoil it. If anyone did that they would be possessed
[*tagoa*]. They would be cursed in their daily living. That is the god
[*tamasa*[33]] of the old people. The god of heaven replaced the god
of our ancestors. Their first god was this [gesturing at the photo-
graph]. . . . Today we see a different god. We get our power from
the Christian god now and from our ancestors. When the mis-

sion came, they stopped worshipping at Sisiata, and they came to Goldie and left everything. But their worship [*vahesia*] stayed on until, after some time, they left the beku and it rotted and people went and spoiled it. When the mission came it had no meaning because people went to the Christian god. When I was small I saw that beku. The old men told me, "That's the beku; don't spoil it." I saw the beku and he was like a human being [*guana tie*[34]]. We paid respect every time we saw him because we were afraid of the beku until the mission came. Resana is the name of that beku. The beku is a spirit [maqomaqo] like the photograph.[35]

What emerges from all these stories is the way in which, through embodiment, artifacts such as beku provide a connection between the beholder and the ancestor; they are manifestations that facilitate access to ancestral power. Makoni recalls how beku were monuments (vina tigono), representations of specific named ancestors who appeared to be like human beings. Beku possess agency and power; they demand something from the viewer and, as David Freedberg argues in relation to beliefs about the agency of a medieval French statue, the *Madonna of Rocamadour*, "what is at issue is the response that is predicated on the assumption of presence, not on the fact of representation. . . . What is represented becomes fully present" (Freedberg 1989, 28). Beku such as figure 3.6, like shrines and a range of artifacts, including photographs, are sites for effective communication with the ancestors; the carvings make the ancestors present. For Roviana people, authority in the world of the living was, and to some extent continues to be, demonstrated "in an ability to commune effectively with power-giving ancestors . . . [, and this] was also effected in a spatial compression, and perhaps even a blurring between the worlds of the ancestors and the living" (Thomas, Sheppard, and Walter 2001, 563). Photographs are intimately entangled in this process. They are entwined with various notions of maqomaqo, and this discourse is bound up with the process of maintaining connections with ancestors and spirits. The photograph is ascribed a place in the scheme of Roviana material culture, and notions of photographic presence play a part in continuing Roviana access to ancestral spirits.

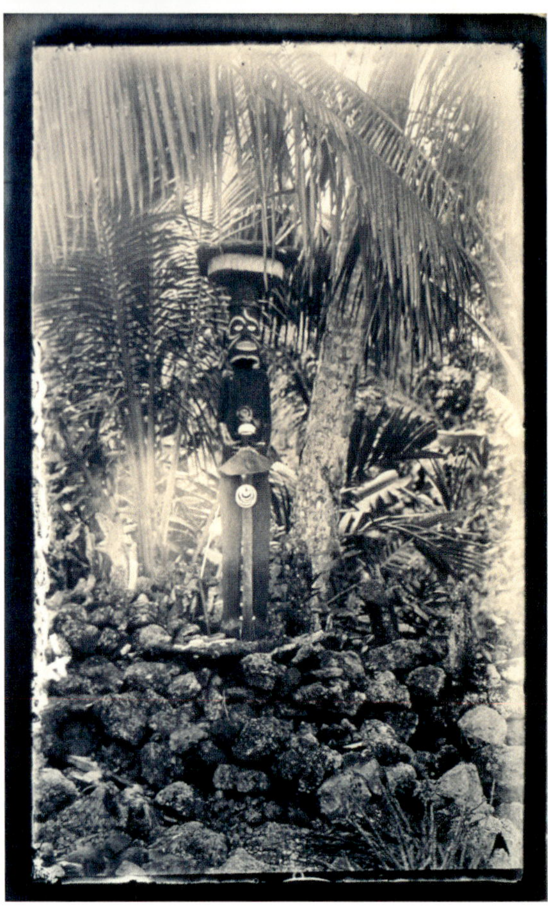

FIGURE 3.5 "A chief's grave with a tall thin black idol, western Rubiana lagoon" Wooden carving (*beku*). Photograph by Robert Ward Williamson, 1910. Courtesy of Royal Anthropological Institute, London. 11359

FIGURE 3.6 "A chief's grave with a very old and worn lichen-covered figure made out of the trunk of a tree, with the face indistinguishable and with two arms hanging on the body, western Rubiana lagoon" Wooden carving (*beku*). Photograph by Robert Ward Williamson, 1910. Courtesy of Royal Anthropological Institute, London. 11367

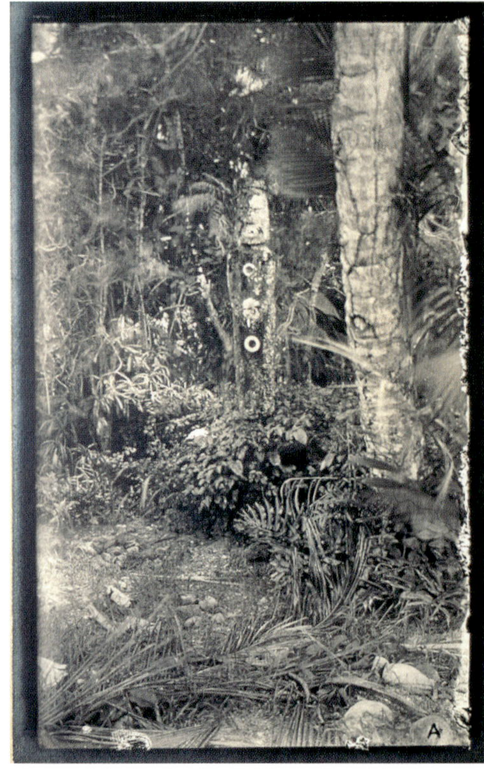

Mimesis

> The photograph is a shadow. It is the true [*hinokara*] shadow of your body.
> It shows hidden [*tome*[36]] things, but it is true. It can imitate [*tavete luli*]. The
> photograph becomes me. The photograph is clever, it can copy [*kumberia*].
> It can make something close [*tata*].
>
> —**Simon Sasae**, March 10, 2001

Simon Sasae, an old man clutching a photograph of himself taken
in the 1970s, delineates a range of Roviana expectations of photographs and suggests that to have one's photograph taken is to be
truthfully imitated (*tavete luli*). *Tavete* translates as "to make," and
luli as "to follow," as in following a path, and together they convey
a sense of "imitation," with the phrase retaining overtones of action
and physical connections. *Hinokara* is used in the sense of "true"
and also "real," as in *tie hinokara* — the real people — often used by
Roviana people to refer to themselves. The use of *tata* invokes not
only closeness as in physical proximity but also the closeness that is
associated with being something else. The use of particular Roviana
terms to describe what a photograph is reveals that Simon's conceptions of photography as a medium are focused on its mimetic possibilities. As he handles the few photographs he possesses and talks
to me about them, it is with a sense of undisguised wonder at their
mimetic magic, their ability to make a double of his world.

Simon, like the majority of older Roviana people (Simon is in
his sixties), has a fragmentary knowledge of photographic processes.
He cannot explain how a photograph is made in terms of any Euro-
American technical model, but he can describe how a photograph is
taken in his own terms. This should not then be interpreted as a defi-
cit of knowledge or a failure to understand the true nature of photography. It is rather a lack of concern with processes that are not
important in establishing the uses of photographs or their authority
in Roviana. The technical processes of negative and positive and the
play of light on film are not necessary features of his understanding
of photography. What is important to him is photography's capacity
for making true copies — a concern with photography as mimesis,
and, as Michael Taussig argues, mimesis concerns not just a copy
or an imitation but "a palpable, sensuous, connection between the
very body of the perceiver and the perceived" (Taussig 1993, 21). In
Roviana the photograph is a material relic that is animated by maqomaqo, but how does it fit with other local mimetic schemes? Simon

traced his outline on a worn photograph of himself with his finger: "I want the photograph [*maqomaqo*] so I can keep [*kopunia*] myself. It is a true picture [*pikisa*]. I can copy [*kumberia*] myself. If I do not have a photograph, I will not see how I was. My children will have nothing to remember me."[37] Here the mimetic expectations of the photograph are linked to its memorial potential, a potential that is underwritten by its status as a true copy. But how is this copy constructed? Simon also talked about how photographs are made: "The photograph [*maqomaqo*] takes something true [*hinokara*] from you. It is a true thing. This camera [*kamera*; pointing at my camera] takes your shadow [*maqomaqo*] and makes [*tavete*] it here [holding up a photograph of himself]."[38] When Simon talks about the camera taking something and then making it in the photograph, it is with the sense of a direct physical continuity between the person in front of the camera and the photographic print—this is the "palpable, sensuous connection" that Taussig refers to as essential to mimetic magic.

Early conceptions of photography in Europe described it as a "mirror with a memory" (Trachtenberg 1989b). To be photographed was like looking in a mirror and having that image fixed. From now on it would be possible to encounter your double. The "mirror" of photography offered the security of possession, an object to be handled, and also created an anxiety around self-possession—others could now get hold of your image. The mimetic faculty concerns the notion that the image can affect what it is an image of—James G. Frazer's "sympathetic magic." Frazer distinguishes between magic that involves similarity and that involves contact. The former contains the notion of the copy and the representation that possesses the same qualities as the thing represented. Regarding the second law, he says that it is based on the assumption that "things which have once been in contact with each other continue to act on each other at a distance after the physical contact has been severed" (Frazer 1923, 11). This is the law of contagion. Both are directly relevant to ideas about photography and to Roviana representational practices.

The mimetic ability of photographs is linked to Roviana histories of imitation or copying (*kumberia*). Although photography is often thought of as modernizing vision, here it relates to Roviana ideas about representation, Roviana "scopic regimes," that preexist photography (Jay 1988). Commenting on Frazer's work, Marcel Mauss and Henri Hubert discuss the lack of realism in magically effective mimetic images: "There is nothing resembling a portrait." The image, doll, or drawing used was only "schematic" (Mauss and Hubert 1972, 68). Any object, as long as it has had the relevant contact with its subject or model, can be made into an effigy. Taussig suggests that "what makes up for this lack of similitude, what makes it a 'faithful' copy, indeed a magically powerful copy . . . are precisely the material connections — those established by attaching hair, nail cuttings, pieces of clothing, and so forth, to the likeness" (1993, 57). This could easily be a description of daguerreotypes which often had lockets of hair attached, and photography would seem to partake of both of Frazer's laws of magic: not just a visual notion of similitude but a performative, physiognomic, and tactile relation.

Objects on shrines that memorialize ancestors span a range between the use of strangely elongated rocks (see figure 3.7), which have not been carved or treated in any way to represent ancestors, and carvings of anthropomorphic figures like beku (see figure 3.8). This suggests a historical movement, or the coexistence of both aniconic forms — nonrepresentative of human or animal — and those that are reliant on notions of visual mimesis. Maqomaqo can be seated (hambotuana) in elongated rocks, but also in more visually recognizable human forms.

The kinds of elongated rocks — basalt columns found in rivers, such as those shown in figure 3.7 — represent ancestors, which reveals one form of mimesis that featured in many stories told to me by contemporary Roviana people. That they were still an active part of Roviana shrines in 1910, clearly maintained and directly adjacent to houses, demonstrates the lack of influence exerted by the mission at this stage. These images of ancestors require ritual activation to empower them, but they *are* ancestors, and do not rely on any kind of visual similitude for their efficacy. The elongated rocks seem to have coexisted with a range of anthropomorphic carvings (beku) of ancestors, such as that shown in figure 3.8, although Roviana people asserted that the rocks were an "old" way of representing ancestors. Beku depicted stylized human forms and were similarly the seats of ancestors. Hocart commented on anthropomorphic carvings on Simbo: "There were several figures in human form called *kimbo* which were said to be representations of *tuturu* [a type of spirit]. . . .

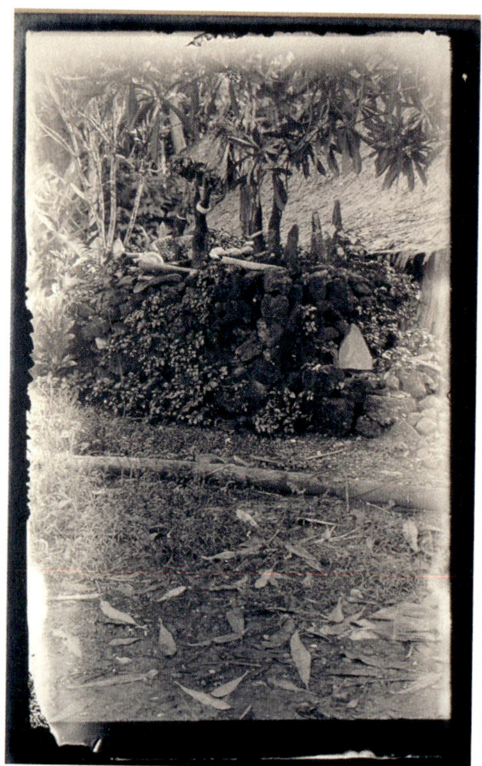 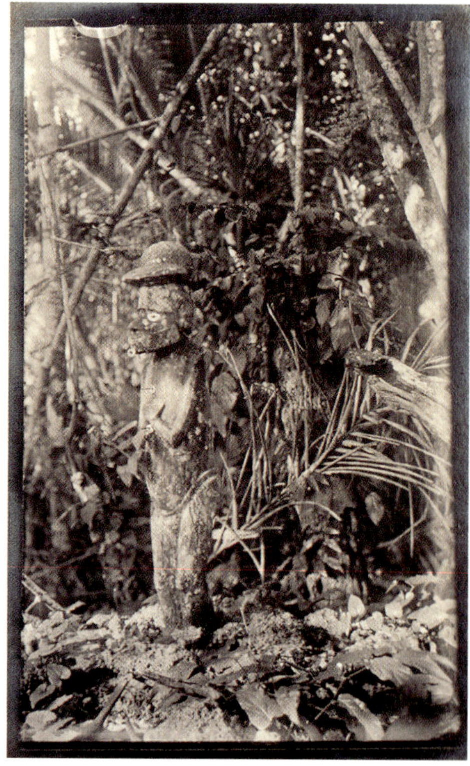

It was a figure carved out of tree fern about four feet high with a shell over the forehead, two shells in the place of ears, mere traces of arms and a very large penis."[39]

Many beku were said by Roviana people to represent "dead relatives," and some people could recognize the specific beku in the prints that I had, despite the fact that many beku share the same stylized features. Beku often have a pronounced prognathic jaw, similar to the carvings on the prows of tomoko called *nuzunuzu*, and often have lines of either lime or inlaid shell on the face, which imitate the decoration applied to the faces of living people (*busa sokovea*). But, although Roviana people said that beku were individualized, the intention was not to copy the faces of specific ancestors. Roviana people often drew an analogy with photographs, praising them for the way they can make a true copy in comparison to beku. But both beku and photographs are considered true in the sense that they are ancestors.

A significant change in Roviana representational practices occurred sometime in the late nineteenth or early twentieth century, when carvings in what the missionary Brown referred to as a more "naturalistic" style began to be made locally (*Australian Methodist Missionary Review*, November 6, 1899, 3). Compared to the elongated rocks, these seem to be at the other end of a mimetic spectrum. Some of these carvings were directly commissioned by Brown, who wanted to prove that so-called savage races actually had abilities that could be improved and were not immutably fixed by race. In particular, Brown was concerned with disproving the theory that Melanesians were incapable of "properly" depicting the human form (see Gardner 1999, 191). Brown saw, and possibly commissioned, one of these new carvings in Roviana in 1899 (figure 3.9). Brown commented that a local carver had produced "a very fine wooden carving of a boy carrying a gun, made by a native, from a life model" (*Australian Methodist Missionary Review*, November 6, 1899, 3). The suggestion that these carvings were made from life perhaps implied for Brown a shift in representational forms, but it also implied a Victorian evolutionary scale in which the elongated rocks form one pole, and realistic or naturalistic sculpture and photographs form the other. The latter were seen by many of Brown's contemporaries as the zenith of European representational and technical prowess — proof of civilized status.

The carving shown in figure 3.10, that we do know was commissioned by Brown (Brown 1901), does seem to represent a totally new form of Roviana representational practice. The figure is overtly naturalistic, like in figure 3.9, and both adopt a more three-dimensional pose than beku. The carving of the woman and baby reveals a strange mixture of the real and the artificial; the lime gourd held in the hand is an actual gourd, and the shell ornament (*hinuili*) around the neck is made from real shell, but the shell rings (*hokata*) on the arms are carved and painted imitations. The delineation of arms and legs, complete with fingers and toes, is not a feature of beku, which possess only rudimentary limbs. This naturalistic style of carving seems to have been adopted for some beku (figure 3.11).

This carving, figure 3.11, probably made just prior to 1910, judging from the condition of the carving and the date of the photograph, is protected by a sheet of corrugated iron, but it stands on a mound of coral cobbles and has several bakiha at its base. Again, it is three-

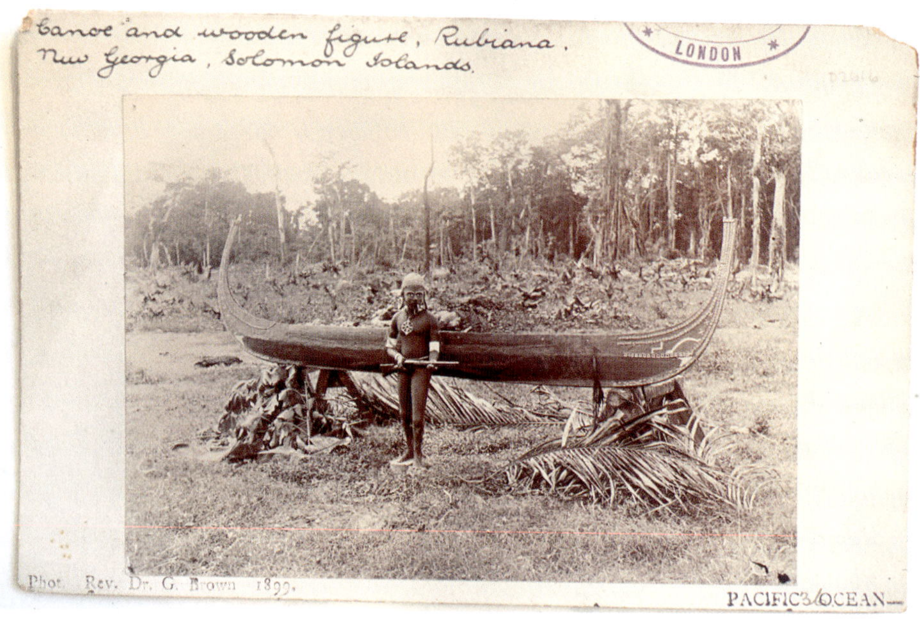

FIGURE 3.9 "Canoe and image"—wooden carving and model canoe. Photograph by Reverend George Brown, 1899. Courtesy of Royal Geographical Society, London. PR 056651

FIGURE 3.10 "Wooden Image of Woman and Baby"—wooden carving of woman and child. Photograph by Reverend George Brown, 1899. Courtesy of Methodist Archives, Auckland. Published in Australian Methodist Missionary Review, October 8, 1902: 75

FIGURE 3.11 "A Roviana idol (still in existence, but more as a curio)," photograph ca. 1910. Courtesy of Methodist Archives, Auckland. de B19a

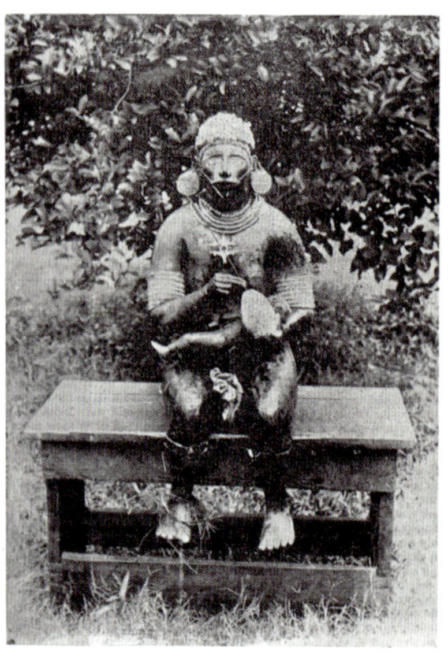

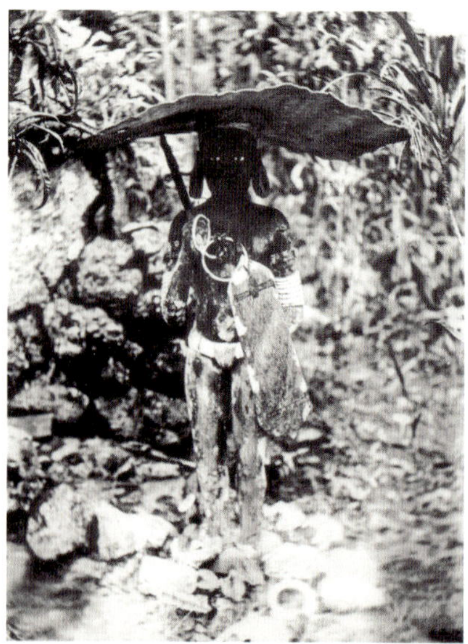

dimensional in a way that beku are usually not and features a combination of real and imitation elements. The stylized prognathic jaw (see figure 3.8) is gone, and the figure adopts a "realistic" pose, demonstrating how Roviana carvers adopted new styles to existing ends. The adoption of European techniques was commented on by early visitors to the western Solomon Islands. Elkington reported: "The natives are very fair draughtsmen, and some of their drawings are surprisingly good. Shark fishing, head-hunting, and scenes of murder, are amongst their favourite pictures. . . . All the drawings are done on wood with a red-hot stick, in much the same way as poker-work is done in England. . . . Nowadays the natives beg a little iron or wire, which they make red hot and go to work with to burn out their designs" (Elkington 1907, 131–32).

Roviana people seem to have been delighted at some Euro-American mimetic technologies, as Elkington and Hardy reported in the first decade of the twentieth century: "We witnessed the delight and wonder of the natives, both here and at Mr. Wickham's, at the phonograph, just introduced, especially when they heard their own speeches reproduced by the machine" (Elkington 1907, 131–32).[40] Early Euro-American responses to new mimetic technologies, including photography in the 1840s, frequently revolved around a dialectic of the strange and the familiar. A sense of wonder, and sometimes fear, mixed with recognition. The nature of the new medium was at issue, as were questions about its social uses. Images in Roviana were concerned with the mimetic possibilities of embodying ancestors and spirits, and the photographic image was readily grasped and understood in these terms. It is important to remember that the process of ascribing power to the mimetic techniques of others worked in both directions. Euro-American reactions to Roviana objects, outside of the Methodist mission's concern with "idols," were often equally strong:

Upon the bookcase of my living-room stands a Roviana head. The features are beautifully modelled with a kind of putty made from the tita-nut. . . . The base is an actual skull, the putty being laid over it. . . . Today it is almost impossible to acquire more of these heads, the art of making them having become a thing of the past. Before I was married I had sent my fiancée a photograph of the interior of my house and in it appeared the head. When the time should come for her to come to the Islands, she told me, the

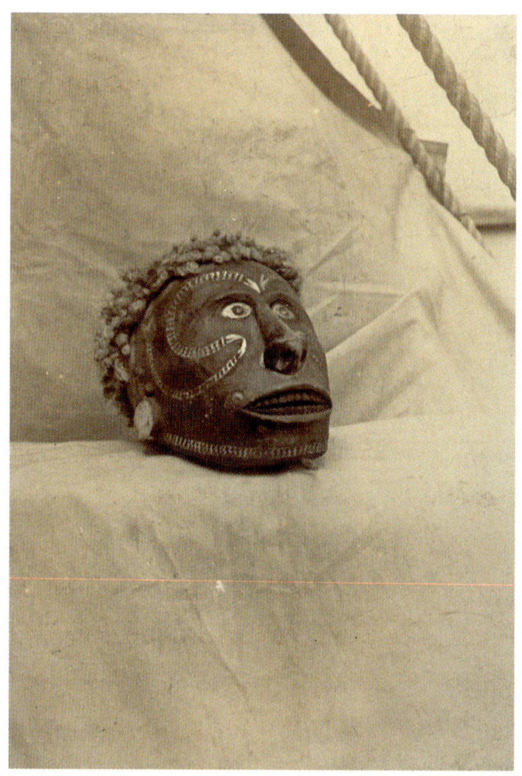

heads would have to go, for she could not tolerate such a grim
spectacle all and every day. When I first acquired it and had it in
my office, set upon a plan case, it often used to startle me when
I looked up, so human was its appearance. . . . After removing it
from my office to my house, in order to prevent the numerous
interruptions of which it had been the cause, I was frequently
momentarily alarmed at the appearance in the living-room of the
black apparition staring wide-eyed into space. . . . All our visitors
comment upon its human appearance, and shudder when they
are told that it really contains a human skull. The bone can be
seen inside, for there is an opening at the base uncovered by the
tita, and an axe-mark may be observed, showing that the victim
met with a sudden and violent death. (Knibbs 1929, 31–32)

The disturbing object that Stanley Knibbs refers to is known in
Roviana as a *kibo* (figure 3.12). These were the overmodeled skulls of
ancestors, complete with tracing eyes made of shell inlay, the lines
of lime (busa sokovea) on the faces of the living, and fiber hair. This

ritual transformation of a bodily relic was sometimes applied to skulls acquired in raids. Although most skulls placed in the canoe house (*paele*) were unidentified, those of prominent leaders or warriors were sometimes transferred to a ritual war house (*zelepade*) and had shell ornaments (hinuili) attached to them or were turned into kibo to allow them to be identified with particular individuals (Aswani 2000, 64). The Roviana people I spoke to said that the practice was carried out to enable people to remember specific individuals more effectively, and stressed that the ability to visualize them was enhanced by the overmodeling. According to contemporary Roviana people, this treatment was only applied to the skulls acquired through raiding and not to the skulls of their own ancestors. Writing about people's memories of earlier practices on Gatokae Island (eastern New Georgia), Jari Kupiainen reports that kibo is the name given to various kinds of carvings and statues of ancestors, and *kibo chalivi* (*chalivi* means "head") is used to refer to what I have been describing here as kibo (Kupiainen 2000, 42). He suggests that kibo chalivi were made from the skulls of particularly venerated ancestors and were kept in people's houses rather than at shrines because of fears that they would be stolen.

In terms of their mimetic properties and desires, kibo can be seen as morphologically related to photographs, particularly daguerreotypes and photo jewelry with human hair. Both involve a combination of visual representation and physical trace that produces a mnemonic object that functions as a relic. James Pitu first saw a photograph when he was a young boy at the Methodist mission in Kokeqolo in the 1930s:

> When I first saw a photograph, I was afraid. I thought they were real [hinokara] people in there. I did not want to make those people angry. I thought they could still move around. They would possess [tagoa] me. The photograph would take me. I thought the photograph was carved [*peqoa*] or they must have done something else on the paper, because the beku I saw is a true one. Some photographs are like beku, others are like people. Photographs are true. They were made by white people [*tie vaka*]. Some were drawn [*doveni*]; others were made to resemble, relive [*titila*[41]].[42]

The mimetic magic of photographs is the focus of attention in Roviana, a concern that directly connects them to earlier forms of mimesis.[43] In Roviana the mimetic powers of photographs are appropriated into local schemes of representation, but in what sense have they replaced earlier forms of representing ancestors?

Skulls

Historically, ancestral spirits and their power were associated with shrines, including those containing ancestral skulls and other material artifacts, and ideas about embodiment in relation to shrines are related to contemporary attitudes toward photography. Roviana shrines (hope) fall into four broad categories: those directly concerned with ancestor worship, usually containing skulls; those for ensuring productivity, which are concerned with magic for gardening, fishing, and hunting; those dedicated to specific nonhuman spirits; and those connected with cleansing and purification. Roviana people continue to personally recall specific ancestors and invoke their power particularly when visiting garden shrines or when practicing various kinds of magic associated with fishing, but my focus here is on shrines solely associated with ancestor worship.[44] These sites, and the material culture associated with them, were those most commonly referred to when relating stories about artifacts that represent or embody individual ancestors, and particularly when discussing the relations between photographs and ancestral spirits.

Skull shrines are dedicated to chiefs and those of chiefly descent—Hocart recorded that "chiefs have a kind of family tomb"[45]—although they also contained the skulls of ancestors other than chiefs.[46] Skulls could be placed in already existing shrines, but a new one was usually built after the death of a prominent chief, and the spirits of dead chiefs formed a special class called *mate mbangara*.[47] The skull house (oru) came into being as a monument or memorial along with a representational complex that involved the veneration of ancestors' skulls and the use of captured heads from headhunting raids, when previously inland populations gradually resettled on the coast of New Georgia in the sixteenth and early seventeenth centuries (Aswani 2000, 44). Earlier inland populations neither used shrines as repositories for skulls nor built skull houses. At the time of this coastal resettlement, new chiefly lineages were established that claimed descent from mateana, a class of divine beings, ancestral connections to which became one of the prerequisites of chiefly power (Aswani 2000, 44). At the same time, a new range of cultural media, such as bakiha and other shell valuables, were developed, which facilitated processes of memorialization and the maintenance of direct connections with ancestors. Through the skulls kept at shrines, the priest (*hiama*[48]) communicated with ancestral spirits and with god (*tamasa*), and the sanction or efficacious blessing (tinamanai) of ancestors was a prerequisite of authority among the living (Aswani 2000, 59). The living and the dead were bound together in a reciprocal relation: "The skulls of chiefs (*bangara*) when conserved in shrines provide material connections to powerful ancestors" (Sheppard, Walter, and Nagaoka 2000, 11). Skull shrines are processual monuments: "Power or efficacy derived from ancestors is materialised, channelled and circulated through an interconnected set of cultural media" (13).

Although many of the skulls in oru were undifferentiated, those of particularly important individuals were sometimes marked by attaching various shell valuables to the skull, occasionally with an elaborate network of plaited string. Brown visited a shrine on Simbo in 1901 that consisted of several skull houses, some of which had twenty to thirty skulls in them, but he found that "one of them had only two which were evidently those of some superior persons, as the skulls were highly ornamented with rings and other valuable shell property" (Brown 1901, 1; also quoted in Waite 2000, 125). After ritual preparation, the skull of the deceased was placed in an oru, a roofed structure of varying size. Roviana skull houses were usually raised off the ground on one or more posts and situated on top of a mound of coral cobbles. They had roofs of thatch, wooden boards, or coral slabs, and many had a wooden board (*leva*) with carved or painted designs. They could also feature small carved figures, like miniature beku, on their supporting posts (figure 3.13). Leva from the late nineteenth and early twentieth centuries often included representations of a human figure, usually taken to be a chief, standing in a war canoe and holding a metal-bladed ax of European origin in one hand and a shell valuable, usually taken to be a bakiha, in the other. According to Deborah Waite, this juxtaposition of representations of Roviana and European artifacts importantly "fused indigenous with imported manifestations of power" (2000, 123). Hocart reported that on one occasion he witnessed on Simbo a European-style coffin that was used to "hide" the body of the deceased immediately after death, although the head was later

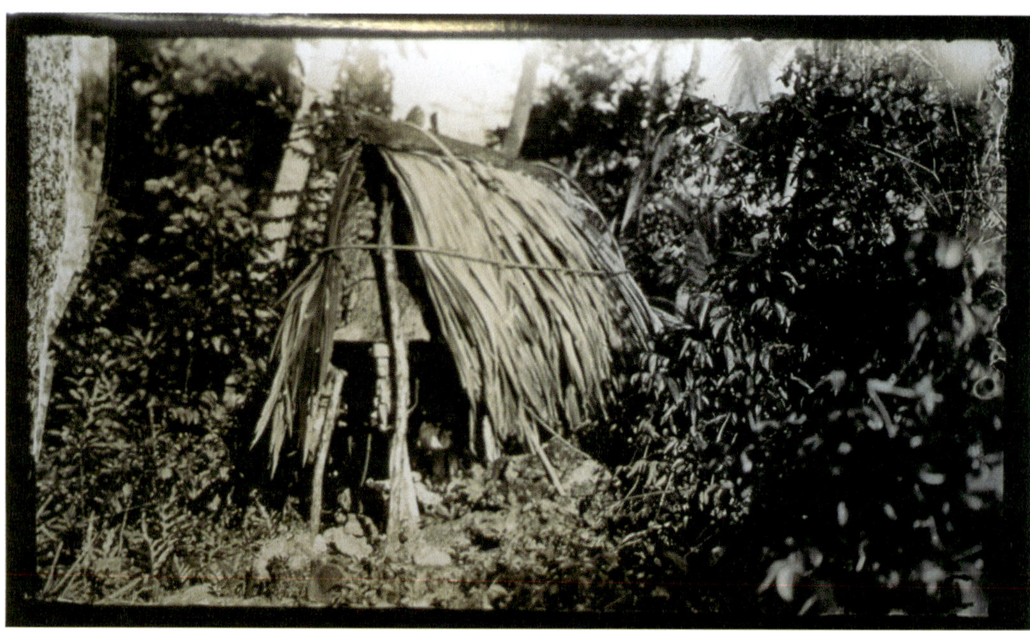

removed, treated, and placed in a skull house (Hocart 1922, part 1, 98). He also talked of corrugated iron replacing thatch as a roofing material for skull houses in 1908 (Hocart 1922, part 1, 104). Artifacts of European origin were frequently incorporated as part of ancestral shrines alongside shell valuables. Several older Roviana people said that photographs were added to ancestral shrines in the 1920s and 1930s, but given the scarcity of indigenous access to photography during this period, it could only have occurred in very isolated cases.

Ancestral shrines are sites that involve, and indeed establish, important connections between embodiment, vision, and ancestral power. Contemporary Roviana people described the small opening on the wooden leva as a door for the spirit or soul, an aperture that allowed it to enter and leave the skull house. Waite suggests that the oval designs depicted on the doors of skull houses resemble the prows of war canoes (2000, 126),[49] but the Roviana people I consulted said that these patterns were eyes. Faletau asserted: "They are big eyes. They are eyes that can bite. The spirit is alive and it looks at you."[50] Visiting an ancestral shrine to leave offerings involved encountering ancestral spirits who could see you, and accounts of earlier practices stress the important role of vision in effective communication between the dead and the living: "When they [people from before, *tie pukerane*] visited a shrine, they saw their ancestors. They could talk to their ancestors. Their ancestors were there and they replied to them. Their ancestors heard them and saw them. When they saw them, their ancestors would give their blessing [tina-manai]."[51]

This reciprocity of seeing, and being seen, resembles Hindu notions of *darsan*, discussed in relation to photography by Pinney (2001) and by Diana Eck: "To stand in the presence of the deity and to behold the image with one's own eyes; to see and be seen by the deity" (Eck 1981, 3). In Hindu belief the deity is present in the image, so seeing the image constitutes an act of worship, and there is a tactility of vision associated with darsan: "Seeing, according to Indian notions, is a going forth of sight towards the object. Sight touches it and acquires its form. Touch is the ultimate connection by which the visible yields to being grasped. While the eye touches the object, the vitality that pulsates in it is communicated" (Kramrisch 1976, 136; quoted in Eck 1981, 9). A similar visual physicality is invoked in Roviana prohibitions against allowing your shadow to fall on skull shrines: "Your shadow [maqomaqo] should not go before you when you go to a shrine. The eyes of the beku can see you, they can trap [*sipata*] you. If you let your shadow fall on the shrine, you will be sick. The spirits [tomate] will take [*palekia*] your shadow. Your shadow [maqomaqo] will get sick and fall [*vuvusu*[52]]."[53]

Such accounts demonstrate that your shadow, your maqomaqo, is susceptible to being taken; it is vulnerable to predation from angry spirits. Older people talk of how they were told not to look directly at the camera when they had their photograph taken; if they did, then the camera would take their maqomaqo. The visual is bound up with obtaining ancestral blessing, but it is also a source of potential danger. When you talked to an ancestral spirit at a shrine, "the spirit answered by shaking you around. This is called *samsambukai* when it happened on land, and *betubetue* on water. This is how the spirits speak to you. You ask a question and they answer you by possessing you and shaking you. You hold the bakiha so you can contact the ancestor's spirit. You had to show the charm to your father before he died, otherwise the charm would not work, he would not answer you." Donald Maepio said, "When I talk to my father's spirit, it touches me and talks to me. I feel like I am standing up in the air; my feet are not on the ground."[54]

The possibilities of embodiment and the association of ancestral skulls with mana are closely tied to Roviana headhunting practices. Headhunting in the western Solomon Islands has been the subject of academic debates. These have generally revolved around the influence, or not, of European contact on the level of raiding and the inflation of the ritual system involved with the taking of heads using the supply of new weapons, like metal axes and rifles.[55] Recent contributions to this debate have suggested that large-scale predatory headhunting was not a direct result of sustained contact with Europeans and other outsiders in the nineteenth century, while acknowledging that the latter undoubtedly did have a significant influence (Aswani 2000, 40). Aswani has argued that through headhunting, "Roviana chiefs and their kin . . . were able to secure their own regional ritual, social, and political hegemony by constructing a quantifiable 'currency of rank' out of persons' detached parts" (2000, 40).[56] After being ritually inactivated, skulls taken in raids were placed in the ritual canoe house (paele).[57] The skulls of prominent victims were kept as heirlooms for display and were sometimes offered as prestations to Roviana ancestors and deities (Aswani 2000, 55).

In relation to headhunting, John McKinnon argues that "one of the most direct ways of obtaining influence was to take the life force residing in another human being, centred in the head. It could therefore be obtained by taking the person's skull" (1975, 301). Taking the heads of your enemies was an opportunity to acquire the "soul value" inherent in them. In contrast, Aswani insists that "keeping the head of a Roviana chief or relative was an act of ritual consecration, a means to subsequently secure the power of the ancestors as vectored through the skull's physical presence. The skulls of enemies however, stood as those of strangers and objectifiable others. Consumed vessels containing nothing that could be supernaturally taken (i.e., *mana*) but, rather, something that could be supernaturally denied" (2000, 55). Headhunting was a way of denying your enemies access to their own ancestral mana. The relatives of someone whose head had been taken in a raid "would replace the captured head by making a statue (*beku*) in the dead person's image (*vina-tigono*) in the hope of propitiating the departed spirit" (Aswani 2000, 68 n.13).[58] This suggests that, like the ritual transformation of enemy skulls into kibo, representation of ancestors is only resorted to if the actual relic, the skull, is unavailable. Presence is the primary aim, not representation.

Successful headhunting raids conducted by chiefs manifested their mana: "Enemy skulls thus acted as *mnemonics* of their power, of their being blessed in warfare, as in other enterprises" (Dureau 2000, 88; my emphasis). The relevance of enemy skulls was not in the mana or soul substance that they contained, but in the channels of "*mana*-ization" they opened up (Aswani 2000, 56; quoting Hviding 1996, 91). Sheppard, Walter, and Nagaoka argue: "Sanction is demonstrated through the successful acquisition of skulls, which became a material token of the efficacy or *mana* bestowed by those ancestors on chiefs who organise, fund and lead head-hunting expeditions. Head-hunting connects the living and the dead and provides material evidence of the will of the ancestors in the decision-making of the living" (2000, 11). Exercising authority in Roviana required the positive sanction of the dead, the ancestors from whom all power ultimately derives, and this continues to be a feature of contemporary politics.

Skull shrines are dynamic media, not just in the sense that they are monuments that were concerned with maintaining active links with ancestors. They are also media that have changed and evolved. The skull shrine associated with Inqava serves as an example of some of the changes that Roviana processes of mana-ization have undergone from the 1900s onward (see figures 3.14, 3.15, and 3.16).

There is a shrine that is situated on a tiny island, Kundu Hite, at the mouth of Vona Vona Lagoon, and it was reportedly moved there from Sisiata in Munda sometime in the early twentieth century. This was possibly a response to the arrival of the Methodist mission—some shrines were relocated to avoid attention from the missionaries—although Brown talked of Inqava "retiring" to Kundu Island (Brown 1908, 517). Today the shrine consists of a carved wooden skull house containing skulls and shell valuables, and the shrine has a leva depicting a chief holding a bakiha and an ax of European origin. The skull house sits on top of a large extended mound of coral cobbles containing many other skulls. One of the skulls it contains is supposedly that of Inqava himself, who died in 1906. Luxton talks of Inqava's skull being placed in "its last resting place in a decorated shelter on an island in the lagoon" (1955, 41). The island and the shrine now feature as "Skull Island" in local tourist tours and, for a *kastom* (custom—as in cultural tradition) fee and the cost of hiring a boat to get there, tourists can visit the island and take photographs of the skulls. Images of the shrine appear in tourist leaflets, and in

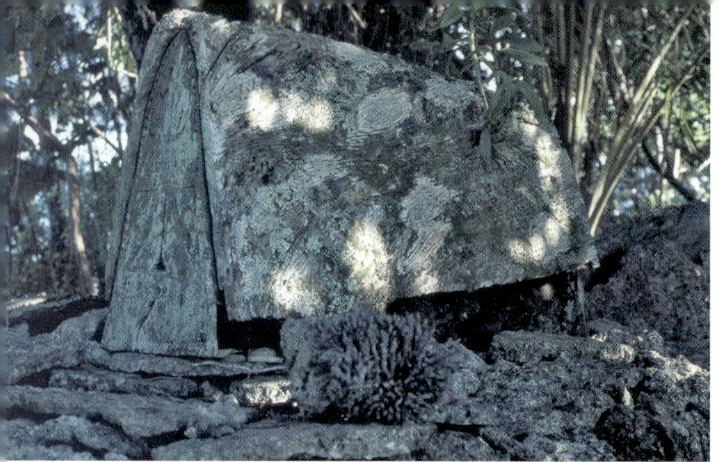

FIGURES 3.14–3.16
Ancestral shrine (*oru*)
on Kudu Hite Island.

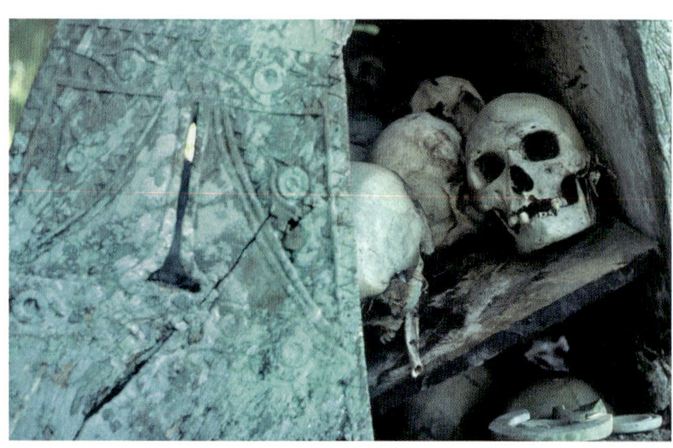

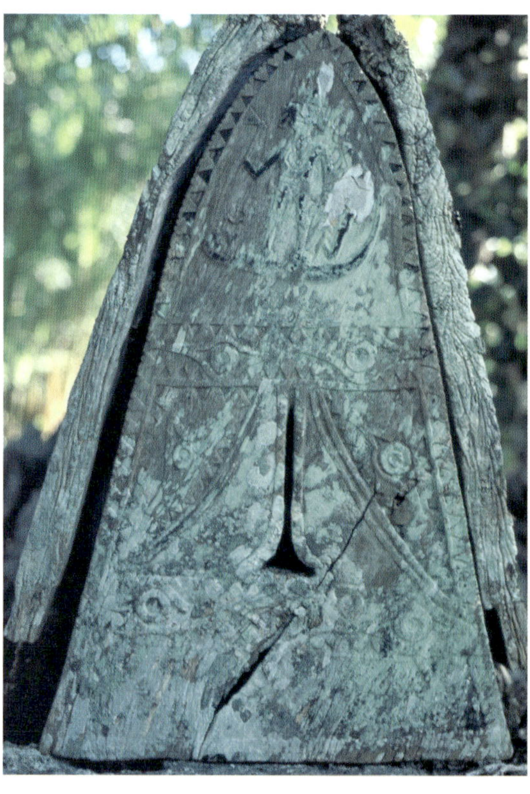

this arena it has become an iconic representation of Roviana history and "headhunting."

There are also several Christian graves close to the skull shrine on Kudu Hite, testimony to the enduring power of proximity and place in Roviana. And the kinds of approaches to embodiment and effective connections to ancestors that are part of the headhunting and skull-shrine complex also continue to be important for contemporary Roviana people. Aswani talks of "the contextual mutability of persons and objects" in relation to attitudes toward ancestral skulls and headhunting and the expectations and uses of photographs in contemporary Roviana display a similar mutability (2000, 65).[59]

Second Resurrection

> Photography has something to do with resurrection: might we not say
> of it what the Byzantines said of the image of Christ which impregnated
> St. Veronica's napkin: that it was not made by the hand of man.
>
> —**Roland Barthes,** *Camera Lucida: Reflections on Photography*

Among the range of images displayed on one wall in Chris Mamupio's house is a framed photograph of his father, Simon Mamupio (figures 3.17 and 3.18). The wall is a display site that confronts anyone visiting Chris; its striking color and the images make it the focal point of the room. For Chris this is an image that is especially "strong," and when he talks about it, he does so in the reverential tone that is a feature of stories about ancestors. The maqomaqo, as Chris calls it, was taken in 1974 by an official from New Zealand when Simon was inaugurated as a chief in Dunde. British, Australian, and New Zealand officials, as well as tourists, all came to the ceremony and feast (*inevana*) that established Simon as a chief "for looking after people," the "last big chief" in Munda.[60] The photograph shows Simon with his "lieutenant" seated behind him. The lieutenant wears a shirt and tie, but Simon wears a woven eye shade (*toropai*), and together with his bakiha and pierced and elongated earlobes, these are visual markers of Simon's connections with "the time before" (he was one of the last generation of Roviana men to have their ears pierced). Chris made the photograph's wooden frame himself after his father died in order to "keep him safe." Simon died in 1991, and "after that there was no respect any more." Chris told me why the photograph was so important: "Some people worry

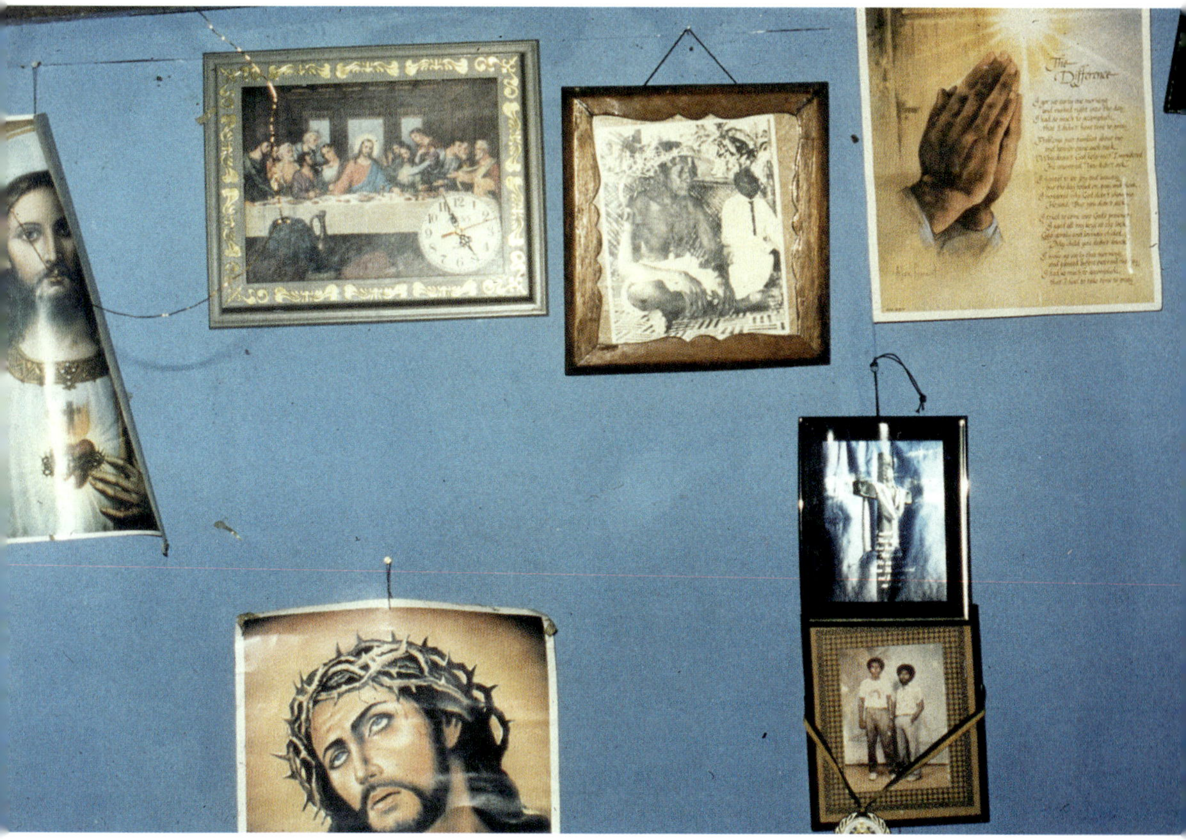

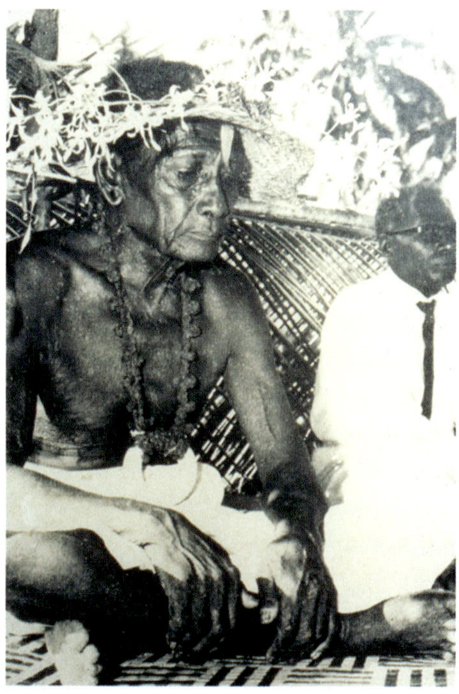

FIGURE 3.17 Images
on the wall of Chris
Mamupio's house,
Munda.

FIGURE 3.18
Photograph of
Simon Mamupio.

about the spirit in the photograph [*debil long pikisa*], but I get power from it. I get blessing [tinamanai] from my father when I look at the photograph. . . . It makes me dream [*putagita*] about him. I talk to the photograph; that is why I put it on the wall. I sit with him. My daughter has a copy of the photograph that she speaks with. The photograph can give a gift; it has power. People can see him."[61]

Chris talks to his father at his Christian grave, and talking to his photograph, which he does daily, is an equivalent process; both allow him access to ancestral sanction. Chris's performance of the photograph includes showing me his drawing of a stepped genealogical pyramid, with earlier generations forming the base and Chris at the apex. He is happy that the photograph shows Simon's whole body, because "you need to see the whole body to make a good photograph. If you only see the head then people cannot see true." Chris has fourteen photographs, and most of them were taken by outsiders. The exceptions were one of him and his father, which was taken by his daughter Sarah, and one or two by other Roviana people. When he first saw a photograph in the 1930s, Chris called it a maqomaqo, and this is also how he refers to the religious prints on his wall, acquired through his daughter, who works in Honiara. For Chris the image of Christ and the photograph of his father both conjure up a presence. David Morgan talks about the use of religious imagery, like the image of Christ on Chris's wall, in late twentiethcentury North America: "When devout viewers see what they imagine to be the actual appearance of the divinity that cares for them, the image becomes an icon. The icon is experienced by believers as presenting some aspect of the real thing[,] . . . as if standing before the image is to enjoy the very presence of its referent" (1998, 43).

For Chris the framed photograph of his father is an icon. He remembers that when he was young having your photograph taken was called being drawn or copied (*kumkumbere*). Chris refers to other photographs as *maqomaqo na pepa* (the shadow on the paper), but his photograph of his father is "a different one":

The camera [kamera] takes something, something inside a person. When someone dies, their soul [maqomaqo] leaves them. You can see it. People before thought that the camera would take something out of your body and you would become weak and sick. The spirit [debil] at a shrine could take your soul if you let your shadow fall on the shrine. People thought that the camera

and the radio were dangerous things and they were frightened
of them when they first saw them. But I think photographs are
strong. With this photograph [maqomaqo] I can remember my
father. When I look at the photograph my father sees me. I ask
him questions and he answers. The photograph is like a beku. You
look at the beku and the beku sees you.[62]

Chris Mamupio's photograph of his father provides him with access
to ancestral sanction and power, and in the sense that it embodies
his fathers spirit, it is a relic that fulfills some of the same roles as
ancestral skulls. The photograph has replaced the monument. But,
although they may be of great importance in connecting individuals
to ancestors, photographs possess little of the public political sanction that was inherent in the veneration of monuments such as skull
shrines. One of the motivations for Chris's display of the photograph of his father is so that "people can see him." The image acts
as evidence of Chris's genealogy. Even though photographs are ad-
dressed as ancestors and maintain a connection for individuals, they
have no connection to places. The topography that is mapped by
photographs in Roviana is social, not geographic, as is the case with
shrines. Individuals get blessings from photographs of their ancestors, and photographs make ancestors present, but they are not public symbols in the sense that shrines were and, to an extent, still are.

Postmortem photography, of the kind discussed by Jay Ruby
(1995) as widely popular in nineteenth-century North American
vernacular photographic practices,[63] is completely unknown in Roviana. Any discussions I initiated on the subject quickly revealed
people's disquiet, sometimes revulsion, at the thought of such a
practice. Some people said that it was *tambu* (taboo) to look at a
photograph of a recently deceased parent, particularly a father. Following the pattern of earlier mortuary practices and also current
Christian ones, both of which involve a period of mourning, Roviana people suggested that this should only occur after a suitable
time had elapsed. To view the photograph before this had happened
was risky because the image was "too strong." Chris's photograph of
his father was safely kept after they received it in 1975, sent by the
New Zealand official. He remembers his father keeping it in a basket
with his shell valuables. After his father's death, Chris did not take
the photograph out until well after the necessary period of mourning. It was only then that he made a frame for it and he referred to it

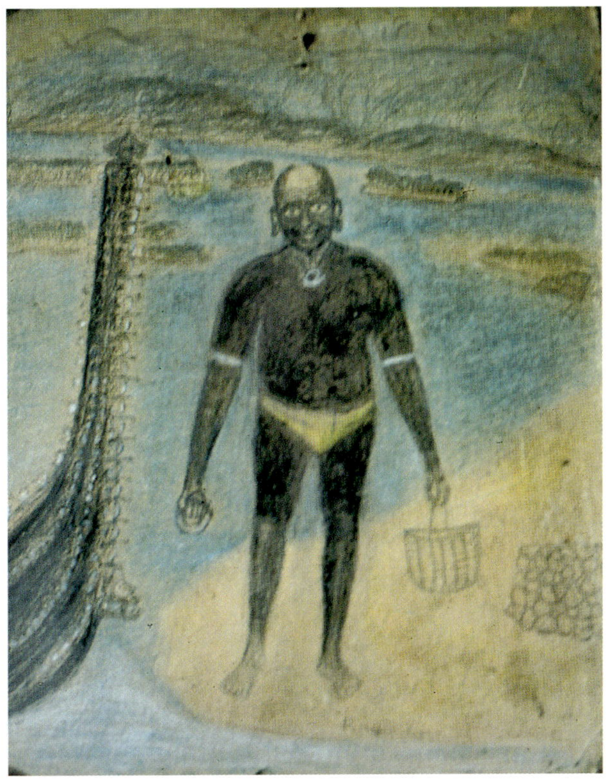

FIGURE 3.19 Drawing of Simon Mamupio, by Chris Mamupio, ca. 1995.

as being fully seated. Although Chris suggested that the photograph was always a maqomaqo—it was always an object that partook of Simon—after the death of its subject it became stronger.

One of the other images on the wall of Chris's house is a picture he drew of his father, Simon (figure 3.19): "I made the picture [pikisa] of my father so I did not lose him. He was a strong man. It is different from the photograph [maqomaqo]. I do not talk to him, but with this [pointing at drawing] I can also remember him. When I first saw a photograph I thought it was a drawing (*kumkubere*[64]).[65] We did not know what a camera [kamera] was, we thought it was like drawing, but now I know it is a different thing."[66]

What is it that makes the photograph of Simon different from the drawing? In a Euro-American frame this would be a function of discourses of realism and technology. Chris also goes to Simon's Christian grave to talk to him there, and has bakiha belonging to him. There is a range of objects available to Chris for staying in contact with his father. However, the discourses of Christian faith that have been adopted by Roviana people effectively disavow the use of physical human remains that function as relics in the way that ancestral shrines once used them. Christian rhetoric maintains a focus on the departure of the soul, rather than its continued presence. The photograph of his father is one form where his presence can be readmitted into the world of the living. It allows Chris to draw on the blessing and sanction of his father, and, although photographs do not play a vital role in the reproduction of Roviana polities in the way that shrines and ancestral relics once did, they do maintain a physical connection at an individual level. The use of photography in Roviana has led to, or perhaps even initiated, an increasing individualization of memory while simultaneously preserving its material dimensions. The display of photographs on the walls of some contemporary Roviana houses is the equivalent of the efficacy once offered to individuals by ancestral shrines. Regarding Maori practices, Binney and Chaplin explain:

> The importance of photographs to all Maori who hold traditional values is that they record the images of their ancestors. They exist as a bond between the living and the dead. Portraits of dead kin are hung in the meeting houses to which they belong, so that the continuity, the line of descent, the *iho*, is retained. Photographs are the contemporary extension of the ancestral carved figures, who support the meeting house and the living, and they have been used in this manner since the late nineteenth century. . . . They are addressed during the speeches as if the person himself was present. (Binney and Chaplin 1991, 442)

Chris's drawing of his father is like a beku in the sense that it fulfills many of the same roles; it is also carved by a human hand. But it does not achieve the presence that the photograph does. The drawing locates his father in an imaginary space—Chris told me that he drew the prow of the tomoko and the body of his father "from memory"—and is located temporally in the time before. When I asked Chris about drawing his father's face, he gave me this account: "When I drew [*kuberia*] the face I thought of him. I can remember him with this. The things he did. It is a picture [pikisa] but not true like the photograph [maqomaqo]. In the photograph I can see him. He is there." The photograph of Simon resembles an ancestral skull in its ability to maintain a physical link. Chris suggests that the drawing allows him to bring forth memories of his father, but it does not function as a relic in the way that the photograph does. Photography holds out a way of Chris remaining in touch with his father; it participates in the common work of memory and mourning, and it acquires the characteristics of earlier rituals that focus on summoning, disclosing, and channeling the presence of the dead.

In the mid-nineteenth century, the novelist Honoré de Balzac explained photography as a process in which the photographic image was formed by membranes that were lifted off the original, whether person or object, and transported through the air to be physically captured by the photographic plate and apparatus (cited in Taussig 1993, 21). As Taussig suggests in relation to Balzac's theory, "who can say we now understand any better?" (1993, 21). There is a Euro-American magic of photography, and in this sense Bruno Latour (1993) is right, "we have never been modern."

James Pitu explains: "People before were afraid of having their photograph taken because they thought it would take away their shadow [maqomaqo]. They would run away. Only some were comforted and stayed. They had their shadow taken. They had to stand still and their shadow was taken."[67] This statement of photography's mimetic power is as relevant to many Euro-American vernacular photographic practices, both historical and contemporary, as it is to Roviana ones. From their inception in Europe in the 1830s, daguerreotypes were considered to be monuments for the self, but their mimetic power was also the source of fears that surrounded early attitudes toward them—they were endowed with a life of their own. Daguerreotypists advertised their services with the slogan "seize the shadow ere the substance fade" (Trachtenberg 1992, 181), and the unique images were endowed with a supernatural force that animated them. People in Europe and North America were scared of having their images "taken" (181). Daguerreotypes were living pictures, and "in sentimental and celebratory verse they are indeed living spirits, animated shadows, or souls of the dead" (Trachtenberg 1989b, 65). In relation to daguerreotypes, Trachtenberg has talked of the "long-repressed belief and feeling that likenesses—shadows as well as reflections in mirror surfaces—are detached portions of living creatures, their soul or spirit" (66). A certain animism continues to haunt Euro-American approaches toward, and uses of, photography despite, or perhaps because of, its disavowal. There was a discourse of animism that revolved around photography's inception in Europe, North America, and elsewhere, alongside any rhetoric of progress and science. Trachtenberg has suggested that the "animistic tropes in [early] written accounts of photography can be taken as a return, at the site of an image, of guilty, repressed beliefs in the old animistic universe expelled by Christianity, reason and science" (1989a, 66). Asked how ghosts or spirits could appear in photographs, Faletau Leve stated: "Using their power spirits can make material forms. Some photographs are very strong like this; they are electric; they take things from the air and make them [gesturing with his hands]. The spirit can make things in the photograph. The spirit can stay in the photograph like it stays in a skull. You can see the shadow of the spirits. Something remains of them, the echo [*kokodala*] of those spirits."[68]

Gillain Beer has discussed European attitudes toward the invisible at the end of the nineteenth century when the great advances made in microscopes, telescopes, and optics of all kinds, including photography, were paradoxically accompanied by a realization that the invisible was "a condition within which we move, and *of* which we are, lateral, extensive, out of human control; worse, not amenable to analysis yet replete with phenomena. The invisible might prove to be a controlling medium, not a place to be explored; a condition of our existence, not a new country to be colonized" (1996, 88). This was the period when studies of the ether were suggesting that it was all-pervading and part of a system in which "'things' themselves proved to be modes of motion rather than stable identities" (85). The mutability that Faletau delineates — a flux between the visible and invisible worlds — suggest that photography in Roviana is a form that can connect the world of the spirits with that of the living. Concerns about invisible worlds and the stability of identities are a feature of both Roviana and Euro-American photographic practices. As Derrida argues, "modern technology, contrary to appearances, although it is scientific, increases tenfold the power of ghosts" (2002, 115).

Disappearance

One of the few photographs that Chris Mamupio owns shows him dressed in a lap-lap, wearing a shell ornament (hinuili) and another necklace around his neck, and shell arm rings (hokata) (figure 3.20). The image was taken by the anthropologist Gerhard Schneider, who carried out fieldwork in Munda in the mid-1990s (Schneider 1996).

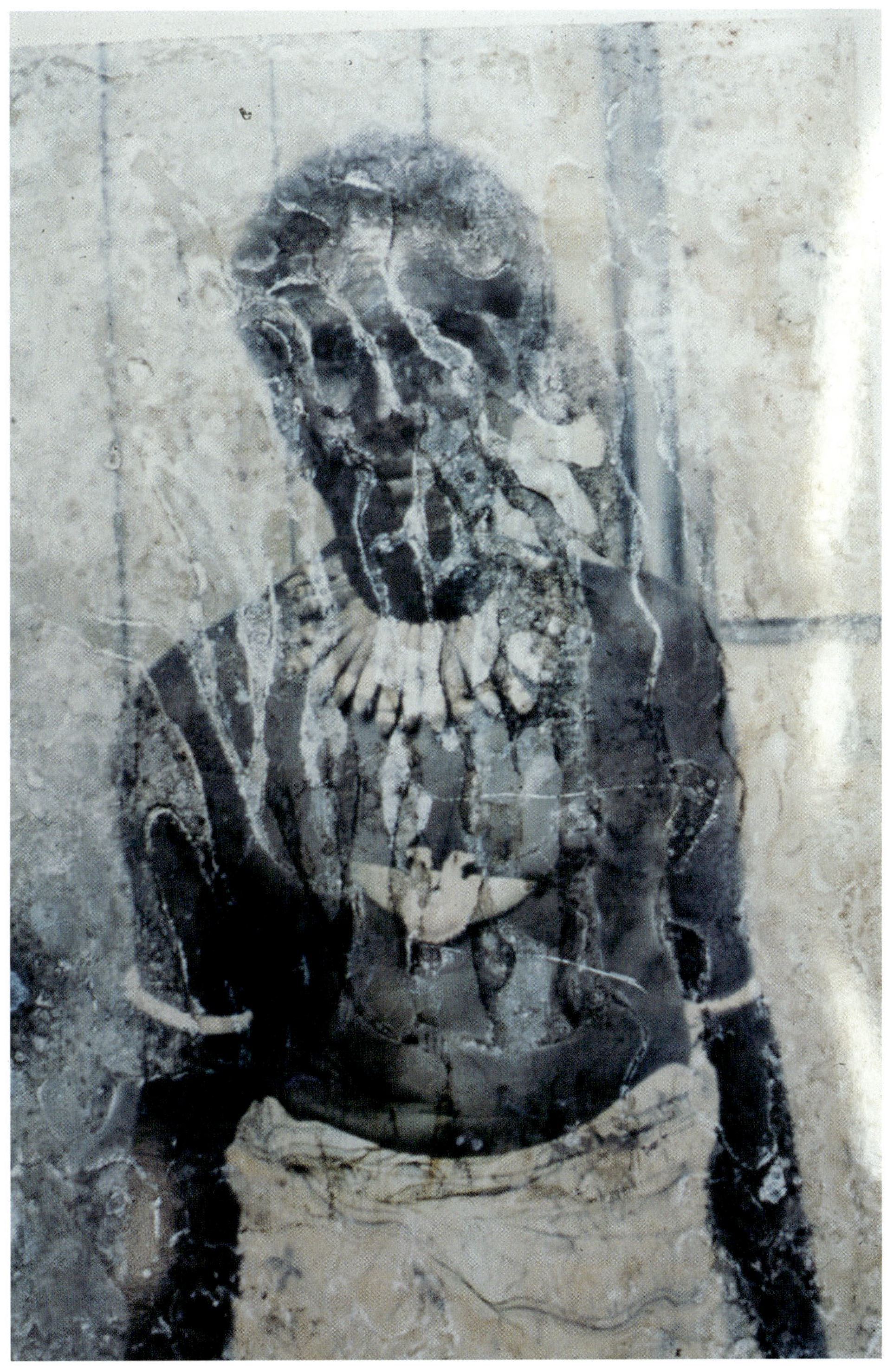

FIGURE 3.20 Chris Mamupio. Photograph by Gerhard Schneider, ca. 1995.

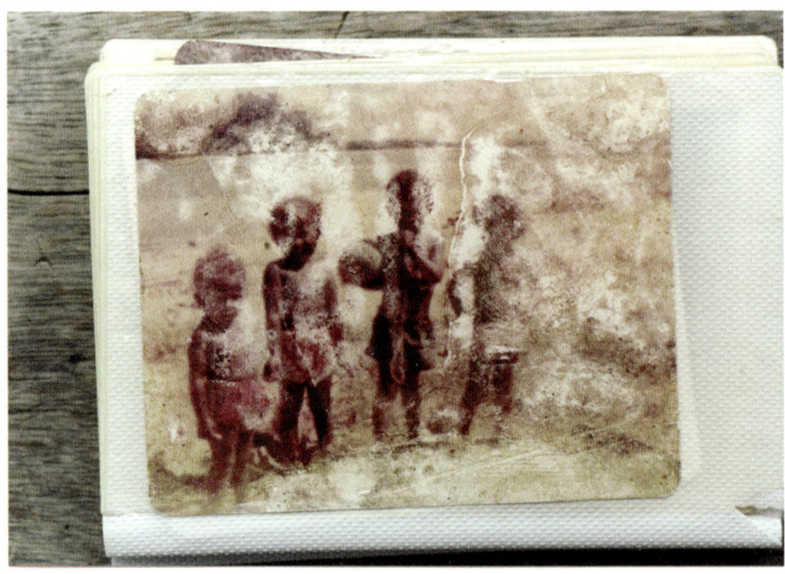

FIGURE 3.21 Illegible photograph, ca. 1998.

FIGURE 3.22 Disappearing photographs in an album.

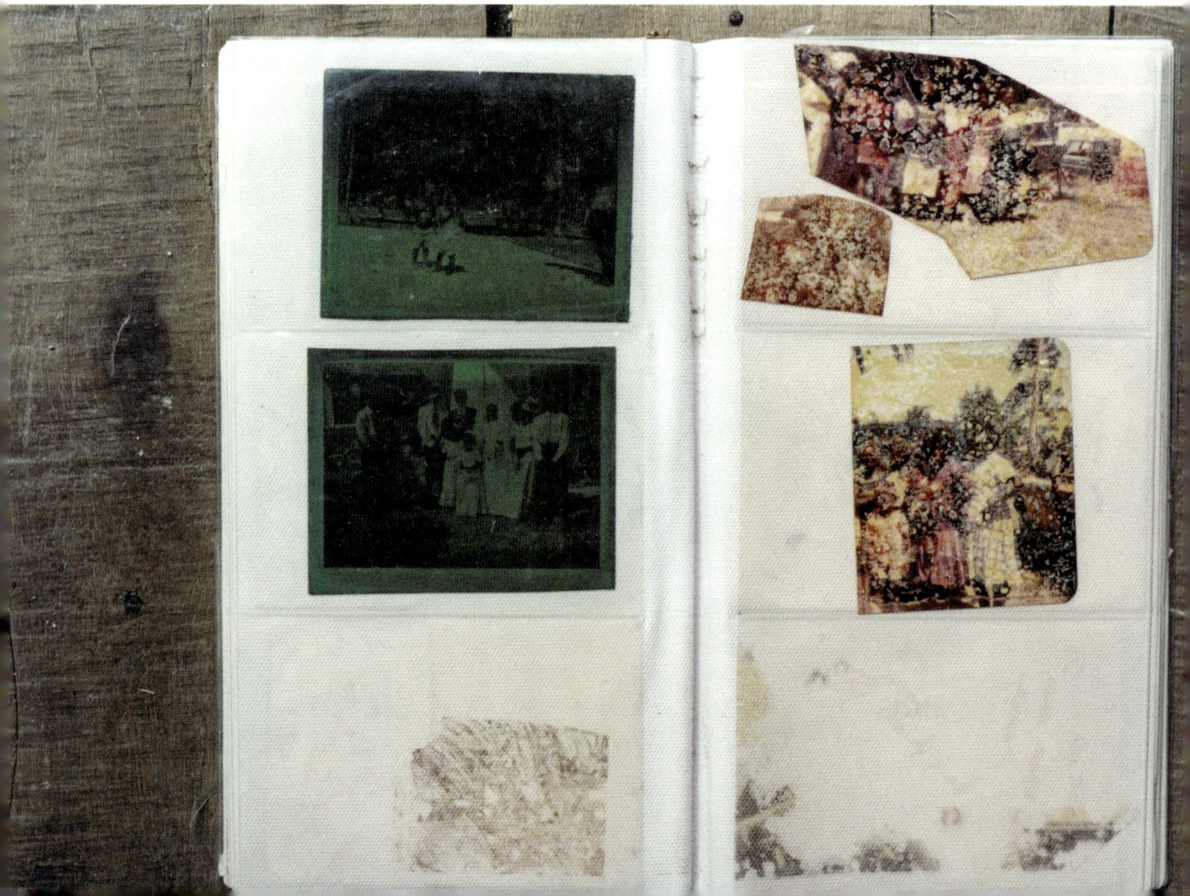

The photograph is slowly disappearing, the colors seemingly melting and distorting the image. This decay and the material flux that it implies is the cause of much anxiety for Chris: "I am not clear in this. I do not come out good. I will not remain [*stap*]. If I do not come out clear, then I can get sick. There is a spirit [maqomaqo] that looks at you. This is called *pela* [a kind of Roviana evil eye]. The devil [debildebil] can eat you."[69]

The disruption of identity that is figured in the photograph concerns a kind of visual ingestion. Earlier Roviana beliefs specified that *kita*—a type of slow wasting disease that reduced the body—was thought to be the work of ghosts. The disappearance of photographs is similarly thought to be the work of malevolent spirits. The concern over the disappearance of photographs and the way in which wholly illegible images could be described to me as "our picnic on the beach," demonstrates the mimetic magic of these photo objects in contemporary Roviana. But the rapid degradation of photographic prints turn the living into ghosts, and the decay of the soul that is prefigured in these photographs threatens the sense of continuing connection to ancestors that photographs can provide in Roviana. Chris complains: "What will I leave behind? I will not remain [stap]. How will those that come after remember me?" The comforting solidity of photographs, a feature that underwrites their memorial function, is replaced here by the fear of being forgotten.

In the uncertainty caused by the civil unrest that affected the Solomon Islands from 1998 to 2001, the decay of contemporary photographs was also seen as symbolic of the current state of affairs in Roviana. The fact that some black-and-white photographic prints (particularly those made between 1930 and 1960) remained "clear" in contrast to color prints of more recent origin that were rapidly disappearing (see figure 3.22), was seen by many Roviana people as a vindication of how things were better "before." Whereas now: "Things are bad. No one listens to kastom. People before were strong and they listened to kastom. Now things are broken [*bagarap*]." Photography is linked to the Roviana past not only through its role as a material relic but also through the ways it is entangled with broader ideas of history; entanglements that connect it very firmly with the present.

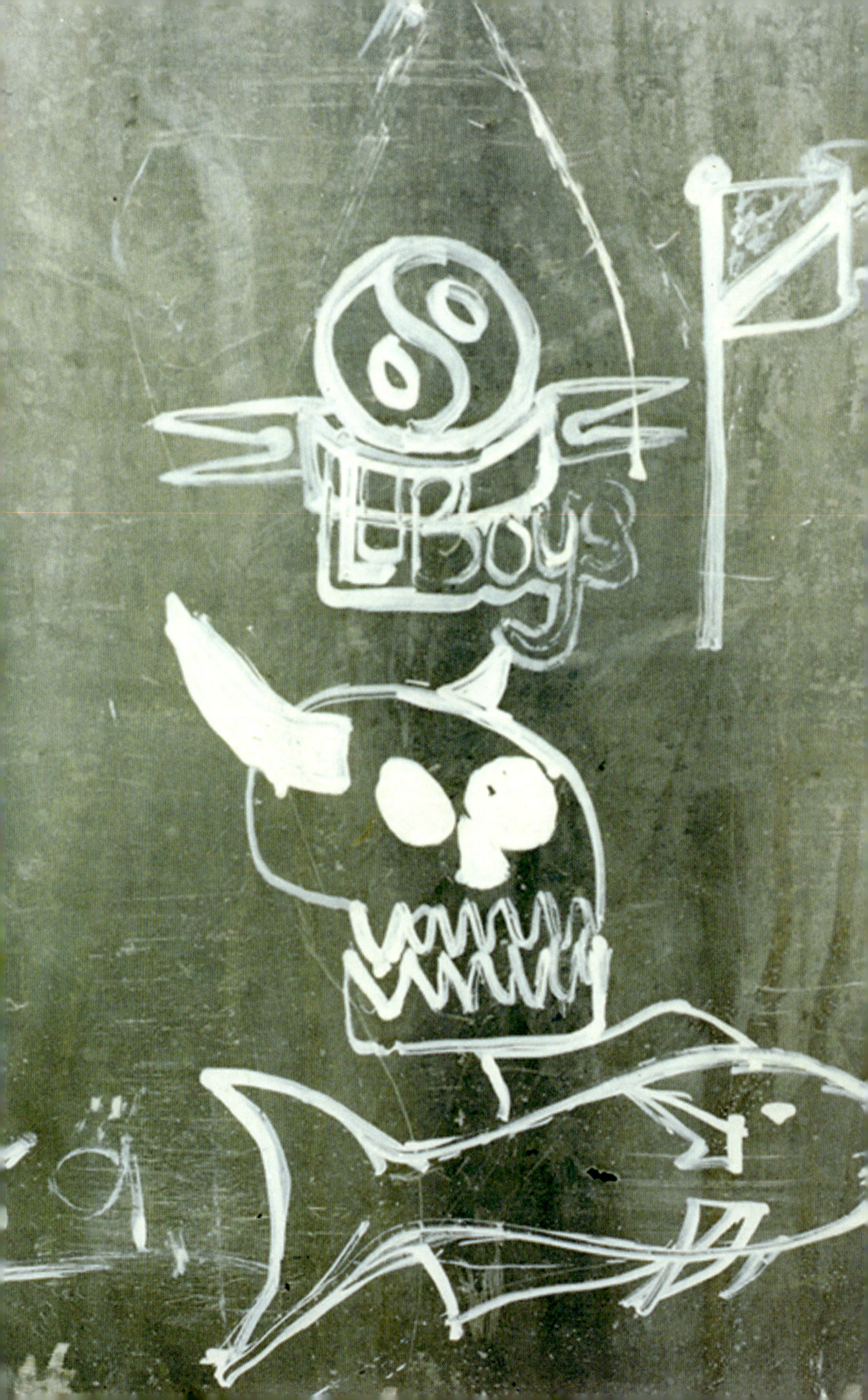

Boys

4

Histories

Faletau Leve's executive-style briefcase was
slowly falling apart. The black fake-leather surface was scuffed and
peeling; the chrome plating on the handle had chipped off; and the
corroded metal underneath left rust stains on your hands when you
held it. Despite the briefcase's dilapidated appearance, it is one of
Faletau's favorite objects. He carries it around the village on important occasions and takes it with him to meetings. When he opens it,
it is often with an air of solemnity, a sense of performative gesture;
it is a ritual. The heavily stained interior gives off the musty, rotting
smell that paper quickly acquires in the intense heat and humidity.
It is where everything is kept:

> Several creased, well-handled photographs: a fading, barely deci-
> pherable image of a young girl standing by some large plants look-
> ing straight at the camera; the color bleached out to a series of
> pastel tones; a blurred black-and-white photograph of a woman
> standing by a bicycle; a color Polaroid photograph, with a name
> and date written on the back, showing a man in a bright red shirt
> standing by a child.

Scraps of paper with hand-written commentaries on particular Bible verses.

Partial genealogies in elaborate geometrical forms drawn on oddly shaped pieces of cardboard.

A cutting—yellowing, torn, and stuck together with tape—from a Solomon Islands newspaper about Faletau's woodcarvings.

A postcard of the Sydney Opera House from an Australian tourist Faletau met in Munda.

Drawings that combine Christian symbolism with local animals—hearts, crosses, and doves with crocodiles and sharks.

After shuffling through these objects, Faletau produced a creased and worn photocopy. It shows ranks of white-uniformed soldiers standing in front of a large western Solomons canoe house (*paele*) (figure 4.1). Faletau, who was aware of my concern with photographs and history, had come to find me and reveal this "important history." The image is hard to make out in any detail, reduced as it is to a stark black and white by several generations of photocopying. Faletau acquired a photocopy of a photocopy that is in the collection of the cultural center in Gizo, a small wooden shed opposite the Gizo Hotel, which has one folder of plastic sleeves containing some twenty or so photocopies and prints of nineteenth-century photographs of the western Solomons. These are part of a larger collection that was collated by an expatriate cultural worker, Barbara Riley, in the late 1980s. The image's lack of legibility in no way diminishes its significance for Faletau. His fingers handle the stained and rapidly disintegrating sheet of paper delicately as he passes it to me.

The photocopy depicts one moment of what British authorities described as a "punitive" raid on Roviana carried out by sailors and marines from HMS *Royalist* in 1891. But for Faletau there is no expectancy or need to ascribe the event a date—no need to secure it chronologically—and only one or two local people know with any precision the actual date of the event depicted. This is not considered important or necessarily relevant knowledge as far as this photocopy, or indeed many historical events, is concerned.[1]

The event is frequently referred to in general discussions about history and contemporary change in Roviana, and it is often used in comparisons between past and present. Unlike the arrival of the

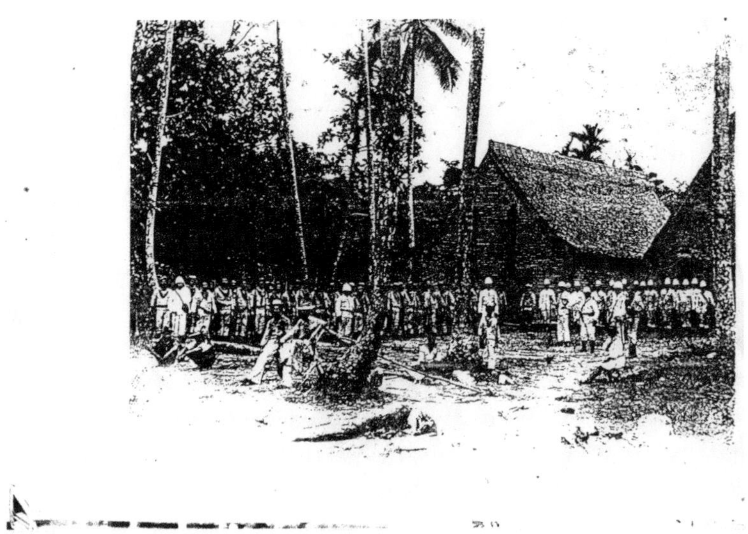

FIGURE 4.1 Faletau's photocopy.

Methodist mission in Roviana on May 23, 1902, a date that many Roviana people know well and celebrate annually, the event in question here is located in broader and more ambiguous terms: people refer to "the time of *Royalist*" rather than making any reference to a specific date. If people do place it in any chronology, the event is said to have happened *bifo lotu*—before the arrival of the mission. The mission is used as a kind of temporal pivot; people talk about the time before the mission and the time behind (after) the mission.[2] Although people do refer to the changes wrought by the *Royalist* event, it is not used as a marker of before and after in the same way. From 2000 to 2001, many conversations and oral histories—both those responses instigated by my questions and those I overheard—that commented on the actions of the crew of HMS *Royalist* did so by making references to the violence, civil unrest, and general disruption caused by the so-called ethnic tensions that affected the Solomon Islands from 1999 onward. The emphasis was less on the *Royalist* event as signaling a major change of epoch and more on the event's relation to current concerns. Why is this image of colonial force in the past seen as saying something about contemporary problems?

Faletau had decided to show me the photocopy because I had expressed interest at an earlier passing allusion he made to the *Royalist* when we were casually talking about how the ethnic tension in Honiara and elsewhere on Guadalcanal was affecting life in Roviana. This brief comment, which linked events in Roviana more than one hundred years ago to those in the capital of Honiara in 2001, and also to events further afield both historically and geographically, was typical of the way in which "the time of *Royalist*" often slipped into normal conversation: "The situation now is very bad. It cannot be solved until it all comes out [until events have run their course]. People will be killed. We have a mafia system in Honiara now. It would be better if we went back to a colonial government. The Solomons is like Croatia; everybody fights each other. Young people are against custom and they have crazy hearts. That is why they drink and fight and steal. It is like the time of *Royalist*. They came and destroyed everything. Everything will change."[3] This kind of brief passing reference to the *Royalist* event — the detritus of history, like the photocopy, is a kind of visual detritus — nevertheless demonstrates its contemporary significance as a means of linking the past and the present. Faletau's reference to Croatia comes from the way in which roadblocks manned by armed members of the self-styled Malaitan Eagle Force in Honiara were known by names such as "Croatia" and "Vietnam." These and other conflicts, some of which feature in videos available in Honiara and to a lesser extent Roviana, as well as in the media more generally (conflicts like the Palestinian intifada, Northern Ireland, and the Balkans were all reported in the *Solomon Star* newspaper), were frequently referred to in relation to the ethnic tensions. During my time in Roviana, the *Royalist* was on occasion the subject of extended oral narratives — particular performances of history (see White 1991a) — and it was also slipped into everyday conversations. This marked a significant change compared to my first visit to Roviana in 1998, when people could recount stories about the *Royalist* when asked but did not relate them to the present day. Since at this point the ethnic tension had yet to make its influence felt, there was perhaps little need for the time of *Royalist* to serve as a point of reference for current events.

This act of colonial violence is discussed in relation to the present, and it is seen to mark, or be indicative of, a period of change and upheaval. In order to understand the image, its relation to history, and its significance for Roviana people, Euro-American expectations demand that we fix the photograph chronologically. This is how photographs and history are linked in most Euro-American discourses. The necessary "forensic" work is done to uncover the history behind or in the photograph (Edwards 2001): archives and collections are consulted, and the photograph has a text or caption attached to it that allows us to understand the image's historical place and importance. This is the Euro-American historical expectation of the photograph.

John Tagg referred to late nineteenth-century photographs in Europe as "'paltry paper signs' that are yet the very stuff of history — as though it were physically scored into their surface" (1988, 7). How can this fragile object support the weight of Faletau's "important history"? What does it keep for him? The event represented in this much-handled photocopy has a continuing significance for Faletau, and tracing the histories that circulate around it reveals Roviana and Euro-American expectations of photography in relation to understandings of the past and the present.

One of my main concerns during the time I spent in Roviana was with the suitability, or not, of photographs as sources for Roviana people to think about their history. Not just to serve as occasions for the recital of formal oral histories but to provoke reminiscences, anecdotes, and personal memories of all kinds. I want to understand Roviana historical expectations of photography, and there is a sense that the detail that anthropologists and historians try to provide through an archival history is irrelevant for contemporary Roviana people; they do not care for exact dates. The details they require and expect are of a different order than those required from this discursive archival history.[4]

Anthropological expectations of history suggest that I should look at oral accounts to see what they can add to the written archival one. In reconstructing the history of an attack by Malaitans on a trading vessel in the late 1800s, Roger Keesing asks how reliable and how illuminating oral historical evidence can be: "How can such oral testimony, encrusted by time, compliment the archival records documenting events from a European perspective?" (1986, 269). He argues that by using the archives, "we can thus reconstruct what actually happened (albeit from the perspective of the crew of a European ship recruiting indentured labour) a century ago; and we can thus compare this scenario with the perspectives of the indigenous attackers, which have been filtered through oral tradition" (269). There is a temptation, following Keesing, to combine the archival and the histories to come up with the complete version — what actually happened — but Roviana attitudes toward history acknowledge that histories are competing accounts constructed in the present with an aim to achieve certain ends. As Elizabeth Edwards argues in relation to photographs and history, "we expect photographs to tell, but find them remarkably resistant, for, like history, they do not lend themselves to being dealt with in any definite way" (2001, 9).

The actions of the men of HMS *Royalist* caused significant changes in the lives of Roviana people, and many of them are able to give some account of this event. The following example comes from someone, Steven Ilo, with a direct genealogical connection to the events — a Roviana measure of the relative authority of an oral account. Steven's story is a direct response to seeing my photocopy, even more illegible, of Faletau's photocopy. The history is not really reliant on any detail in the photocopy, but is nonetheless prompted by it; like a *bakiha* (shell valuable) with a story attached to it, the photocopy functions as a mnemonic device. The history was recounted to an attentive crowd of adults and children who had been looking through the collection of prints I had taken with me to Kokorapa village on Nusa Roviana — one of Roviana Lagoon's many barrier islands:

> I am Steven Ilo of Kokorapa, Nusa Roviana. I can only tell you what I know. How that burning happened. It is the story of the three people who killed the white man at Hombuhombu. It happened because the white men were buying copra. There was a trader who lived on Hombuhombu. The people of Vuragare [a settlement area of Nusa Roviana] would dry their coconut and take it to the trader to sell it. The buying price was bad from Peter [Edmund] Pratt, so these people were not happy. They said this man lives on our island and that island belongs to us. He did not buy the island from us to operate his business there. He was not doing well for us. So the anger came from there. So the three men — warriors — went to Hombuhombu and killed [*sekea*, literally, "whipped"] the manager. After that there was an investigation by the white men. And that was how it became known that Vuragare people were responsible. That was when the man-o-war [*maneroa*] came and they bombed [*gona*] this place. This side of the island is deep and they stopped there to shoot at us.

The people here had already heard the ship was coming. When they knew about it, they left. They went to the shore [Munda]. Because there were people living near Bebea [a small island directly to the west of Nusa Roviana], they came to bomb around Bebea. They also bombed Nusa Roviana. They burnt all the houses and war canoes and all the warriors belongings. There was nothing left. They [the people of Nusa Roviana] moved to those villages, Dunde, Kindu, Mono [all hamlets of Munda]. That is how the steamer [*sitima*] came to bomb Nusa Roviana, because these three men had killed a white man. I do not know them all, but one of them is Lotana. He was the person who got those other two and planned the killing. They were the ones who went and killed the white man at Hombuhombu. Lotana's father was Avosia from Bilua [Vella Lavella], and he married a woman from Vuragare who bore Lotana. Lotana married a Simbo woman called Atunaru, and she bore Sibapitu. Sibapitu married Dae, and she bore Siope, Nemo, Kele, Isiah, Buta, Pozelmali. Those were their children. That was how we are related to Lotana. That was how we came to be and remain here today. They all ran away from here to Munda. Only Taqala remained here. They were just hiding everywhere. Then they left and stayed at Buala, Kepekepe, Langoro [all hamlets on the mainland opposite Nusa Roviana]. These were the places they settled. They lived along the Ilangana coast up to Dunde. That was how they came to live there. The people here came from Kazukuru and when the bombing from the man-o-war took place they left and went to the coast. Those from Kalikoqo [a settlement area on Nusa Roviana] were at Nusa Banga, Sasavele, and Bethlehem [other villages around Roviana lagoon]. That is the story about how they came to be.[5]

Steven is not concerned with the kinds of accuracy that might be required of an archival history. His history is an explanation of how groups of people got to be where they are now, how those living in the present are directly connected to those in the past. Steven recounts the impact of the *Royalist* attack on the temporary movement of his extended kin group (*butubutu*) from Kokorapa to the mainland of New Georgia. This was the direct effect that the *Royalist* event had for many Roviana people. The actions of HMS *Royalist* caused the relocation of one of the main butubutu of Kokorapa to found the village of Dunde on the Munda coast. The event also possibly had an effect on the position of Nusa Roviana as the political center of the confederation of Roviana peoples. Steven's history starts with a declaration of identity—this is a history that starts from where one person is in the present; it is history from one "side" (Hviding 1996). Steven also includes references to Kazukuru, an area in the interior of New Georgia from which populations moved to the coast in the sixteenth and seventeenth centuries. The *Royalist* incident is one juncture in a series of population movements and changing relations to land that took place in Roviana over hundreds of years. Steven's oral account is a performance of history that uses a photograph, here in the form of a photocopy, as a starting point but is not exhausted by it. His history is one that is unconcerned with the details that would most likely form the focus of Euro-American endeavors in regard to the photograph's relation to history.

There are concerns with committing oral accounts to paper. Walter Ong has discussed the transient reality of the spoken versus the permanent unreality of the written word (Ong 1982), but perhaps even a tape recording would preserve the phonocentrism of a Euro-American approach (see Derrida 2002). For some contemporary Pacific historians, it is precisely the "transient reality" of the oral account that needs to be preserved in contrast to written histories (Neumann 1992, 14). Photographs seem to hold out the promise of a permanent historical inscription, that such and such an event actually took place, but they are also resistant to fixed readings. However, this makes them particularly useful tools for Roviana histories. There is an equation made by many Pacific historians that a peoples' ability to know its past is a necessary prerequisite to its ability to control its future (Borofsky 2000). My arrival in Roviana with a large number of historical photographs, at a time when there were significant changes occurring, meant that this equation was at the forefront of many discussions about what the photographs meant to Roviana people.

The photograph that is the source of Faletau's photocopy and the starting point of Steven's history was possibly taken by Captain Edward H. M. Davis, who was in command of HMS *Royalist* at the time of the attack on Roviana villages. It is one of a series of photographs—now held by the Macleay Museum in Sydney—that reveals an act of colonial violence (figures 4.2 and 4.3). There is a text-based

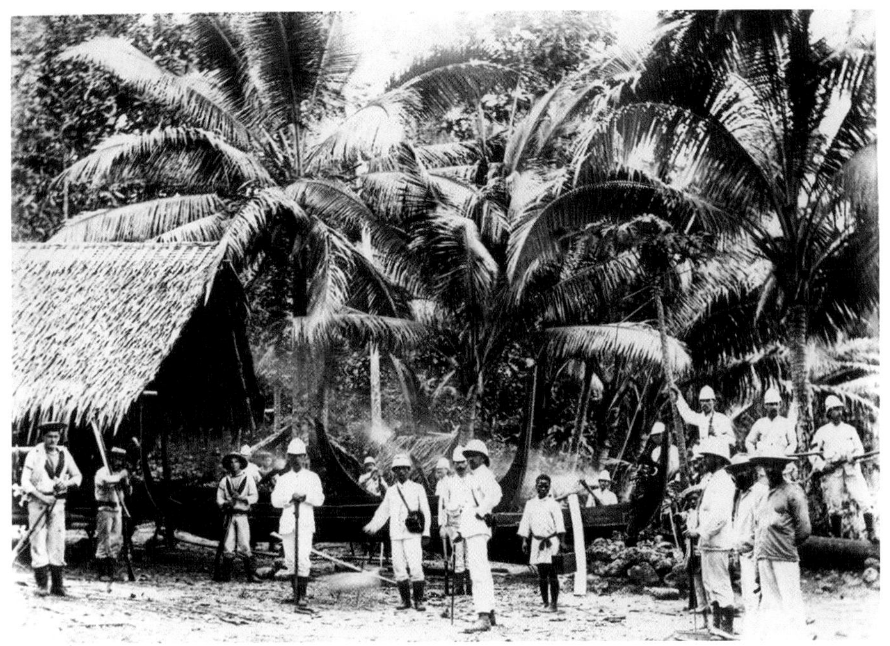

FIGURE 4.2 Officers and marines of HMS *Royalist* on the shore at Sisiata, 1891. Courtesy of
Macleay Museum, University of Sydney. HP87.14.24

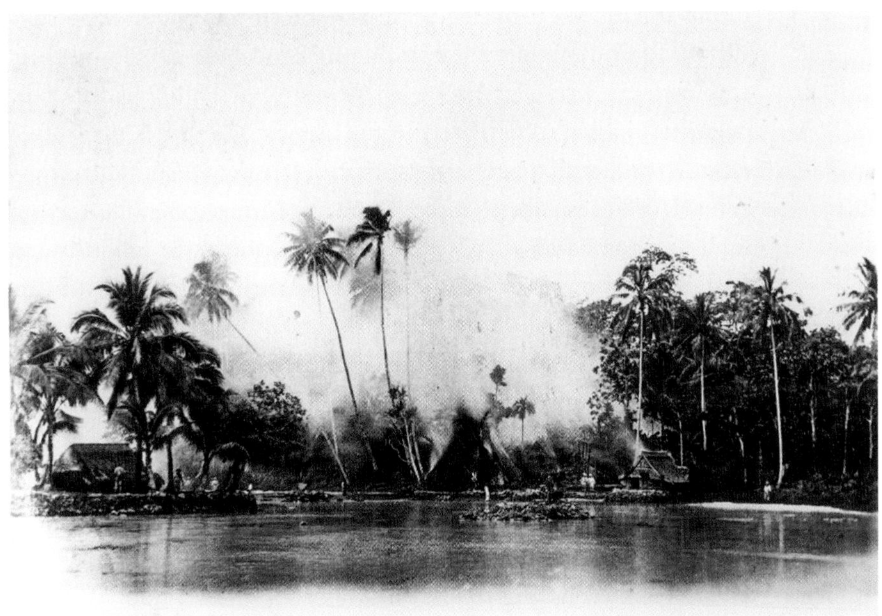

FIGURE 4.3 Buildings burning on Nusa Roviana island, 1891. Courtesy of Macleay Museum,
University of Sydney. HP87.14.21

history that could be attached to Faletau's photocopy. This history comes from the "printed papers," the archival records left behind by the colonial administration and old newspaper reports of the incident. There are many histories that revolve around Faletau's photocopy, and, as Greg Dening points out, the relations between history and the contexts of its preservation are in one sense the text that has to be dealt with (Dening 1988, 26). The side from which this textual history is written must remain clear.

One of the archival traces left by the *Royalist* incident begins with the written report in the British Admiralty records of Case No. 32: "20th June 1889, on an island near Rubiana Island. Death, at the hands of natives, of Mr. William Dabelle, a trader, and two native boys, in the employ of Mr. Edmunds, a trader." The account of the actions carried out by the men of HMS *Royalist* in Roviana Lagoon, and the events leading up to it, is constructed from the official reports and letters that can be found in the Royal Navy records that are housed in the National Library of Australia and also in the Public Records Office in London.[6] The events referred to as "the time of *Royalist*" took place in a period when relations between Roviana people and Europeans had shifted from relatively few sporadic contacts to more sustained and often permanent interaction.[7] As a result of a series of "outrages" against European traders settled in various locations around the Solomon Islands, and attacks on their employees and vessels, the Royal Navy's Australian Squadron had begun to expand its activities in the islands during the 1870s. But despite the fact that between 1867 and 1879 thirty-four Europeans and thirty-five islanders employed by Europeans were killed, along with £24,000 of property reported as lost within the Solomons as a whole, only one such incident was reported in the western Solomons (Jackson 1978, 76).

The trading vessel *Marion Rennie* was attacked off the coast of Rendova Island in 1867. And, in a pattern that was later to become common practice for the Royal Navy in the western Solomons, a full year after the attack, HMS *Blanche*, under the command of Captain John Montgomerie, shelled the islands of Roviana Lagoon (Jackson 1978, 76–77). Although the organizer of the attack on the *Marion Rennie* was, according to the admiralty reports, Londo, a *banara* (chief) from Rendova, the decision was made to attack villages in Roviana. And, after failing to apprehend Londo, Montgomerie imposed a fine of three tons of tortoise shell on Londo in his absence—

a huge fine that was clearly impossible to actually pay.[8] The *Marion Rennie* incident and the various punitive measures taken by the British reveal the lack of any coherent official stance on dealing with "outrages" against European (primarily British) interests. The case also shows that long intervals could occur between events and subsequent policing actions carried out by the Royal Navy.

Although villages could easily be shelled from the safety of Royal Navy warships, creating a spectacular display, the best method of inflicting real and lasting damage was to send a landing party to burn houses and chop down coconut trees. Since the trees took six years to reach maturity and bear fruit, their destruction was a severe blow at a time when most trade with Europeans was rapidly shifting to copra. But the Royal Navy was also obliged to protect the interests of traders and was under instructions to avoid the wholesale destruction of plantations (Jackson 1978, 99). The other great loss that could be inflicted on Roviana people was the destruction of their large trading and raiding canoes (*tomoko*). These represented a significant material and spiritual investment, the loss of which restricted the efficacy of local banara and polities.[9] After the shelling by the navy in 1868, it was another twenty years before a similar incident reportedly took place in Roviana, despite the arrival of one or two Europeans who began to set up permanent trading posts in the lagoon.

Throughout the 1870s, Royal Navy ships frequently called at Roviana, mostly Nusa Zonga, a small island off Munda (see map P.1) to gather information from traders and to recruit interpreters and guides. The island was also a coal depot for Royal Navy ships and a point where they could pick up orders conveyed by trading vessels plying their trade between northern Queensland and the Solomons. For information about events in Roviana, the captains of Royal Navy ships were totally dependent on traders and local banara, particularly Inqava, who could speak pidgin English well and had gradually acquired a reputation as the "king of Rubiana."

Although relations between Roviana people and traders who had settled there were a potential source of arguments, Kim Jackson suggests that there were relatively few violent incidents in the 1870s because it was a period when the copra trade was blossoming (Jackson 1978, 82). Roviana people were to a large extent able to dictate the terms of this trade,[10] and increasingly demanded rifles, as well as the more acceptable ax blades, in return for copra. And some expatriate traders had a reputation for trading firearms, despite it being illegal under Queen's Regulation No. 1 of 1884 (Jackson 1978, 83). Outside of the changes caused by trade, the traders themselves, almost all of whom married local women, were figures of some influence and power, able to act as intermediaries in the flow of European commodities. They participated in local networks of exchange and generosity, and when the naturalist and colonial official Charles Woodford spent several weeks in Munda in 1886, he complained that headhunting, ritual sacrifice, and cannibalism were regularly being practiced in the presence of Europeans.[11] Although only eleven Europeans were killed in the western Solomons between 1880 and 1896, the consequences of these outrages had a significant effect on the lives of Roviana people (Bennett 1986, 395–97).

The *Royalist* incident was a punitive action carried out by the British in retaliation for two attacks on the English trader Edmund Pratt's trading station on Hombuhombu Island in Roviana. A raid in October 1888 resulted in the death of two islander employees and the loss of £200 of goods (Jackson 1978, 83). The islanders working directly for European traders in the western Solomons were usually from elsewhere in the group, often Malaita. Roviana people were particularly averse to working for Europeans at this stage, and islander employees were outsiders who may well have been considered easier targets for local people as they had no relatives nearby who might avenge the death or demand compensation. In the first attack on Pratt's station, the killers came from Simbo, and they may have had a personal reason for the attack; they were mistreated by Pratt in the past. Pratt wrote a letter concerning this attack to the *Sydney Morning Herald*, which was published on March 29, 1889, under the headline "Atrocities at Rubiana." Pratt's station was attacked again on June 20, 1889, and two islander employees and one European working for Pratt, William Dabelle,[12] were killed and their heads taken. The second attack, referred to in the official correspondence as "Case No. 32,"[13] was understood to have been carried out by "renegades" from Mbilua (Vella Lavella island), according to inquiries carried out by Captain Hand.[14] However, as a response to these two outrages and insistent requests from traders, the Royal Navy decided to take punitive measures.

On August 15, 1891, Davis, in command of HMS *Royalist*, was at Nusa Zonga where he found a Mr. Atkinson in charge, because the regular officer in charge, Captain Woodhouse, had gone to Sydney to deliver a load of copra. Atkinson reported that four of Woodhouse's islander employees had recently been murdered at Ndovele village (Vella Lavella island) and Davis agreed to look into the matter and to apprehend the killers of Dabelle and the two islander employees. He anchored off Ndovele on August 17 and sent a message to deliver the killers. After getting no response, Davis landed with twenty-five men and proceeded into the bush to Ndovele and destroyed it. He then advanced to Mbilua and took on board—although exactly how this was achieved is unclear—"Tooloo, the chief, and two other natives of that place until the murderers of Dabelle (case 32) [were] delivered up."[15] The taking of hostages in cases like this was a recognized Royal Navy practice.

After a brief return visit to Nusa Zonga to refuel with coal, Davis was back at Mbilua on August 20 and again sent demands for the killers of Woodhouse's employees to be handed over. He was met with a series of excuses and left, threatening to "make war on the whole of [Mbilua]" if those wanted for the various killings were not surrendered on his next visit.[16] In his reports to his commander in chief (Sir J. B. Thurston), Davis wrote that HMS *Royalist* anchored at Hathorn Sound at 7:45 on the morning of September 24. Davis then proceeded with thirty armed men in rowing boats to Nusa Zonga where he ascertained—although the source of his information is not clear—that the five men wanted for Dabelle's murder were in "Rubiana."[17]

While at Nusa Zonga, Davis sent for Banara Wonge, but he refused to comply and Inqava was apparently away fishing. Davis then sent a message back to HMS *Royalist* to order Lieutenant Luscombe to bring all the "small-arms men and marines" to Nusa Roviana at daylight the following morning. Then, having assembled many local banara on Nusa Zonga, Davis warned "all the villages in the vicinity" that they should give up the killers or he would "make war against all the villages in the district." In the evening Davis went to "Cocorappa" (Kokorapa) on "Rubiana Island" (Nusa Roviana) and told the villagers that he and a small contingent of marines were going to camp there for the night. He repeated his warning that "if the seven murderers, whom they were harbouring, were not given up by the following morning, [he] should make war against all the villages."[18]

Following Davis, Luscombe arrived at Nusa Roviana at 8 a.m. on September 25 with all the ship's men (eighty in total) and, since there was no sign of the murderers by 10 a.m., Davis and his men "proceeded to destroy all the villages on and near Rubiana." That night Davis, perhaps feeling it unwise to stay on Nusa Roviana, camped at Inqava's village (Sisiata) and on September 26 proceeded with the destruction of villages along the shoreline at Munda. Due to the long-standing relation between Inqava and the British, he left Inqava's two canoe sheds and own house intact, "in hopes that, on his return from his fishing expedition, he would endeavour to have the men given up."[19] By 3 p.m. Davis had stopped burning villages in the Munda area and returned to Nusa Zonga. He left there with his men to rejoin HMS *Royalist* in Hathorn Sound at 4 p.m.

Davis wrote of the attack:

In all I estimate 400 houses, 150 canoes, and 1,000 heads were destroyed. In one house I found twenty-four heads ranged along one side, but it was too dark to see the rest of the house. In Goolie's house [presumably his paele, as this is where heads would have been kept], the chief who murdered Dabelle, I found several guns, spears etc. and from ten to fifteen heads. The big war canoes had been removed into the shallow lagoons, where, with the small force at my disposal, it was quite impossible to get at them, but this severe punishment will not be lost on the noted Rubiana head-hunters, who for years have considered themselves safe in their strongholds.[20]

In his surveying expedition of 1893–94, Henry Somerville recorded that Roviana people saw the beaches of the lagoon "absolutely littered" with smashed skulls (Somerville 1897, 399). Davis returned to Nusa Zonga on October 11 and "ascertained that [his] action of 25 and 26 September had had a great effect on the natives of Rubiana and Munda, and that there was some talk amongst them of delivering up some of the murderers." He continued: "They were anxious to know what I intended to do, and I sent word to them that if they gave up the murderers I would do no more, but if they persisted in keeping them I should continue to make war on them" (Somerville 1897, 399). The *Sydney Morning Herald* echoed Davis's sentiments on December 10, 1891: "It is to be hoped that these savages, the noted Rubiana head-hunters, who have depopulated all the surrounding islands by their cruel practices, will not soon forget their well-merited punishment."

When the Royal Navy returned to Roviana in 1892, the islanders asked if they could now rebuild their houses,[21] and in 1895 Commander Rason reported that HMS *Royalist* is "a name to conjure by, owing to the strong action of Captain Davis, and his name is still respected throughout the group" (Jackson 1978, 102). Reverend George Brown visited Roviana in August 1899 and commented that "many of the villages in that part were destroyed some years ago by H.M.S. Royalist, for some outrages committed against white men, and they do not yet appear to have recovered" (*Australian Methodist Missionary Review*, November 6, 1899, 2). Brown noticed a significant decrease in the population compared to his previous visit twenty years earlier and, when visiting some religious sites, declared, "the best of these had been destroyed by the ship of war, some years ago" (3).

In his account of Roviana in *The Savage South Seas*, E. Way Elkington wrote about Inqava's paele:

> Fifteen years or more ago, old Ingova [Inqava], the notorious head-hunting chief of Rubiana lagoon, was about at the height of his power, and his raids of slaughter to neighbouring islands were of dreadful frequency. It was to this canoe house that he returned after a successful expedition in his great TOMAKO (war canoes) laden with ghastly trophies, but ever since Rear-Admiral Davis, then of H.M.S.Royalist, sacked this place in 1891, all has been comparatively quiet, though I did hear, while I was there, that Ingova had led a head-hunting raid or two. . . .
>
> One day, soon after one of Ingova's rash ventures amongst white men, Commander . . . Davis played havoc with his village, burning and sacking it. It was no ordinary attack but a clean sweep he made of Rubiana, and then the shore was littered with Ingova's skulls: skulls that he and his fathers had collected for generations were scattered in all directions, and lay bleaching on the beach, some half burnt and others cracked and broken. (Elkington 1907, 90, 99)

In addition to burning paele and smashing the skulls of victims from headhunting raids, skulls that would have been hung up inside paele and inside ritual war houses (*zelepade*), Davis also destroyed ancestral skull shrines (*hope*). He also took lots of Roviana material culture away with him — so much of it that several years later in London he had a small catalogue printed that offered this collection for sale — some of this is now in the British Museum in London.[22] The actions of Davis and the crew of HMS *Royalist* reverberate, or echo, through the printed records, archives, and museum collections of Europe and Australia. Woodford commented on a series of "funerary ornaments" that had appeared as illustrations in an article by Thomas Edge-Partington and Thomas Joyce in the anthropological journal *Man* in 1904:[23] "At the time I received the magazine I happened to be on a short official visit to Gizo, and as Inqava, the chief of Rubiana mentioned in the article, happened to be in the neighbourhood, I sent for him and showed him the plate. The old man was delighted and recognized every article illustrated. He told me that Figs. 1–5 were taken away by Captain, now Rear-Admiral Davis, from the natives of the village of Kolokongo at the time he visited Rubiana in 1891, and that the 'bakeha' illustrated in Fig. 6 was presented to Captain Davis by himself" (Woodford 1905, 38).

Elkington reported: "[Inqava] wears no necklace round his neck now, for Admiral Davis has it, it having been given him by Ingova many years after that little visit as a kind of peace offering" (1907, 100). The photograph of Inqava included with the obituary that Edge-Partington wrote for him, published in *Man*, was reproduced from a copy in Davis's possession (Edge-Partington 1907, 22). Davis also took a food trough from Kaliqogo on Nusa Roviana. These were usually kept in a paele and used for ritual feasts, and this is now the only surviving example of a whole Roviana trough in existence (Edge-Partington 1906, 21; see also Waite 2000). The artifacts that Davis took are now in the collections of the Auckland Museum, the British Museum, and the Rautenstrauch Joest Museum in Germany. In desecrating shrines and smashing or taking away ancestral skulls, Davis denied people access to their ancestral power and efficacy. In some ways it was an assault on Roviana history.[24]

As Steven Ilo pointed out, the destruction wrought by the men of HMS *Royalist* had long-term effects in the sense of the relocation of people and the disruption of political forms of power channeled through access to ancestral relics, but in other respects the event was ineffectual. Although the British officially recorded the attack as a punitive action for the murder of Dabelle and others, it is likely that it was also an attempt at the suppression of headhunting and the reduction of local resistance prior to the establishment of the British protectorate in 1893 (see Aswani 2000; McKinnon 1975; Zelenietz 1979). As an attempt at pacification, its impact was minimal. It failed to destroy many tomoko. And during a head-hunting raid on Choiseul three years later, in 1894, Inqava allegedly mustered five hundred men and twenty-two tomoko from his and another chief's resources, and with help from traders he was able to use two English boats, three hundred to four hundred rifles, and five thousand rounds of ammunition (Bennett 1986, 91). In 1894, a year after the declaration of the British protectorate, traders complained that people in the western Solomons were too busy either headhunting or dealing with its consequences to gather copra, and as a result, the trade was suffering (*Sydney Morning Herald*, June 11, 1894).

Although many Roviana people today know some stories about the *Royalist* incident, particularly stories related to the history of their own kin group, there is no strong sense of moral outrage at the actions of Captain Davis and his men. According to Roviana accounts, the attacks did not result in the loss of life, nor were any of the prestigious and important tomoko canoes destroyed. And the violence was seemingly directed at the *mana* of the victims, at their ability to function as powerful political lineages through access to ancestral relics. With the destruction and capture of human remains and important religious items, the incident was perhaps seen as a strange form of British headhunting. This was certainly how Roviana people referred to it when I discussed the existence of human remains taken during the raid in the collections of the British Museum and other European institutions.

The *Royalist* incident did have an effect on Inqava's relative local position, improving his situation in both economic and political terms. The destruction wrought to others left him in a favorable position, and the increased reliance of the British on him as an intermediary — reinforcing his image as the king of Roviana to outsiders — meant that he was able to enlarge his standing locally through better access to trade and influence.[25] Pratt was involved in a land dispute with Inqava in 1893, after Inqava made a complaint to the British authorities. Inqava won his case through the newly implemented British legal system.[26]

The account of the *Royalist* incident pieced together from the "printed papers" constructs a narrative chain of events and dates.

It fixes a precise chronological sequence in a style that fulfills Euro-American genre expectations of a history that is behind the photograph. But this is not a form of history within which the photocopy kept in Faletau's briefcase is embedded. This history from the printed papers has little relevance for Faletau. The context that leaves its mark on this history is the archive. The act of inscription that I have carried out performs a history that links the Royal Navy records to the photograph. The text possesses an authority—all those footnotes giving the exact archival references—but it is an authority of which I am wary. Although individual Roviana people frequently requested that I write down their history, "to make it straight," they were very much aware that history has a side: history is constructed from a certain position, and people have different shifting positions.[27] They are aware of history's manipulation by people in order to make themselves "come up," to advance their own positions, and having their history committed to paper is one way of enabling this, because in Roviana, the written word has increasingly been seen to possess more authority than an oral account.

Do we understand Faletau's photocopy any better for knowing this archival history, or do we find what we already knew? Carlo Ginzburg warns, "The historian reads into them [images] *what he has already learned* by other means, or what he believes he knows, and wants to demonstrate" (Ginzburg 1989, 35). The archival history positions the photograph as a document and performance of colonial power, but this reading forms another pacification of Roviana histories (Aswani 2000). We must consider the possibility of other histories, what Klaus Neumann has called "savage histories" that are linked to the photograph (2000, 72).

Before the advent of the written word, Roviana oral history was channeled through mnemonic objects such as shrines and the topography of a religious landscape, shell valuables, and ancestral relics, all of which had histories associated with them (Thomas, Sheppard, and Walter 2001). What do the details of the photograph that is the source of Faletau's photocopy tell us? The photograph (figure 4.4)—reproduced more legibly here from a print from the Macleay Museum in Sydney—has had a history constructed for it, laid down like the sediment in which it is embedded. We know it was taken on September 25 or 26, 1891, and we know something about what Davis thought he was doing. The photograph shows a large contingent of

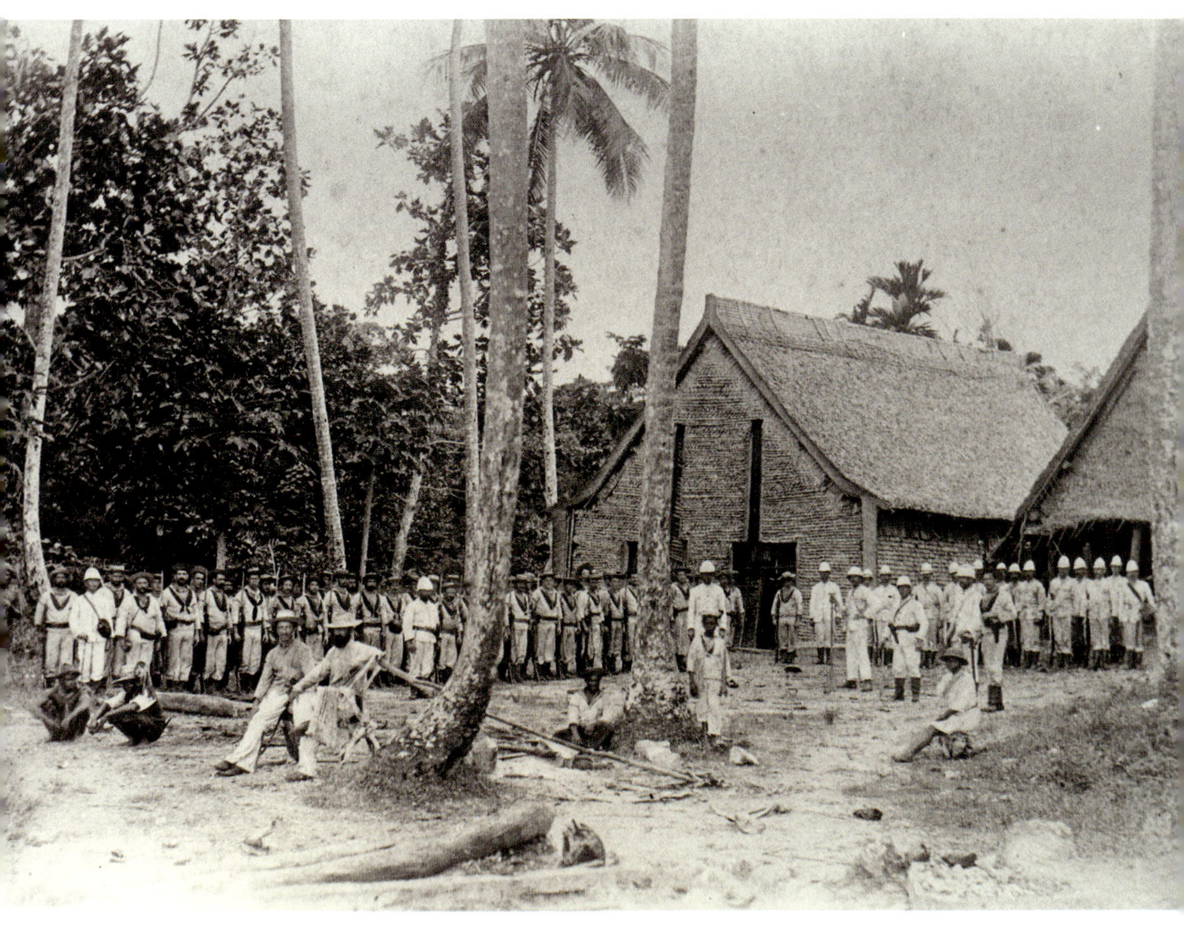

FIGURE 4.4 Officers and marines of HMS *Royalist* on the shore at Sisiata, 1891.
Courtesy of Macleay Museum, University of Sydney. HP87.14.13

British sailors and marines from HMS *Royalist* standing in ranks in front of two paele, which, from other photographs I have seen, can be identified as belonging to Inqava. These buildings, along with houses in Inqava's hamlet of Sisiata, were the only ones to be left untouched by Davis and his men. The photograph bears the stamp of colonial performance; it seems to perfectly fit Foucauldian readings of a mutually supportive network that connects power, photography, and the state (Tagg 1988). It has the feel of a ritual, such as those enacted by the commander and crew of HMS *Curacao* several years later, in 1893, when declaring the Solomon Islands a British protectorate and raising the Union Jack flag on Nusa Zonga. It is a staged, almost theatrical, event, although for Roviana people the destruction was real enough.

The paele are at Sisiata, Inqava's hamlet within Munda, and the detail available in the digital scan from the photograph in the Macleay Museum reveals details of the house on the left. A comparison with other photographs of these two buildings suggests that the paele on the left must have been built in the intervening period between a photograph taken by Woodford in 1886 (see Woodford 1890b, 159), which shows a single paele, and that taken by the photographer from HMS *Royalist* in 1891.[28] The good condition of the thatch on the building also marks it out as being of relatively recent construction. This demonstrates the active expansion of at least one Roviana polity in the period leading up to the declaration of the British Protectorate in 1893. The building of a second paele demonstrates the relative success in economic terms that was being enjoyed by Inqava and his butubutu during this period. This is certainly forensic evidence, but does the increased legibility of the print actually enhance its historical potential for Roviana people? Our expectations of photography and history have been fulfilled — the detail has been filled in — in the same way that the print is more legible than the photocopy.

But Dipesh Chakrabarty (1992) argues that history, as a discourse produced at the institutional site of the university, remains European history. Only Europe is theoretically knowable; all other histories are matters of empirical research that flesh out a theoretical skeleton that is substantially "Europe" (Chakrabarty 1992, 3). "History" is precisely the site where the struggle goes on to appropriate, on behalf of the modern, other forms of memory. Chakrabarty goes on to argue that Europe needs to be provincialized, and what is at stake here is precisely a Roviana history that is not based around a European model. History, certainly of the kind constructed from the printed papers, is firmly embedded in institutional practices that invoke the state. But in the same way that photographs taken by colonial officials can contain within them indigenous spaces — they are the result of various encounters — histories have all kinds of absences and ambiguities that allow counterhistories to surface (see Edwards 2001, 107–31). Europe must not be overprivileged. Constructing a colonial history can amount to perpetuating that past specifically through a certain way of constructing that history.[29] For Judith Binney and Gillian Chaplin, their project of "taking photos home" to Maori communities was successful because "the photographs conveyed a past that had not died in individual memories, but which had been suppressed in the European-recorded historiography. They became the means by which a people's history was recovered and their particular understanding of it brought into the world of light" (Binney and Chaplin 1991, 431).

Keesing has written about the way that he was co-opted into the Kwaio project of "straightening out" and "writing down" the people's history from the early days of his fieldwork on the island of Malaita in the Solomons in 1962 (Keesing 1990, 296). He was pleased when the Kwaio "learnt to write down their genealogies in proper anthropological fashion rather than in Biblical 'begats'" (Keesing 1990, 296). In Roviana the histories that can be "recovered" from nineteenth- and early twentieth-century photographs are essentially those of extended kin groups and particular ancestors, but the writing down of genealogies causes significant problems, and there is a tacit realization that a single, uncontested history is not possible — it is contingent.

Rubbis

In relating the *Royalist* incident to the movements of his butubutu, Steven Ilo's account also demonstrates one reason why the incident is referred to in conversations about problems caused by the recent ethnic tensions in the Solomons. In 2000 and 2001, the influx of "refugees" into Roviana from the troubles in the capital, Honiara, on Guadalcanal Island had exacerbated long-standing arguments about land rights as people built new houses and made new claims for land or reinstated dormant ones. The actions of HMS *Royalist* in 1891 caused a significant shift in residence patterns and land ownership, just as the problems in Honiara in 2000, which caused many Roviana people living in the capital to return home, entailed shifts in residence and reawakened land issues.

The troubles also affected Roviana people in other ways. In addition to making more firearms physically available, as people brought these back with them from the capital, events in Honiara had an impact on local conceptions of violence in the past and the present. A series of violent incidents in Munda and elsewhere in Roviana—including the attempted killing of an expatriate, rape, and armed robbery—threatened local people's ideas of acceptable behavior and cultural continuity. The disappearance of respect in the younger generations, and other perennial concerns, were thrown into sharp focus and became the subject of many heated debates. Donald Maepio's comment is typical of many I heard: "Before people had respect. *Kastom* [custom] was strong. If you did something wrong, you had to pay a fine. People had respect for their elders. Now it has all finished. Now young people smoke [marijuana] and drink—they have guns—there is nothing for them. We need to make kastom strong again. Otherwise it will all be lost. Everything now is *rubbis* [rubbish]."[30]

Munda is now home to two local youth gangs, Westside and Tupac (after the rap singer Tupac Shakur), and marijuana is grown and smoked by teenagers, although currently not in large enough quantities to initiate the drugs-for-guns trade that is now widespread in Papua New Guinea. But people did express grave concerns that unless action was taken, the kinds of crime and violence (rascalism) that they associated with Papua New Guinea would soon spread to Roviana. Munda gangs mark out their territory through graffiti (figures 4.5, 4.6, and 4.7), mimicking styles they encounter in the few videos and music magazines they see. As a result of one particular generational dispute, Faletau was beaten up by a much younger relative. He spent several days in the local hospital, shaken by the collapse of respect that such an action signaled as much as he was physically injured. The attack represented an assault on his conceptions of how things should be. It was against a backdrop of this kind of violence that discussions of history and HMS *Royalist* took place. For Faletau the violence of current events was beyond

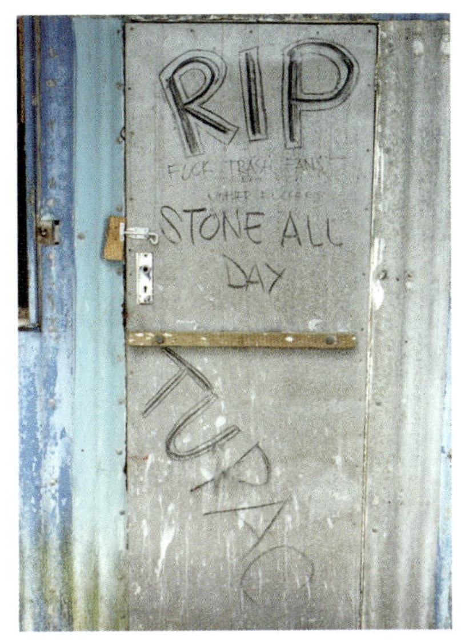

FIGURES 4.5–4.7
Graffiti in Munda.

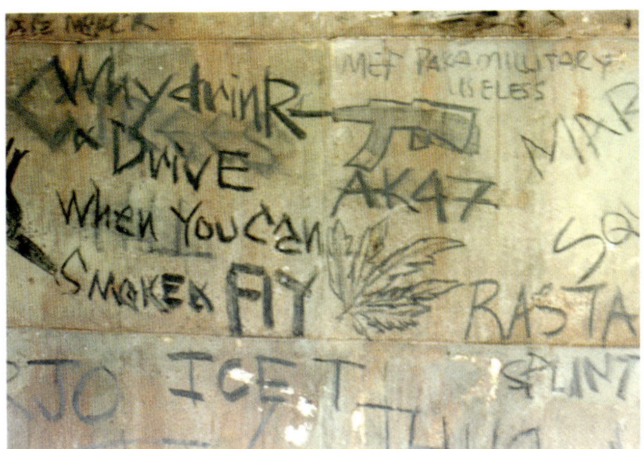

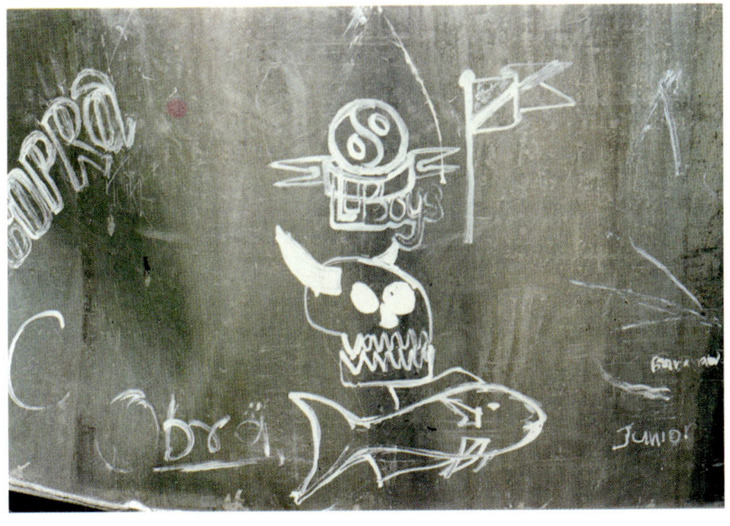

his understanding: "the youth are crazy in their hearts," he said. Relating recent incidents to the *Royalist* attack was a way for Faletau to make some sense of them. Histories often reveal more about the present of their telling than any past events, and Faletau's reactions to violent events in Munda were concerned with change and the ability to control change. The violence threatened Faletau's image of a "peaceful" Christianized Roviana, differentiated from the "time before."

The actions of youths also represent a threat to memory for a particular generation of Roviana people who have some knowledge of kastom. The lack of interest shown in kastom creates fear about its disappearance. Many older people complained that their knowledge was not interesting to young people, and they would not listen to oral histories. The population growth rate of the Solomon Islands has steadily increased over the last two or three decades and, as a result, a large proportion of the population is now aged under twenty.[31] There are very few job opportunities for those graduating from secondary school and, particularly when young people have been to Honiara for their education, there is little or no interest in returning to Roviana and taking up a subsistence living based on fishing and gardening. Large numbers of bored teenagers are turning to marijuana and, in the absence of money to buy imported alcohol, are making a local moonshine called *kwaso*. In Honiara there is a growing problem with street crime and drug and alcohol use, and this was replicated on a smaller scale in Munda with the sudden influx of people fleeing the capital in 2000.

In comparison to contemporary events, the actions of the officers and men of HMS *Royalist* are understandable. British pacification did not result in the death of large numbers of Roviana people. As Christine Dureau points out, although they destroyed tomoko and religious relics, actions that undoubtedly had a significant impact, the British did not leave a "legacy of death that could contribute to resistance and assertive identity building" (2001, 143). There is a sense of loss, but there is surprisingly little anger about the actions of the men of HMS *Royalist*. The incident is recounted in the same way as stories about raids on Roviana carried out by people from Vella Lavella. It is seen as a retaliation for the murder of one person from a particular side; Roviana people reportedly saw all white men (*tie vaka* — people of the ship) as belonging to the same side.[32] Although elements of both the *Royalist* incident and current events are beyond the control of Roviana people, the *Royalist* incident is knowable in the sense that the actions of those involved are explainable in terms of local models, and, because it happened in the past, the outcomes are known. The violent incidents in Munda in 2001 demonstrated the uncertainty of the future. Older Roviana people recall the colonial past in favorable terms, at least rhetorically, and although Independence Day is now celebrated in Roviana, it also provides an occasion for forms of colonial nostalgia. It is not that the events depicted in Faletau's photocopy are seen in a positive light — they are not — but there is an ambivalence that surrounds the image that mitigates against it being seen solely in negative terms.[33]

The other mitigating factor against negative readings of the *Royalist* incident is the way that notions of savagery were displaced onto Malaitans. This was a feature of Roviana reactions to the violence in Honiara that was associated with the ethnic tensions. The perceived threat of Malaitan aggression was a part of daily life in 2000 and 2001. There were regular rumors that members of the Malaitan Eagle Force were planning an attack on Munda or Gizo in which they would arrive in high-powered speedboats from Honiara and would loot, kill, and burn. There is a sense that Roviana people have ideas about so-called Malaitan pagans that align them with colonial attitudes (see Keesing 1990), but these views are also informed by local oral histories of violent encounters between Roviana people and Malaitans working for European traders in the nineteenth century. Several Malaitan families were evicted from Munda directly after the armed coup in March 2000, and their burned houses were potent symbols of the disorder.[34] The displacement of savagery onto others allows a more favorable perception of powerful ancestors who, despite being bifo lotu, were even then "not as violent" as Malaitans. In this context the actions of the British are seen as negative, but not because they were in essence bad people.

If we return to Faletau's passing comment that linked the events of the attack by H.M.S. *Royalist* with upheaval caused by the "ethnic tensions," both this, and his photocopy, can now be seen in a new light. Despite its relative illegibility, the photocopy endows the *Royalist* event with a visibility that enhances its significance. The visibility it enables is not a product of any visual clarity in the image, but the image functions like an object of memory. Both Faletau's comment and his photocopy are integral to understandings and expectations of history in contemporary Roviana. Faletau's conflation of past and present is itself photographic.[35] Edwards argues, after Eduardo Cadava (1997, 61), that "photographs interrupt history and open up another possibility of history, one that spatialises time and temporalises space," and photographs are "points of fracture," points that allow an "opening out" and the possibility of new histories (Edwards 2001, 116, 6). The kinds of creativity that can result from shifting photographs from archives into other spaces reveals their historical usefulness to be myriad rather than singular.

Photographs are not valued as historical evidence in Roviana, at least not in the way dictated by any Euro-American model. Although there is an interest in the kinds of material culture photographs depict, their use extends far beyond this. Their efficacy resides in their ability to suggest a plenitude of memories and histories.[36] Nicholas Thomas's notion of "double vision" seems appropriate here: "Indigenous historical consciousness is not necessarily defined around the same events or chronologies as European narrative. It may occupy a different ground altogether" (Thomas 1999, 4). Edwards argues against decoding the photographic image to reveal a truth, and suggests that, in approaching its relation to history, the focus should be on "how photographic meaning is made in the precise intersections of ethnography, history and the past, both as a confrontation with the past and as an active and constituent part of the present" (Edwards 2001, 7).

As Neumann has written in relation to Pacific histories, there is a need "to subvert History with histories, no longer their grandiose history as an alternative to the colonial one, but breaking down the category history" (2000, 75). In Roviana, committing a history to paper is seen as a way of making it strong, of fixing it in an authoritative form. Histories will undoubtedly continue to be written in some form in Roviana, but photographs are better suited to the more fluid and mobile work of Roviana histories. They can provoke histories and memories that are not immobilized by being written down. Photographs seem to offer the promise of historical fixity, of certainty, but they do not do this, and it is precisely because they don't that they are such useful tools for Roviana histories. What does Faletau keep in his briefcase? He keeps the possibility of bringing forth a whole range of histories, and of opening up memories. He keeps a photo object that does the work of remembering, and that holds out the possibility of what Neumann calls a "savage history" (2000, 72). This is the alchemy of Faletau's photocopy.

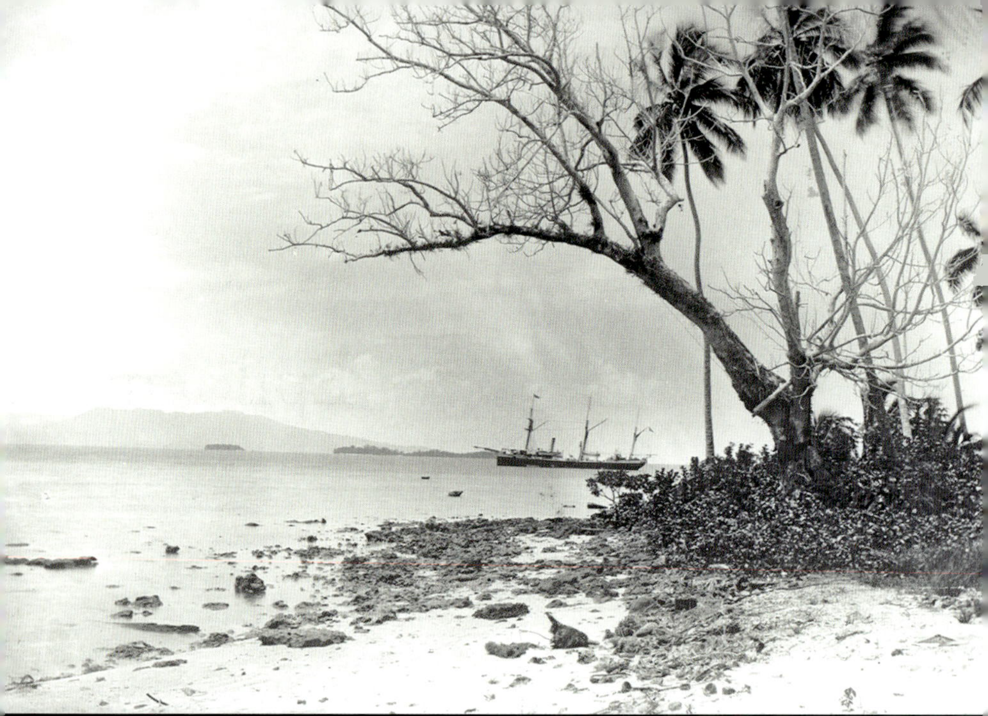

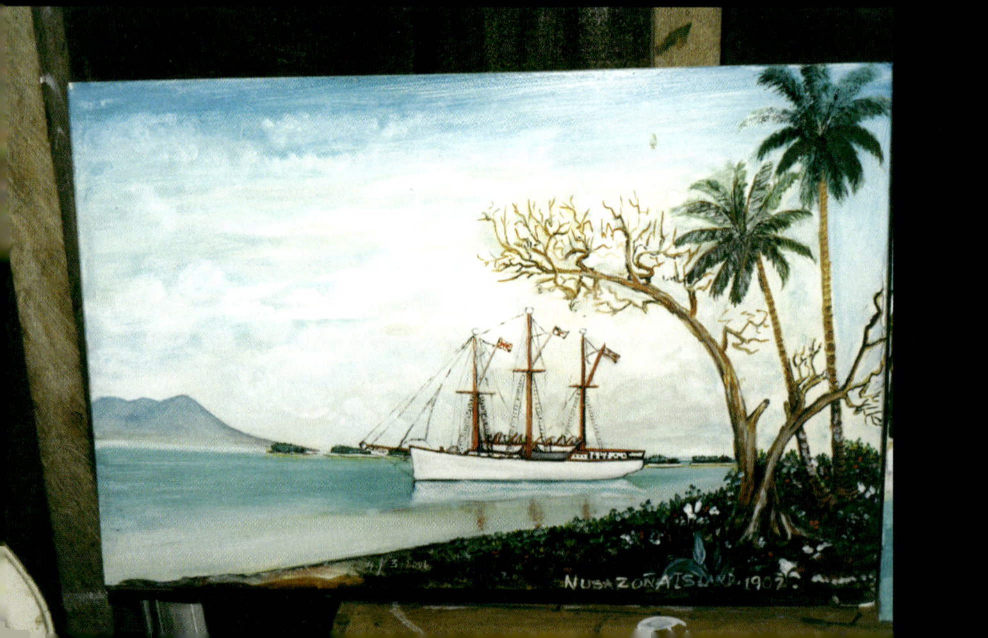

NUSA ZONA ISLAND. 1907.

Epilogue

ONE OF THE COPY PRINTS THAT I TOOK WITH ME TO
Roviana in 2000 was of a photograph taken by Sir John Thurston
on a visit to Roviana in 1894, when he presided over the first major
land-rights cases to go through the newly imposed colonial legal
system. The case was brought by Inqava against the trader Edmund
Pratt (see Jackson 1978, 115). The photograph shows HMS *Royalist*
off the shore of Nusa Zonga Island, and was taken looking southeast
toward Rendova island with Hombuhombu Island in the middle
distance (figure E.1). When I showed the photograph to Faletau, he
expressed no concern for who the photographer was, or the date the
image was made. Instead we engaged in a short discussion about the
possible location from which the photograph was taken. Faletau's
first priority was to orientate himself within the landscape depicted.
Having established this, he then announced that the ship depicted
must be SS *Titus*, the ship that brought Reverend John Goldie and
the other Methodists from Australia on May 23, 1902, to set up the
mission in Roviana. Faletau asked for a copy of the image and subsequently used it as the model for a painting he made, which he
called *The Coming of Lotu* [the coming of the mission] (figure E.2).

FIGURE E.1 (*opposite*)
HMS *Royalist* off the
shore of Nusa Zonga
island. Photograph
by Sir John Bates
Thurston, 1894.
Courtesy of Royal
Geographical Society,
London. B8047

FIGURE E.2 (*opposite*)
Faletau's painting, *The
Coming of Lotu*, 2001.

Faletau was intent on copying (*kumkumbere*) the photograph—a process that took him several days—but he was unconcerned by any idea of historical accuracy that would have constrained the photograph's use within a Euro-American context. According to the archival records, the newly arrived missionaries stayed with the trader Frank Wickham at his house on Hombupeka Island before constructing mission buildings on Nusa Zonga. Faletau insisted that his painting was a "true history" and that the copying process was a matter of bringing out what was strong in the photograph, rather than adhering to any absolute sense of indexical or historical fidelity. His painting is a visual and temporal refashioning. Importantly, he decided to change the color of the ship, from black to white, to show the coming of the "light" of lotu.

Thurston's photograph is transformed and incorporated into another history, one that demonstrates the fluidity of Roviana historio-visual, as opposed to historio-graphical, processes. The irony of HMS *Royalist* being transformed into SS *Titus* was not lost on Faletau, and he would break into a wry smile at the thought of it; the notion of history making as transformation and appropriation was one that he liked. Both the actions of Captain Edward Davis and his men and the arrival of lotu have had effects on Roviana culture and history. The *Royalist* incident has histories that, through images like Faletau's photocopy, are accessible to Roviana people, but there are no photographs that adequately depict the arrival of lotu—even in the Methodist archives in Auckland. The photograph that was published in the *Australian Methodist Missionary Review* on July 7, 1902—showing the "embarkation party on the wharf"—is not known in Roviana, nor would it necessarily do the work required of a Roviana history of the coming of lotu. In the absence of an appropriate image, Faletau created one for himself. That the person behind the camera was the High Commissioner of the western Pacific is of no interest to Faletau, for him the image shows the arrival of lotu from *his* perspective. It is transformed into his history. There is a sense of revelation, that surface appearances and meanings are only a starting point for a series of emergent histories. It is an example of what Arjun Appadurai has called "visual decolonization" (1997, 6), and reveals the copying as an act of appropriation—part of the continuous struggle over mimesis that often defines colonial and postcolonial contexts. There is a reworking of European culture here: Faletau has fashioned his own history by getting hold of the photograph.

For Roviana people photography is one way of mediating modernity through mimetic practices, but there is a sense in which photography is not new for them. It is connected to previously existing visual and memorial formations. In Roviana there is an insistence on the materiality of memory, and the photograph — the singular photo object — fits into this scheme. The photograph has an ability to summon up presences and confer a blessing (*tinamanai*) in ways that ancestral relics had previously done. The reciprocity of vision that is provided by the photograph — to be in front of the photograph of an ancestor is to be watched by him or her — allows this blessing to be effective, to be *mana*.

It is hard to separate subjects and objects in Roviana, and photo objects make particular demands that cannot be refused (see Pinney 2001). I have argued that, in addition to differences, there are certain similarities between Roviana and Euro-American photographic practices: photography has a metaphysic that both the West and Roviana are equally subject to. But Roviana photography does not represent a primitive form from which Euro-American practices have evolved. Instead, Euro-American photographies come to resemble those of Roviana, rather than the reverse. Ideas and practices of materiality and embodiment, although culturally configured in different ways and inflected through particular historical contexts, are enduring features of photography. Walter Benjamin argues that photography "make[s] the difference between technology and magic visible as a thoroughly historical variable" (1985, 244), and although it has certainly contributed to a modern culture of realism, photography has extended the fantastic and the magical in myriad ways. Far from banishing magic, photography has actively enhanced and multiplied its hold over us; it is productive of social formations, not merely a reflection of them. In Roviana photography maintains a series of bodily connections and affects that suggest that we need to pay attention, not only to a closer ethnographic understanding of various photographies in practice but also to photography's role as a particular kind of magic and enchantment. Both Roviana and Euro-American practices reveal a widespread network of corporeality — bodies made of paper, of shell, and of flesh — a network that reveals something of photography's savage identity.

Prologue

1. All interviews and conversations with Roviana people were translated in the field with the individuals involved and, wherever necessary, I have retained words or phrases in either Roviana dialect or Solomons Pijin. No names have been changed.

2. Interview with Faletau Leve, Dunde, April 3, 2001.

3. Interview with Faletau Leve, Dunde, November 17, 2000.

4. See Poignant 1992 for a brilliantly illuminating account of similar processes in an Australian Aboriginal community.

5. Edwards 1995 and 2001 exemplify a more productive approach.

CHAPTER 1. Tie Vaka—*The Men of the Boat*

1. Paele were also used as communal houses for men, and as places where male visitors would stay and where various kinds of ritual and economic transactions took place.

2. UK Royal Navy Australian Station Correspondence, 18 Pacific Islands, Confidential 379, 9–11. National Library of Australia mfm G 1799–1843.

3. It also set up some longer-term problems over land in Munda as Inqava's reputation with the British grew out of proportion to his actual standing in relation to local extended family groups (*butubutu*) and as his successors tried to maintain an authority over land in the face of other local banara trying to reassert their rights. See Schneider 1996.

4. In addition to trading in European manufactured goods, the whalers also introduced various venereal diseases to the western Solomons.

5. Unlike other previously colonial territories in the Pacific, like Fiji or Samoa, the photographic representation of the western Solomon Islands and Roviana does not constitute a large corpus of images. Roviana is better represented than other areas or islands generally considered part of the New Georgia group, such as Simbo Island, but even here the numbers of photographs from the late nineteenth century kept in institutions in the United Kingdom, Europe, and the United States are in the region of 2,500 and higher. In contrast, Alison Devine Nordström reports that more than fifteen thousand photographs of Samoa made between 1870 and 1925 are held in U.S. institutions alone (Nordström 1995, 11).

6. See Powerhouse Museum 1993, 72, for an example printed by Kerry & Co.

7. The latter are housed in the Tyrrell Collection of Kerry & Co. photographs and postcards at the Powerhouse Museum, Sydney. There is a set of twenty stereographs of Roviana published by George Rose in Sydney in the late 1890s that are now in the collection of the Metropolitan Museum of Art, New York.

8. See 'Sketches in the Solomon Islands by F.P.Fairfax' Album PXD 255 Mitchell Library, Sydney.

9. This is a Pijin adoption of a Polynesian word that reflects the influence of South Seas teachers.

10. Faletau Leve, Dunde, March 28, 2001.

11. Faletau Leve, ibid.

CHAPTER 2. *"A Devil's Engine"*

1. Interview with Josephine Wheatley, Dunde, January 23, 2001.

2. Carpenter (1995) reports a similar action of covering the mouth among people who first encounter the camera in Papua New Guinea.

3. Buckley (2000) reports the joking stories told by Gambians about naïve people from the country who come to town and wear perfume to have their photographs taken.

4. Interview with Sesolo Makoni, Buni, April 8, 2001.

5. Interview with Joyce Kevisi, Kokeqolo, October 19, 2000.

6. Christine Dureau (2001) has contrasted three narratives of first contact between Europeans and Simbo islanders in the western Solomons; one based on an account written by Lieutenant John Shortland in 1788, another recorded by the anthropologist Arthur Hocart in 1908, and one she recorded herself in 1990.

7. Unpublished transcript of Hocart's fieldnotes compiled by Christine Dureau, University of Auckland.

8. Woodford was a botanist and a geographer and took microscopes and other surveying devices with him when he visited Roviana in 1886.

9. On Japanese reactions to European optical devices, see Screech 1996. See also Benjamin 1985, 1992; Jay 1988; Slater 1995.

10. Interview with Voli Gasimata, Dunde, March 26, 2001.

11. *Debil-debil* is a Pijin term that refers to dangerous and malevolent spirits usually referred to as *tomate* in Roviana. Interview with Voli Gasimata, Dunde April 26, 2001.

12. Interview with Donald Maepio, Dunde January 5, 2001.

13. Interview with Josephine Wheatley, Dunde, March 15, 2001.

14. Interview with Josephine Wheatley, Dunde, April 6, 2001.

15. Interview with Josephine Wheatley, Dunde, April 6, 2001.

16. Interview with Simon Sasae, Dunde, April 27, 2001.

17. Interview with Voli Gasimata, Dunde, March 26, 2001.

18. Donald still keeps this camera carefully in its original plastic box despite not having used it for more than fifteen years. After it broke he reverted to using a Kodak Box Brownie that he bought in the 1960s.

19. Interview with Rosemary Maepio, Dunde, April 3, 2001.

20. Interview with Donald Maepio, Dunde, January 1, 2001.

21. The term *maqomaqo* is used for "shadow," "soul," etc. but is also used to refer to a photograph.

22. Interview with Idadao, Buni, January 26, 2001.

CHAPTER 3. *Photographic Resurrection*

1. The Roviana word *hope*, although generally taken as meaning "shrine," actually contains the broader meanings of "forbidden" and stems from the word *hopena* (sacred). John Waterhouse translates *hope* as "the general name for sacred places especially where skulls are placed, hence *hopena*, sacred, taboo; *va hopena*, to make sacred; *hope nedara*, a skull repository built of flat stones" (1928, 30). The Pijin phrase *tambu ples* is often used today to refer in a more generalized, and occasionally vague way, to any old sites or features connected with prohibitions. Some sites associated with ancestors are considered hope, while others are not, and distinctions between mythological or sacred sites and actual shrines for worship are often hard to make, since the former do not necessarily require manmade structures in order to qualify as hope.

2. Interview with Joni Kia, Nusa Gele, March 9, 2001.

3. The term *tinamanai* is used in the context of Christian beliefs as well as referring to ancestors and spirits. See Waterhouse 1928, 61.

4. The complexities of maqomaqo will be discussed later.

5. For a recent reappraisal of Barthes's theories of photography, see Batchen 2009. For a further discussion of mana, see Hocart 1925, 260–61; Keesing 1982, 46–49; and Williamson 1914, 71–72, 80.

6. Wonge is wearing a kolekole, a "traditional" style of men's loincloth previously made of bark cloth. *Kabilato* is a Pijin term of Malaitan origin for loincloth, which is now often used to refer to all types of traditional men's clothing.

7. See Prologue.

8. This is a dilemma faced by institutions housing collections of nineteenth- and early twentieth-century photographs of other peoples. For example, photographs in Australian collections, although they may contain valuable ethnographic information about Koori and Murri peoples, are simultaneously photographs of peoples' dead relatives, and as such they are accompanied by a range of restrictions and taboos.

9. In the 1970s Tibetan guerrillas fighting the occupying Chinese forces wore amulets containing a photograph of the Dalai Lama, whereas previously they would have carried an image of the Buddha to protect themselves against bullets and arrows. The photograph of the Dalai Lama was kept on the body as a sign of solidarity, and it became a photo icon. By wearing the photo icon, Tibetans partake in the Dalai Lama's personhood and risk arrest by having this icon on their bodies. See Harris 2001, 187.

10. There is, however, a real desire among sections of the contemporary Roviana population to reconstruct a coherent vision of their past.

11. Some shrines may well have been moved soon after the arrival of the Methodist mission.

12. However, skulls were also kept in caves. There are similarities between oru and the *zelepade*, a ritual men's house (see Aswani 1998 for an account of the zelepade).

13. See also Dureau 2000, 79, because Rivers also reports that inanimate objects have souls.

14. Unpublished transcript of Hocart's fieldnotes compiled by Christine Dureau, University of Auckland, page 3.

15. Lattas explains that similarly, among the Kaliai of New Britain, the word for "soul," *ano*, is the same word for "reflection." See Lattas 1998, 21.

16. Interview with Donald Maepio, Dunde, February 25, 2001.

17. *Beku* is translated as "idol" or "image," although Waterhouse qualifies this as "one that is not necessarily worshipped" (1928, 6). It is also used to refer to a photograph.

18. Interview with Sesolo Makoni, Buni village, Vona Vona Lagoon, March 26, 2001.

19. Other terms used on occasions were *maqomaqo rimata* (sun), meaning the shadow caused by the sun, and *maqomaqo zuke* (lamp), meaning the shadow caused by a lamp or torch. *Zuke* was originally a type of New Georgian torch made of resin wrapped in palm leaves, but it is now used to refer to all kinds of lamps (see Waterhouse 1928, 135).

20. Interview with Simon Sasae, Munda, March 10, 2001.

21. This following account is summarized from Hocart 1922, part 1, 71–112.

22. Note that the word *tomate* is used here, rather than *galagala*. *Tomate* is also used in reference to photography, and Waterhouse translates it as "a corpse; a ghost or spirit" (1928, 114).

23. Hocart recounts a visit to a skull cave, an alternative to the skull house, in which a flat boulder near the entrance is referred to as "the ghosts' seat" (Hocart 1922, part 1, 100). Importantly, *habotuana* is not used solely in relation to *tomate*, but in relation to seats of all kinds, reinforcing notions of presence.

24. Kokorapa is one of the three main settled areas on Nusa Roviana.

25. *Vina* is a prefix that transforms an adjective into a noun, and *tigono* is used to refer to a statue, idol, monument, or memorial. *Vina tigono* is used to refer to a statue of a named ancestor.

26. Waterhouse translates *vukivukihi* as "to make an offering to a *tomate*" (spirit) (1928, 132).

27. *Tie* (human being) *pukerane* ("before" or "formerly") is used to refer to people living before the arrival of the Methodist mission or, more generally, to people who practiced kastom.

28 Interview with James Pitu, Nusa Roviana, April 12, 2001. The site of the hope is still visible in Sidevele but, according to Pitu, the beku itself was destroyed by bombs during World War II.

29. In this case the storyteller, James Pitu, is in his seventies.

30. Olobuki shrine on Nusa Roviana, the most important shrine on the island because it contains the skulls of many important ancestors, was vandalized by a Christian group in 1993 and many of the skulls were thrown away or broken (Sheppard, Walter, and Nagaoka 2000, 22).

31. *Mama* is an endearing term for "father."

32. Waterhouse translates this as "to call upon to accompany" (1928, 93).

33. The use of *tamasa* in relation to *tomate* is complex and will be explored later in this chapter.

34. *Guana* also has the sense of "resembling."

35. Interview with Sesolo Makoni, Buni village, Vona Vona Lagoon, March 12, 2001.

36. *Tome* refers to a general sense of out of sight.

37. Interview with Simon Sasae, Dunde, March 10, 2001.

38. Interview with Simon Sasae, Dunde, March 10, 2001.

39. Unpublished transcript of Hocart fieldnotes compiled by Christine Dureau, University of Auckland, page 20.

40. See also Elkington 1907, 109, which mentions a Roviana chief having an old musical box, which he asks Hardy to "make him sing." See also Taussig 1993 for more on reactions to gramaphones.

41. *Titila* refers to a sense of repeating an action in order to relive it. It is said to have originally been a term for shooting an arrow in the approximate position of a missing one in order to find it.

42. Interview with James Pitu, Nusa Roviana, May 5, 2001.

43. Sprague (1978) has discussed the way that in Nigeria photographs replaced earlier Yoruba carved twin figures, *ibeji*.

44. Contemporary Roviana people, particularly those of the older generation, frequently call on the help of specific ancestors when they are out fishing or working in their gardens. These practices, which often include the physical intervention of the ancestor through actions such as rocking the canoe (*betuebetue*) when asked to indicate which areas might be good for fishing, are differentiated from those involved with ancestral spirits that are tied to specific sites or objects. Christian graves have replaced skull shrines, but in terms of material culture, nothing has replaced garden and fishing magic. Shrines are both things of the past and a part of everyday life. Although they may not be actively maintained, shrines remain important in establishing ancestral sanctions and are bound up with land disputes and approaches to landscape (see Thomas, Sheppard, and Walter 2001).

45. Unpublished transcript of Hocart's fieldnotes compiled by Christine Dureau, University of Auckland, page 13.

46. Hocart reports that, although female chiefs (*bangara maqota*) certainly existed prior to the coming of the mission and, although they may have been able to order their building, the skulls of female ancestors were not placed in shrines (unpublished transcript of Hocart's fieldnotes compiled by Christine Dureau, University of Auckland, page 13). However, Hocart 1922, part 2, 263, reports that the heads of women who had committed suicide by hanging were kept.

47. Unpublished transcript of Hocart's fieldnotes compiled by Christine Dureau, University of Auckland, page 13. Dureau suggests that *mate* is a mistranscription of *tomate*.

48. There were two types of hiama: those associated solely with the ritual preparation of ancestral skulls and those concerned with other less hazardous ritual functions. The former were usually foreigners from other islands because of the dangerous nature of their tasks (Aswani 2000, 69 n.21).

49. Eyes were a feature of leve and zelepade.

50. Interview with Faletau Leve, Dunde, April 11, 2001.

51. Interview with Pitim Bule, Kokeqolo, January 1, 2001.

52. *Vuvusu* contains a sense of dispersal and dissolution—Waterhouse translates it as "to fall, as dust from a dirty roof; to fall, as leaves" (1928, 133)—as opposed to *hoqa*, which is used in reference to an object falling.

53. Interview with Faletau Leve, Dunde, April 27, 2001.

54. Interview with Donald Maepio, Dunde, February 3, 2001.

55. For a summary of the arguments involved, see Aswani 2000.

56. The process involved a blurring of persons and things; human beings were sometimes referred to as "pigs" or "bonito" when recording the number of victims taken in headhunting raids. The jaws of pigs and the skulls of frigate birds and turtles were also kept and displayed in the paele.

57. The skulls of prominent chiefs or warriors were sometimes placed in the zelepade, and those of common people were sometimes buried under paths, where walking over them constituted a further desecration and also had the effect of preventing revenge-seeking spirits from reemerging from the skulls.

58. Although special plants were attached to the beku to aid in the transfer of ancestral power, the power it channeled was not as strong as that effected by the actual skull.

59. T. W. Edge-Partington's obituary for Inqava in the anthropological journal *Man*, complete with photographic portrait obtained from Captain Edward Davis of HMS *Royalist*, is another kind of monument to him. See Edge-Partington 1907.

60. There have been problems with appointing a successor to Simon Mamupio.

61. Interview with Chris Mamupio, Dunde, February 24, 2001.

62. Interview with Chris Mamupio, Dunde, March 1, 2001.

63. This is in contrast to Harris (1999) who says that in pre-1959 Tibet, photos were only made of the dead; while someone was living there was no need to duplicate their presence.

64. Waterhouse translates *kuberia* as "to draw, to write[;] . . . *kinube kubere*, a picture" (1928, 49).

65. Chris said that the first time he saw a photograph was in the late 1930s. It showed Roviana people with Goldie and belonged to one of the Methodist missionaries in Kokeqolo.

66. Interview with Chris Mamupio, Dunde, May 7, 2001.

67. Interview with James Pitu, February 19, 2001.

68. Interview with Faletau Leve, Dunde, April 22, 2001. It would be interesting to consider Faletau's assertions in the light of the contemporary practice of Kirlian "aura photography."

69. Interview with Chris Mamupio, Dunde, May 7, 2001.

CHAPTER 4. *Histories*

1. Klaus Neumann (2000, 67) reports that, similarly, the Tolai people of Papua New Guinea are vague about dates, where a Western historian would strive for the utmost precision.

2. In Pijin the phrases *bifo lotu* and *bihaen lotu* are used to indicate broad historical epochs; particularly the former, which is the ubiquitous phrase to historically locate all sorts of events and artifacts.

3. Interview with Faletau Leve, Dunde, November 4, 2000.

4. See also Aswani 2000 for a discussion of oral history in Roviana.

5. Interview with Steven Ilo, Nusa Roviana, November 18, 2000.

6. UK Royal Navy Australian Station (UK RNAS) 18–23 National Library of Australia mfm G 1799–1843.

7. See Prologue.

8. UK RNAS 23, 2

9. The attacks were to a large extent ineffective at reducing the scale of headhunting. See Aswani 2000; McKinnon 1975; Zelenietz 1979.

10. See Prologue.

11. Woodford 1879–1927 *Woodford Papers*. Australian National University Pacific Manuscripts Bureau, 1288. Five microfilm reels. Libraries Australia ID — 43048991 diary entry for September 1, 1886.

12. William Dabelle's brother Tom, had been murdered on Yanuta Island, west of San Cristoval, on March 26, 1889. UK RNAS 23, 2.

13. UK RNAS 23, 1.

14. UK RNAS 23, 3.

15. UK RNAS 23, 8.

16. UK RNAS 23, 15.

17. UK RNAS 23, 11. The ship the *Marshall S* was attacked in Roviana in May 1891, and two Savo members of its crew were killed. One of the killers, Buko, was caught and flogged. This was a contributing factor to the decision to attack Roviana. See Bennett 1986, appendix 6, 395. The term *Rubiana* was used in at least two ways in British accounts of the area: to refer to Roviana Lagoon generally and to refer specifically to the island of Nusa Roviana. It is sometimes unclear in which sense it is being used.

18. UK RNAS 23, 11. Tooloo, who had been kept as a handcuffed hostage since August to identify the murderers, escaped during the night (of the twenty-fifth to the twenty-sixth) and went alongside the English schooner *Saucy Lass* (a ship belonging to the European trader Frank Wickham), with the hope of getting his handcuffs filed off, but Wickham returned him to Davis at Nusa Zonga later the following day.

19. UK RNAS 23, 11.

20. UK RNAS 23, 12. Having wrought so much destruction in Roviana, Davis proceeded to San Cristoval island, where he executed a local man named Taiemi: "Having previously satisfied myself as to his guilt, from the evidence of natives who witnessed the murder, and he himself having confessed to the crime. I shot him on the same spot he murdered Craig in January last, in the presence of Chief Wasinghow and other natives" (13). There is a photograph of the moment before this execution in the Fiji Museum. Here state terror and photography come together.

21. UK RNAS 23, 12.

22. BM Ethno 1894–188.

23. See Edge-Partington and Joyce 1904.

24. Keesing describes how the Malaitan police involved in punitive raids after an infamous event in colonial history known as the Bell massacre desecrated ancestral shrines in order to systematically destroy other Malaitans' relationships with their ancestors (1990, 282).

25. There are many other banara who are of equal, or more, importance to Roviana people historically.

26. See Prologue.

27. Similar requests are a feature of relations between anthropologists and Melanesians. See Neumann 1992, 249.

28. See Festetics von Tolna 1903, 327, for another photograph of the second canoe house.

29. See Taussig 1992, 38, for an account of this in relation to the Columbus quincentenary.

30. Interview with Donald Maepio, Dunde, February 2, 2001.

31. Statistics from UNICEF.

32. Keesing has argued that Malaitans viewed Europeans as a single group, and as such they were responsible for each other's actions, and therefore vengeance could be taken on any one of them (1986, 270 n.8).

33. So we should not read it as solely about the imposition of colonial power.

34. Many Malaitan "squatters" were evicted from their homes on the road between Munda and Noro. However, some long-term Malaitan residents of Munda were allowed to stay, but only those married to local women or temporarily working in the bank.

35. As Walter Benjamin suggests, "to articulate the past historically does not mean to recognise it 'as it really was.' It means to seize a memory as it flashes up at a moment of danger" (Benjamin 1992, 255).

36. See Lippard 1992 for a series of diverse responses to photographs of native North Americans.

Alloula, Malek. 1987. *The Colonial Harem*. Minneapolis: University of Minnesota Press.

Appadurai, Arjun. 1997. "The Colonial Backdrop." *AfterImage* 24 (5): 4–7.

Arens, William. 1979. *The Man-Eating Myth: Anthropology and Anthropophagy*. Oxford: Oxford University Press.

Aswani, Shankar. 1998. "Ethnohistorical Reconstruction of a Roviana Zelepade." In *New Georgia Archaeological Survey Report Year 3*.

———. 2000. "Changing Identities: The Ethnohistory of Roviana Predatory Head-Hunting." *Journal of the Polynesian Society* 109 (1): 39–70.

Banks, Marcus, and Howard Morphy, eds. 1997. "Introduction" in *Rethinking Visual Anthropology*. New Haven and London: Yale University Press.

Barthes, Roland. 1982. *Roland Barthes: Selected Writings*, Susan Sontag, ed. London: Fontana Press.

———. 1984. *Camera Lucida: Reflections on Photography*. London: Flamingo.

Batchen, Geoffrey. 1997. *Burning with Desire: The Conception of Photography*. Cambridge: MIT Press.

———. 2001. *Each Wild Idea: Writing, Photography, History*. Cambridge: MIT Press.

———. 2004a. "Ere the Substance Fade." In *Photographs Objects Histories: On the Materiality of Images*, Elizabeth Edwards and Janice Hart, eds. New York: Routledge. 32–48.

———. 2004b. *Forget Me Not: Photography and Remembrance*. Princeton: Princeton Architectural Press.

———, ed. 2009. *Photography Degree Zero: Reflections on Roland Barthes's Camera Lucida*. Cambridge: MIT Press.

Beer, Gillian. 1996. "Authentic Tidings of Invisible Things: Vision and the Invisible in the Later Nineteenth Century." In *Vision in Context: Historical and Contemporary Perspectives on Sight*, Teresa Brennan and Martin Jay, eds. New York: Routledge. 83–101.

Behrend, Heike. 2003. "Photo Magic: Photographs in Practices of Healing and Harming in East Africa." *Journal of Religion in Africa* 33 (2): 129–45.

Benjamin, Walter. 1985. "A Small History of Photography." In *One Way Street and Other Writings*, E. Jephcott and K. Shorter, trans. London: Verso. 172–93.

———. 1992. *Illuminations*. New York: Schocken Books.

Bennett, Judith A. 1986. *Wealth of the Solomons: A History of a Pacific Archipelago, 1800–1978*. Honolulu: University of Hawaiʻi Press.

Binney, Judith, and Gillian Chaplin. 1991. "Taking the Photographs Home: The Recovery of a Maori History." *Visual Anthropology* 4 (3–4): 431–42.

Black, Eileen. 1979. "A Painter Voyaging to the South Seas." In *Country Life* (February), 8. Published by the Ulster Museum.

Borofsky, Robert, ed. 2000. *Remembrance of Pacific Pasts: An Invitation to Remake History*. Honolulu: University of Hawaiʻi Press.

Bourdieu, Pierre. 1990. *Photography: A Middle-Brow Art*. Cambridge: Cambridge University Press.

Brown, Rev. George. 1901. *Australian Methodist Missionary Review XL*. 1

———. 1908. *Pioneer Missionary and Explorer: An Autobiography*. London: Hodder and Stoughton.

———. 1910. *Melanesians and Polynesians: Their Life-Histories Described and Compared*. London: Macmillan.

Buckley, Liam. 2000. "Self and Accessory in Gambian Studio Photography." *Visual Anthropology Review* 16 (2): 71–91.

Burgin, Victor, ed. 1982. *Thinking Photography*. London: Macmillan.

Burns, Philp. 1903. *All about Burns Philp & Co.* Sydney: Burns Philp.

Carpenter, Edmund. 1995. "The Tribal Terror of Self-Awareness." In *Principles of Visual Anthropology*. Paul Hockings, ed. 2nd edition. The Hague: Mouton.

Chakrabarty, Dipesh. 1992. "Postcoloniality and the Artifice of History: Who Speaks for 'Indian' Pasts?" *Representations* 37: 1–26.

Chandra, Mohini. 2000. "Pacific Album: Vernacular Photography of the Fiji Indian Diaspora." *History of Photography* 24 (3): 236–42.

Dening, Greg. 1988. *History's Anthropology: The Death of William Gooch*. New York: University Press of America.

Derrida, Jacques, with Bernard Stiegler. 2002. *Echographies of Television: Filmed Interviews*. Cambridge, U.K.: Polity Press.

Douglas, Bronwen. 1999. "Art as Ethno-Historical Text: Science, Representation and Indigenous Presence in Eighteenth and Nineteenth Century Oceanic Voyage Literature." In *Double Vision: Art Histories and Colonial Histories in the Pacific*, Nicholas Thomas and Diane Losche, eds. Cambridge: Cambridge University Press: 65–103.

Dureau, Christine. 1998. "Decreed Affinities: Nationhood and the Western Solomon Islands." *Journal of Pacific History* 33 (2): 197–219.

———. 2000. "Skulls, Mana and Causality: Essays on Head-Hunting in the Western Solomon Islands." Special issue of *Journal of the Polynesian Society* 109 (1): 71–98.

———. 2001. "Recounting and Remembering 'First Contact' on Simbo." In *Cultural Memory: Reconfiguring History and Identity in the Postcolonial Pacific*, Jeannette Marie Mageo, ed. Honolulu: University of Hawai'i Press. 130–61.

Eck, Diana. 1981. *Darsan: Seeing the Divine Image in India*. Charmersburg, Penn.: Anima Books.

Edge-Partington, James. 1906. "Note on the Food Bowl from Rubiana." *Man*. 6: 21.

———. 1907. "Ingava, Chief of Rubiana, Solomon Islands: Died 1906." *Man* 7: 22–23.

Edge-Partington, James and Thomas Joyce. 1904. "Note on Funerary Ornaments from Rubiana and a Coffin from Santa Anna, Solomon Islands." *Man* 4: 129–31.

Edwards, Elizabeth, ed. 1992. *Anthropology and Photography 1860–1920*. New Haven: Yale University Press.

———. 1995. "Visualizing History: A Contemplation of Two Photographs by Captain W. D. Acland." In *Picturing Paradise: Colonial Photography of Samoa, 1875 to 1925*, C. Blanton, ed. Daytona Beach: Southeast Museum of Photography. 49–58.

———. 2001. *Raw Histories: Photographs, Anthropology and Museums.* Oxford: Berg.

———. 2005 "Photographs and the Sound of History." *Visual Anthropology Review* 21 (1–2): 27–46.

Edwards, Elizabeth and Janice Hart. 2004. "Introduction: Photographs as Objects." In *Photographs Objects Histories: On the Materiality of Images*, Elizabeth Edwards and Janice Hart, eds. New York: Routledge. 1–15.

Elkington, Ernest Way. 1907. *The Savage South Seas: Painted by Norman Hardy and Described by E. Way Elkington.* London: A & C Black.

Eves, Richard. 1996. "Colonialism, Corporeality and Character: Methodist Missions and the Refashioning of Bodies in the Pacific." *History and Anthropology* 10 (1): 85–138.

Faris, James. 1992. "Anthropological Transparency: Film, Representation and Politics." In *Film as Ethnography*, Peter Crawford and David Turton, eds. Manchester: University of Manchester Press. 171–83.

———. 1993. "A Response to Terence Turner." *Anthropology Today* 9 (1): 12–13.

———. 1997. *Navajo and Photography: A Critical History of the Representation of an American People.* Albuquerque: University of New Mexico Press.

Festetics von Tolna, Rudolphe. 1903. *Chez les Cannibals: Huit ans de croiserie dans l'Ocean Pacifique et Indien a bord du yacht* Tolna. Paris: Plous Nourrit.

Flower, William Henry. 1882. "President's Address." *Journal of the Anthropological Institute* 11: 184.

Forge, Anthony. 1970. "Learning to See in New Guinea." In *Socialization: The Approach from Social Anthropology*, Philip Mayer, ed. London: Tavistock. 269–91.

Frazer, James George. 1923. *The Golden Bough: A Study in Magic and Religion.* London: Macmillan and Co.

Freedberg, David. 1989. *The Power of Images: Studies in the History and Theory of Response.* Chicago: University of Chicago Press.

Galassi, Peter. 1981. *Before Photography: Painting and the Invention of Photography.* New York: Museum of Modern Art.

Gardner, Helen. 1999. "Cultures, Christians and Colonial Subjects: George Brown's Representations of Islanders from Samoa and the Bismarck Archipelago." PhD dissertation, La Trobe University.

Ginsburg, Faye. 1994. "Culture/Media: A (Mild) Polemic." *Anthropology Today* 10 (2): 5–15.

Ginzburg, Carlo. 1992. "From Aby Warburg to E. H. Gombrich: A Problem of Method." In *Clues, Myths, and the Historical Method*, John Tedeschi and Anne C. Tedeschi, trans. Baltimore: Johns Hopkins University Press. 17–59.

Goldie, John F. 1908. "The People of New Georgia: Their Manners and Customs and Religious Beliefs." *Proceedings of the Royal Society of Queensland* 22 (1): 23–30.

———. 1912. "Industrial Training in our Pacific Missions." *Australian Methodist Missionary Review* (July 4): 2.

———. 1915. "The Solomon Islands." In *A Century in the Pacific*, James Colwell, ed. Sydney: Methodist Book Room. 563–74.

Green, David. 1984. "Classified Subjects—Photography and Anthropology." *Ten-8* 14: 30–37.

Guppy, Henry Brougham. 1887. *The Solomon Islands and Their Natives*. London: Swan, Sonnenschein, Lowery & Co.

Hallam, Elizabeth, and Jenny Hockey, eds. 2001. *Death, Memory and Material Culture*. Oxford: Berg.

Harris, Clare. 2001. "The Politics and Personhood of Tibetan Buddhist Icons." In *Beyond Aesthetics*, N. Thomas and C. Pinney, eds. Oxford: Berg. 181–201.

Harwood, Frances Hine. 1971. "The Christian Fellowship Church: A Revitalization Movement in Melanesia." PhD thesis, University of Chicago.

Heidegger, Martin. 1977. "The Age of the World Picture." In *The Question Concerning Technology and Other Essays*, William Lovitt, trans. 115–54. New York: Harper.

Henisch, Heinz. 1994. *The Photographic Experience, 1838–1914: Images and Attitudes*. University Park: Pennsylvania State University Press.

Hirsch, Eric. 2004. "Techniques of Vision: Photography, Disco and Renderings of Present Perceptions in Highland Papua." *Journal of the Royal Anthropological Institute* 10 (1): 19–39.

Hocart, A. M. 1922. "The Cult of the Dead In Eddystone of the Solomons." Parts 1 and 2. *Journal of the Royal Anthropological Institute* 52: Part 1: 71–112, Part 2: 259–305.

———. 1925. "Medicine and Witchcraft in Eddystone of the Solomons." *Journal of the Royal Anthropological Institute* 55: 229–70.

Holland, Patricia. 1997. "Sweet It Is to Scan . . . : Personal Photographs and Popular Photography." In *Photography: A Critical Introduction*, Liz Wells, ed. New York: Routledge. 115–58.

Houlberg, Marilyn. 1992. "Haitian Studio Photography: A Hidden World of Images." *Aperture* 126: 59–65.

Hulme, Peter. 1986. *Colonial Encounters: Europe and the Native Caribbean 1492–1797*. London: Methuen.

Hviding, Edvard. 1996. *Guardians of Marovo Lagoon: Practice, Place and Politics in Maritime Melanesia*. Honolulu: University of Hawai'i Press.

Jackson, Kim B. 1978. "Tie Hokara, Tie Vaka: Black Man, White Man; A Study of the New Georgia Group to 1930." PhD thesis, Australian National University.

Jay, Martin. 1988. "The Scopic Regimes of Modernity." In *Vision and Visuality*, Hal Foster, ed. Seattle: Bay Press DIA Art Foundation. 3–23.

Jeffrey, Ian. 1999. *Revisions: An Alternative History of Photography*. Bradford, U.K.: National Museum of Photography, Film and Television.

Keenan, Catherine. 1998. "On the Relationship between Personal Photographs and Individual Memory." *History of Photography* 22 (1): 60–64.

Keesing, Roger M. 1982. *Kwaio Religion: The Living and the Dead in a Solomon Island Society*. New York: Columbia University Press.

———. 1986. "The Young Dick Attack: Oral and Documentary History on the Colonial Frontier." *Ethnohistory* 33 (3): 268–92.

———. 1990. "Colonial History as Contested Ground: The Bell Massacre in the Solomons." *History and Anthropology* 4 (2): 279–301.

Knibbs, Stanley George 1929. *The Savage Solomons, as They Were & Are: A Record of a Head-Hunting People Gradually Emerging from a Life of Savage Cruelty and Bloody Customs, with a Description of Their Manners and Ways and of the Beauties and Potentialities of the Islands*. London: Seeley Service & Co.

Kracauer, Siegfried. 1980. "Photography." In *Classic Essays on Photography*, Alan Trachtenberg, ed. New Haven: Leete's Island Books. 245–69.

Kramrisch, Stella. 1976. *The Hindu Temple*. 2 vols. Delhi: Motilal Banarsidass.

Krauss, Rosalind. 1985. "The Photographic Conditions of Surrealism." In *The Originality of the Avant-garde and Other Modernist Myths*. Cambridge: MIT Press. 87–119.

Kupiainen, Jari. 2000. *Tradition, Trade and Woodcarving in the Solomon Islands*. Aarhus: Intervention Press.

Landau, Paul. 1994. "The Illumination of Christ in the Kalahari Desert." *Representations* 45 (Winter): 26–40.

Latour, Bruno. 1993. *We Have Never Been Modern*. Cambridge: Harvard University Press.

Lattas, Andrew. 1996a. "Introduction: Mnemonic Regimes and Strategies of Subversion." *Oceania* 66 (4): 257–65.

———. 1996b. "Memory, Forgetting and the New Tribes Mission in West New Britain." *Oceania* 66 (4): 286–304.

———. 1998. *Cultures of Secrecy: Reinventing Race in Bush Kaliai Cargo Cults*. Madison: University of Wisconsin Press.

Levy-Bruhl, Lucien. 1928. *The "Soul" of the Primitive*. London: Macmillan.

Lippard, Lucy, ed. 1992. *Partial Recall*. New York: The New Press.

Luxton, Clarence. 1955. *Isles of Solomon: A Tale of Missionary Adventures*. Auckland: Methodist Foreign Missionary Society.

MacDougall, David. 1992. "Photo Hierarchicus: Signs and Mirrors in Indian Photography." *Visual Anthropology* 5 (2): 103–29.

Mauss, Marcel, and Henri Hubert. 1972. *A General Theory of Magic*. New York: Norton.

Maynard, Patrick. 1997. *The Engine of Visualization: Thinking through Photography*. Ithaca: Cornell University Press.

McCauley, Elizabeth. 1985. *A.A.E. Disdéri and the Cartes de Visite Portrait Photograph*. New Haven: Yale University Press.

McKinnon, John M. 1975. "Tomahawks, Turtles and Traders: A Reconstruction of the Circular Causation of Warfare in the New Georgia Group." *Oceania* 45: 290–307.

Michaels, Eric. 1991. "A Primer of Restrictions on Picture-Taking in Traditional Areas of Aboriginal Australia." *Visual Anthropology* 4: 259–75.

———. 1994. *Bad Aboriginal Art: Tradition, Media, and Technological Horizons*. Minneapolis: University of Minnesota Press.

Moore, Rachel. 2000. *Savage Theory: Cinema as Modern Magic*. Durham: Duke University Press.

Morgan, David. 1998. *Visual Piety: A History and Theory of Popular Religious Images*. Berkeley: University of California Press.

Neumann, Klaus. 1992. *Not the Way It Really Was: Constructing the Tolai Past*. Honolulu: University of Hawai'i Press.

———. 2000. "Starting from Trash." In *Remembrance of Pacific Pasts: An Invitation to Remake History*, Robert Borofsky, ed. Honolulu: University of Hawai'i Press. 62–78.

New Georgia Archaeological Survey. 1996. *Roviana Lagoon Year 1 Annual Report*, Peter Sheppard, Shankar Aswani, Matthew Felgate, Takuya Nagaoka, eds. Auckland: Centre for Archaeological Research, University of Auckland.

———. 1997. *Roviana Lagoon Year 2 Annual Report*, Peter Sheppard, Shankar Aswani, Matthew Felgate, Takuya Nagaoka, eds. Auckland: Centre for Archaeological Research, University of Auckland.

———. 1998. *Roviana Lagoon Year 3 Annual Report*, Peter Sheppard, Shankar Aswani, Matthew Felgate, Takuya Nagaoka, eds. Auckland: Centre for Archaeological Research, University of Auckland.

Nordström, Alison Devine. 1991. "Early Photography in Samoa: Marketing Stereotypes of Paradise." *History of Photography* 15 (4): 272–86.

———. 1995. "Popular Photography of Samoa: Production, Dissemination and Use" in *Picturing Paradise: Colonial Photography of Samoa 1875–1925*. C. Blanton, ed. Daytona Beach: Southeast Museum of Photography. 11–41.

Obeyesekere, Gananath. 1998. "Cannibal Feasts in Nineteenth-Century Fiji: Seaman's Yarns and the Ethnographic Imagination." In *Cannibalism and the Colonial World*, Francis Barker, Peter Hulme, and Margaret Iversen, eds. Cambridge: Cambridge University Press. 63–87.

Ong, Walter. 1982. *Orality and Literacy: The Technologizing of the Word*. London and New York; Methuen.

d'Ozouville, Brigitte. 1997. "F.H. Dufty in Fiji, 1871–92: The Social Role of a Colonial Photographer." *History of Photography* 21 (1): 32–41.

Pinney, Christopher. 1992. "The Parallel Histories of Anthropology and Photography." In *Anthropology and Photography, 1860–1920*, Elizabeth Edwards, ed. New Haven: Yale University Press. 165–73.

———. 1997. *Camera Indica: The Social Life of Indian Photographs*. London: Reaktion Books.

———. 2001. "Piercing the Skin of the Idol." In *Beyond Aesthetics*, Nicholas Thomas and Christopher Pinney, eds. Oxford: Berg. 157–80.

Poignant, Roslyn. 1992. "Wurdayak/Baman (Life History) Photo Collection: Report on the Setting up of a Life History Collection at the Djomi Museum, Maningrida." *Australian Aboriginal Studies* 2: 71–78.

Powerhouse Museum. 1993. *Pirating the Pacific: Images of Trade, Travel and Tourism*. Exhibition catalogue. Sydney: Powerhouse Museum.

Premdas, R., J. Steeves, and P. Laramour. 1983. "The Western Breakaway Movement." In *Solomon Islands Politics*, P. Laramour and S. Tarua, eds. Suva: University of the South Pacific.

Quanchi, Max. 1997. "Thomas McMahon: Photography as Propaganda in the Pacific Islands." *History of Photography* 27 (1): 42–53.

Richards, Thomas. 1993. *The Imperial Archive: Knowledge and the Fantasy of Empire*. London: Verso.

Root, Marcus Aurelius. 1864. *The Camera and the Pencil*. Philadelphia: M.A. Root.

Ruby, Jay. 1995. *Secure the Shadow: Death and Photography in America*. Cambridge: MIT Press.

Scarr, Deryck. 1967. *Fragments of Empire: A History of the Western Pacific High Commission 1877–1914*. Canberra: ANU Press.

Scheiffelin, Edward, and Robert Crittenden. 1991. *Like People You See in a Dream*. Stanford: Stanford University Press.

Schneider, Gerhard. 1996. "Land Dispute and Tradition in Munda, Roviana Lagoon, New Georgia, Solomon Islands." PhD dissertation, University of Cambridge.

Screech, Timon. 1996. *The Western Scientific Gaze and Popular Imagery in Later Edo Japan*. Cambridge: Cambridge University Press.

Sekula, Allan. 1982. "On the Invention of Photographic Meaning." In *Thinking Photography*, Victor Burgin, ed. London: Macmillan. 84–109.

Serres, Michel. 1982. *Hermes: Literature, Science, Philosophy*. Baltimore: Johns Hopkins University Press.

Sheppard, Peter, Richard Walter, and Takuya Nagaoka. 2000. "The Archaeology of Head-hunting in Roviana Lagoon." *Journal of the Polynesian Society* 109 (1): 9–37.

Shineberg, Dorothy. 1971. *The Trading Voyages of Andrew Cheyne 1841–1844*. Canberra: ANU Press.

Slater, Don. 1995. "Photography and Modern Vision: The Spectacle of 'Natural Magic.'" In *Visual Culture*, Chris Jenks, ed. New York: Routledge. 218–36.

Smith, Bernard. 1992. *Imagining the Pacific in the Wake of the Cook Voyages*. Melbourne: Melbourne University Press.

Smith, Bernard, and Richard Vokes, eds. 2008. "Haunting Images: The Affective Power of Photography." Special edition of *Visual Anthropology* 21 (4).

Somerville, Henry Boyle. 1897. "Ethnographical Notes in New Georgia, Solomon Islands." *Journal of the Royal Anthropological Institute* 26: 357–413.

————. 1928. "Surveying the South Seas." Lecture notes. Royal Anthropological Institute Manuscripts Collection.

Sprague, Stephen. 1978. "Yoruba Photography: How the Yoruba See Themselves." *African Arts* 12 (1): 52–60.

Tagg, John. 1988. *The Burden of Representation: Essays on Photographies and Histories*. London: Macmillan.

Taussig, Michael. 1992. *The Nervous System*. New York: Routledge.

————. 1993. *Mimesis and Alterity: A Particular History of the Senses*. New York: Routledge.

Thomas, Nicholas. 1991. *Entangled Objects: Exchange, Material Culture, and Colonialism in the Pacific*. Cambridge: Harvard University Press.

————. 1993. "The Beautiful and the Damned." In *Pirating the Pacific: Images of Trade, Travel and Tourism*. Exhibition catalogue. Sydney: Powerhouse Museum. 42–59.

————. 1994. *Colonialism's Culture: Anthropology, Travel and Government*. Cambridge: Polity Press.

————. 1995. "Exchange Systems, Political Dynamics, and Colonial Transformations in Nineteenth Century Oceania." In *The Austronesians: Historical and Comparative Perspectives*, P. Bellwood, J. Fox, and D. Tryon, eds. Canberra: Australian National University Press. 287–308.

————. 1999. "Introduction" in Losche, Diane, and Nicholas Thomas, eds. *Double Vision: Art Histories and Colonial Histories in the Pacific*. Cambridge: Cambridge University Press.

Thomas, Tim, Peter Sheppard, and Richard Walter. 2001. "Landscape, Violence and Social Bodies: Ritualized Architecture in a Solomon Islands Society." *Journal of the Royal Anthropological Institute* 7 (3): 545–72.

Trachtenberg, Alan. 1989. *Reading American Photographs: Images as History, Mathew Brady to Walker Evans*. New York: Hill and Wang.

————. 1989b. "Mirror in the Marketplace: American Responses to the Daguerreotype, 1839–1851." In *The Daguerreotype: A Sesquicentennial Celebration*. John Wood, ed. Iowa City: University of Iowa Press. 60–73.

————. 1992. "Likeness as Identity: Reflections on the Daguerrean Mystique." In *The Portrait in Photography*, Graham Clarke, ed. London: Reaktion Books. 188–212.

Waite, Deborah. 2000. "An Artefact/Image Text of Head-Hunting Motifs." *Journal of the Polynesian Society* 109 (1): 115–44.

Waterhouse, John Henry Lawry. 1928. *A Roviana and English Dictionary, with English-Roviana Index and List of Natural History Objects and Appendix of Old Customs*. Taroaniara, British Solomon Islands: Melanesian Mission Press.

Weiner, James. 1997. "Televisualist Anthropology: Representation, Aesthetics, Politics." *Current Anthropology* 38 (2): 197–235.

White, Geoffrey. 1991a. *Identity through History: Living Stories in a Solomon Islands Society*. Cambridge: Cambridge University Press.

————. 1991b. "Village Videos and Custom Chiefs: The Politics of Tradition." *Cultural Survival Quarterly* 15: 56–60.

Williamson, Richard W. 1912. *Mafulu Mountain People of British New Guinea*. London: Seeley, Service and Co.

————. 1914. *The Ways of the South Sea Savage: A Record of Travel and Observation Amongst the Savages of the Solomon Islands and Primitive Coast and Mountain Peoples of New Guinea*. London: Seeley, Service and Co.

Woodford, Charles M. 1879–1927 *Woodford Papers*. Australian National University Pacific Manuscripts Bureau, 1288. Five microfilm reels. Libraries Australia ID — 43048991.

————. 1888. "Exploration of the Solomon Islands." *Proceedings of the Royal Geographical Society* 10: 351–76.

————. 1890a. "Further Exploration of the Solomon Islands." *Proceedings of the Royal Geographical Society* 12: 393–418.

————. 1890b. *A Naturalist Among the Headhunters*. London: G. Philip.

————. 1905. "Further Note on Funerary Ornaments from the Solomon Islands" in *Man* 5: 38–39.

Wright, Christopher. 2003. "Supple Bodies: The Papua New Guinea Photographs of Captain Francis R. Barton." In *Photography's Other Histories*, Christopher Pinney and Nicholas Peterson, eds. Durham: Duke University Press. 146–73.

Zelenietz, Marty. 1979. "The End of Headhunting in New Georgia." In *The Pacification of Melanesia*, Margaret Rodman and Matthew Cooper, eds., 91–108. Lanham, MD: University Press of America.